How to Grandparent

Also by Fitzhugh Dodson

How to Grandparent

Dr. Fitzhugh Dodson
with Paula Reuben

1817
HARPER & ROW, PUBLISHERS, New York
Cambridge, Hagerstown, Philadelphia, San Francisco,
London, Mexico City, São Paulo, Sydney

22974

FIRST EDITION

Designer: Ginger Legato

U.S. Library of Congress Cataloging in Publication Data

Dodson, Fitzhugh, birth date
  How to grandparent.

  Includes index.
  1. Grandparents—United States. 2. Children—Management. 3. Parenting—United States. I. Reuben, Paula, joint author. II. Title.
HQ759.9.D62   306.8'7   80–7849
ISBN 0–690–01874–6

---

81 82 83 84 85 10 9 8 7 6 5 4 3 2 1

To Howard and Hazel Goheen
who are the wonderful grandparents
of
Robin, Randy, and Rusty Dodson
and to
Nathalie P. Agronick
a great mother
a great grandmother
and a great great-grandmother

Contents

Contents

Part Four: Appendixes

Part One

Becoming a Grandparent

❧ 1 ❧

The New Extended Family

"A grandma is old on the outside and young on the inside."
John Wright, age 7½

I've been thinking a lot about grandparents lately.

For a long time I've had the idea from my own observation and my professional counseling experience that older people have a lot to give to younger people, and younger people have a lot to give to older ones, particularly within the same family.

These thoughts have led me to realize that the experience of being a grandparent could and should be a lot more rewarding and enriching than it is for most grandparents. By the time a person reaches grandparent age, he or she has a lot of life wisdom, as well as a lot of love to give, and usually plenty of time to give it in.

And for a person who loves her grandchildren and wants to keep alive, alert, growing, and giving, grandparenting is a marvelous opportunity for just that. I think that any grandparents who are now experiencing some degree of loneliness or alienation from their families could be having a wonderful time instead, as full-fledged, loved, and loving family members. Even grandparents who are already enjoying their families could probably be having an even better time, if they learned a little more about how to go about it.

The experience of being a grandparent varies widely from person to person, of course. So when I decided to write this book about the rewards of grandparenting, I began interviewing people in different sections of the country, to find out as much as I could about what grandparenting means to grandparents.

One of my most interesting interviews was with a couple I met while camping in the Angeles National Forest in California. My family and I do a lot of camping, and I've discovered that the relaxed outdoor atmosphere is especially good for getting people to talk freely about themselves. This particular couple were both in their fifties. They were camped with their grandson, aged eight, and their granddaughter, aged ten, who were fishing in the river while I talked to their grandparents. I'll repeat the conversation as nearly as I can.

"Do I enjoy being a grandfather? You better believe I do! I think I actually

3

enjoy my grandchildren more than I did my own children."

"Why is that?"

"Well, I don't have the full responsibility for my grandchildren. That eases things up considerably. What's even greater, we can enjoy the children for a day or a weekend or a week and then give them back to their parents. Wonderful! Kids for rent, and no charge!

"We take them camping and fishing a lot. I taught both of 'em how to fish. And do they love it! I'm teaching them to clean and cook their fish, too, and they do a pretty good job at it."

"Yes," his wife chimed in, "we really enjoy them. Of course, they cut up every now and then and give us a hard time. Sometimes we have to land on them when they get out of hand. But that's just the way children are.

"I'm teaching them to cook. They can already bake cookies and cupcakes. And it's a big help to their parents for us to take them. We live only thirty minutes' drive away. If they want to take a weekend or a week's vacation or just an evening, we can take care of the kids. And with the cost of baby-sitting for a weekend these days, that's no small thing."

From time to time throughout the weekend on the river, I would see the two grandchildren fishing or swimming. I also occasionally glimpsed the grandmother and grandfather playing cards or Monopoly with them. It was obvious that they all really enjoyed being together.

Quite a different attitude was expressed by a grandfather I interviewed while camping at a park in Utah. He and his wife lived in Arizona. His son, the son's wife, and the grandchildren lived in southern Oregon. I asked him if it didn't bother him living so far away from his grandchildren.

"Bother me? Absolutely not. That's the best thing about it. We only see them at Christmas. And that's the way I like it. I don't want to get too involved in raising my grandchildren. It was enough blood, sweat, and tears getting my own children raised. I don't want to go through it again with my grandchildren. They're in Oregon and I'm in Arizona, and that's just fine with me."

A third grandfather, this one a taxi driver in Washington, D.C., expressed a still another viewpoint. His only grandchild, a three-year-old boy, also lived in Washington.

"I'm really looking forward to when he's older, like about six," he said.

"Why so?"

"Well, I don't know what to do with a three-year-old. I can jounce him up and down on my knee and play Ride the Horsey with him for a couple of minutes, but that's about all. But when he gets to be six, I can take him to the ball game and play catch with him and things like that."

The outstanding impression I got from my interviews with grandparents of different socioeconomic classes in different sections of the country is that grandparents are remarkably like parents in their understanding, or lack of understanding, of children, and in their ability or inability to enjoy the company of children.

Some find children an irksome burden. Others wish they knew how to understand and interact with them, but confess frankly that they don't. A minority of grandparents, like a minority of parents, really understand children and enjoy spending time with them.

Although this book is entitled *How to Grandparent*, I want to do more than merely discuss the role of the grandparent in today's society. I want to sound a trumpet for establishing what I call "the new extended family."

This, I believe, is the key to a more rewarding life not only for grandparents, but for parents and grandchildren as well. This *new extended family* can help give maturity, enrichment, and stability to the family as a unit. That is extremely important in this bewildering age of change.

A bit of history will help to explain this idea of a new type of family.

Many years ago, everybody grew up in the old-fashioned extended family. This was the name given to a family that included not only parents and children, but grandparents as well. Most of the time all three generations lived under the same roof. I myself grew up in just such a family. My grandparents lived with us from the time I was born until my late teens, when they died.

In some cases the extended family included other relatives, such as uncles and aunts and cousins. They usually did not live under the same roof with the parents and grandparents and children. But they visited frequently and were part of a close-knit family structure.

There were some definite psychological advantages to living as a member of an extended family. For one thing, help of many kinds was built into the very structure of your family. When a mother had her first child, for example, and was unsure about taking care of a baby, she could always get information and emotional support from her mother or mother-in-law, or another more experienced female relative. If a teenager got in trouble, various family members could rally, with his parents, to aid him. If there was a financial crisis in the extended family, the various members of the family would band together to try to provide financial help and emotional support. Being a member of an extended family gave a person the secure feeling of belonging to a group of people who cared.

Sociologist Leontine Young recently interviewed groups of parents, grandparents, and young unmarried adults on the subject of the family. One of the surprising things she discovered was that when the young adults talked about families, they frequently talked about something they felt they had missed:

> For some it was family rituals like turkey at home on Thanksgiving, for others it was relatives living close by and filling the

house with noise and security, for still others the continuity of neighborhood and house and familiar routines. For all there was a wistful longing, a feeling of something important missed but still vaguely sensed and symbolized by family as an ideal, an inchoate dream.

These were not young people in trouble. Nor were they, as far as one could see, alienated from their own families. They were thoughtful, well educated, alert to the surges and conflicts of the day. Yet they seemed more aware than their parents or grandparents that some deeply important quality had gone out of the family, and they felt a loneliness for it.[1]

One youngster said to her mother, "I wish we had more relatives close by. It would be so nice to have a big family to walk down the street with, to do things with."[2]

A naïve eighteen-year-old commented wistfully, "The Depression must have been wonderful. I've heard my parents talk about it, and everyone was together; the whole family was in one place."[3]

One grandmother in Dr. Young's study made this comment: "I feel sorry for my grandchildren because they can never remember what it was like to grow up in a family in a small town, as I did. They've lost so much."[4]

But not everything about the extended family was psychologically beneficial. There were disadvantages as well, and these ultimately brought about the downfall of the extended family.

In many cases it proved to be psychologically unworkable for three generations to live and interact together in the same house. Perhaps that statement will become more meaningful when I illustrate it with the story of a couple I am currently counseling.

The couple have two sons, ages four and seven. The wife's mother lives with them; her husband is deceased.

There is an enormous amount of tension between the grandmother and the parents, most of it due to a constant stream of advice coming from the grandmother. The parents are raising their children in ways considerably at variance with those the grandmother approves. And she does not hesitate to tell them so.

Her advice is not confined to child-raising. If the couple, for example, are relaxing—reading or watching TV—she tells them that the front yard is a mess and they should be out doing yard work. In fact, any time either of them is *not* doing some kind of work around the house, she reminds them that they should be.

The husband is furious at this 50,000-watt Broadcaster of Advice and wants to give her her walking papers. His wife is terrified of her mother and will not hear of her being turned out. She tries to overlook her mother's interference and to act as a buffer between her mother and her husband. The couple's marriage is foundering on the rocks of the grandmother's constant interference, and it was this marital crisis that brought them into counseling with me.

Unfortunately, this kind of conflict is typical of many parent-grandparent interactions, particularly if the parents and grandparents live under the same roof. Here is what one young woman says:

> "My grandmother grew up in Europe and now that she's alone, she lives with us. She thinks we should behave just as she did when she was young. She's always interfering, always telling us what to do. My mother tries to stop her, to explain that things are different now, but that only causes arguments. My brother won't even speak to my grandmother half the time, and then she cries and feels hurt. I feel sorry for my mother. She's always in the middle."[5]

Another girl remarks with distaste, "I had to share a room with my grandmother when I was growing up. It was *awful.*"[6]

And a young mother says angrily, "I wish my mother-in-law would stop telling me what to do about my children. I want to do things my way, not hers. I wish we lived a long way from her, and then I'd be free."[7]

It is precisely this sort of psychological sand in the gears that brought about the downfall of the extended family. There were also other factors—such as the shift from a rural to an urban society, the increasing number of women in the work force, and the much greater mobility of families—that began to exert a pressure on the extended family which it was not able to withstand. But I believe that the *major* reason the extended family broke down was that in some ways it just didn't work very well, in spite of its benefits.

Everybody is familiar with the phrase "generation gap," referring to the difficulties in communication between parents and their teenagers. But few people speak of the other very important "generation gap" that exists—the one between grandparents and parents. Where there should be an easy and fruitful contribution of grandparents to the raising of grandchildren, all too often we find only alienation and suspicion.

Grandparents may feel that parents shut them out from a healthy enjoyment of their grandchildren. Parents may believe that grandparents are interfering with the raising of their children. Both sides need help in bridging this gap.

In this book, I hope to help you, as grandparents and parents, to open up channels of communication among yourselves, your children, and their children so that all of you may enjoy the satisfactions and enrichment of the new extended family. The possibilities are enormous for family and individual fulfillment and for raising children to be happy, successful adults. Although this book is addressed primarily to grandparents, Chapter 19 is written especially for parents. And the whole book could be read profitably by both grandparents and parents, since both are vital parts of the extended family.

Each segment of the family, because of its age and its psychological position in the family structure, has unique qualities to contribute to the total group. Parents, grandparents, and children each have something to teach the others and something to learn from them, if they can learn how to communicate in a free and nondefensive way.

I am *not* proposing that we go back to the system of three generations living under the same roof. There are too many obstacles to communication in such a situation. I am talking about a new form of extended family that would operate in today's usual situation, in which parents and children live under the same roof, while grandparents live elsewhere.

Unfortunately, many families are only disastrous caricatures of the potentials inherent in the family structure. Parents and grandparents generally think their role is to teach and mold the children. It seldom occurs to them that they have anything to *learn* from the children. Although children may absorb what they are taught by their parents and grandparents, when they become teenagers they usually believe that grown-ups have nothing worthwhile to offer them. And parents often don't believe they can learn much from their own parents about raising children. So they do not think of them as important auxiliaries in raising children.

The result of such a set of erroneous beliefs is that many families realize only a small part of their potential for learning and loving and growth.

This book focuses primarily on your role and function as a grandparent. While books on parenting are as numerous as the lilies of the field, books on grandparenting are practically nonexistent. I believe that you, as a grandparent, are very important in the raising and guidance of children, but that you have been sadly neglected. One well-dressed grandfather in his sixties spoke bitterly to me about this situation. "I think grandparents are the most forgotten people in the country," he said.

So far, I have been writing about grandparents as if everyone knows what a grandparent is. But that may not be true.

So let's look for a minute at the definition of a grandparent. When I asked my fourteen-year-old son Rusty for a definition, he said, "A grandparent is a parent whose children have children." This is, of course, quite correct if we are limiting ourselves to a purely biological definition. But a *psychological* definition would go something like this: A grandparent is a unique kind of *emotionally involved, part-time parent without pressure.*

Suppose a couple are taking a weekend vacation, leaving the grandparents in charge of the children. What the grandparents are doing during this weekend is acting as part-time parents. There is a Latin phrase that describes the teachers and principal of a school: *in loco parentis,* "in place of the parents." When a grandparent is acting in place of the parents, she is fulfilling the role of a parent to the children, whether she is aware of it or not.

But grandparents are not part-time parents in the same way baby-sitters are. Grandparents are *emotionally involved,* while baby-sitters usually are not. And being emotionally involved with the grandchildren has both positive and negative aspects for all concerned.

Because of this emotional involvement, grandparents will take the job of caring for their grandchildren much more seriously and responsibly than the average baby-sitter. But, on the negative side, they are not likely to be as objective about the children as an outsider would. And grandparents are much more likely to be defensive about the way they handle the children. I will be discussing both the positive and negative sides of the grandparents' role throughout this book.

The phrase "without pressure" needs a little explanation. Grandparents are without pressure, as compared to parents, in several ways. For one thing, as the grandfather I spoke of earlier pointed out, grandparents do not have to bear the full responsibility for raising the children. They can enjoy them for a brief time and then hand them back to the parents.

Grandparents are comparatively without pressure in other ways, too. Since they are not in charge of raising the children, they ordinarily do not get involved in setting goals for them, goals such as "to be good," or "to be successful." This means that they are free simply to enjoy the children. In addition, grandparents, whether they are still working or retired, usually have ample leisure time to spend with their grandchildren if they wish to do so.

Many grandparents assume they do not need any special information or training in the complex skills required to raise a child. When I ask grandparents what they need to know in order to be good grandparents, I often get an answer like, "What an absurd question! You don't need to know anything special. You just do what comes naturally. You see your grandchildren when you want to see them. You enjoy them without feeling a sense of responsibility for them. And you spoil them a little, because that's your privilege." They tend to subscribe to the theory of "doing what comes naturally." They feel that "nature" and love are enough. I disagree. In addition to natural instincts and love, I believe grandparents (and parents) need *information* in two basic areas:

1. Child psychology, because every parent and every grandparent is a child psychologist, whether she is aware of it or not.
2. Teaching methods, because parents and grandparents are the most important teachers of their children.

That is why this book gives you information about both child psychology and teaching—so that you can achieve maximum pleasure and satisfaction from enriching your grandchildren's lives. I will present this information in chronological sequence, from birth to age twenty-one, discussing each stage of psychological development your grandchild goes through.

What specifically can you, as a grandparent, gain by becoming a successful part of the new extended family?

First, you will be able to establish a closer, warmer relationship with both your adult children and your grandchildren.

Second, you'll find that grandchildren can quite literally make you feel younger again. Being in close touch with your grandchildren as they grow up can be like drinking at some psychological Fountain of Youth. And that is certainly preferable to shuffling along glumly on the sidelines of life as you grow older!

Third, you can have the satisfaction of teaching your grandchildren things that will stay with them the rest of their lives. Margaret Mead, the famous anthropologist, has paid tribute to her maternal grandmother for being the most important personal influence in her life. From her grandmother Ms. Mead learned the careful habits of scientific observation that she later used in her research work in the South Seas. Bertrand Russell, the philosopher, has also spoken of the immense influence of his grandmother on him.

There are many grandparents who are full of love and goodwill and want to guide and influence their grandchildren. But they make the mistake of thinking that all they need to do when they are relating to a ten-year-old grandson is to remember what *their* son was like when he was ten. Usually this does not work out too well, because both children and families today are vastly different from children and families of yesterday.

In what ways are children different?

Well, for one thing, our children are much more sophisticated today. To a great extent this is due to the influence of the media, particularly television.

In the old days, you could convince a child that a person needed to be moral and upright in order to succeed in life. But today's children have seen with their own eyes on a TV screen a President and Vice-President who chose to resign rather than go to prison. The same TV screen also informs them of the illegal activities of governors, senators, union officials, and corporation executives.

Our television-era children are the first to grow up truly aware of the entire world. When something newsworthy happens in Africa or China or Saudi Arabia, children are likely to comment on it the next day to their friends or parents or schoolteachers.

The bits of information picked up by our children at an early age are truly mind-boggling. After seeing a TV program, they may discourse knowingly about undersea exploration or anthropological digs or Freudian defense mechanisms. And this at the age of nine or ten!

This fantastically increased sophistication of children is summed up in the comment "If Booth Tarkington wrote his novel *Seventeen* today, he'd have to call it *Twelve!*"

In what ways are families different?

Not only are children more sophisticated, but men and women are beginning to see themselves quite differently. This is due to the impact of new social forces, especially the feminist movement.

In days gone by, husbands went out to work; wives stayed at home and took care of the house and children. This stereotype was perpetuated in children's books, in which little girls saw women portrayed mainly as homemakers and nothing else. Or if women were portrayed in other occupations, they were nurses but not doctors, secretaries but not lawyers.

Obviously, the situation is different today. Of course there are still fields in which women are subtly discriminated against, and in many cases women are paid less than men for the same work. But the old "comfortable" roles and role models for men and women are gone. More and more mothers now work outside the home. Women today are becoming more assertive and independent in their thinking and acting.

And today's men are beginning to allow themselves to experience and express feelings that in past generations would have been labeled "feminine." Today's men allow themselves to be tender, soft, and caring. More and more, today's fathers are involved with their babies and young children, giving them baths or bottle feedings, or changing their diapers.

The old rigid division between work for men and homemaking for women has broken down. In many families, both mother and father work outside the home, and both share in the care of the children and the house.

A new crop of children's books is making its appearance in libraries and bookstores. In these, little girls can read about women who have many more options in life than their grandmothers did.

We are still in the turbulent midstream of the changing roles of men and women in our society. We have not yet reached a point where the new roles have become stabilized. But we know we can never go back to the old stereotyped roles.

The changing roles of men and women are not the only things affecting the family today. Divorce is having an increasingly powerful impact on our society. Currently, one out of three American marriages ends in divorce; this figure is edging up toward one out of two. Today there are many more single-parent families than there used to be, and more stepparents and stepchildren. All of this can mean grandparents may be forced out of "traditional" roles, as I will point out presently.

I have said that today's children are highly sophisticated. That goes double for today's teenagers—and particularly in terms of sexuality. This fact is summed up tidily in the witticism "Parents, have a good heart-to-heart talk with your sixteen-year-old about sex. You'll learn a lot!"

Today's teenagers can generally talk more freely about sex than their parents, and they also act more freely. According to a study by Dr. Robert Sorensen, 52 percent of all thirteen- to nineteen-year-olds in the United States have had sexual intercourse before they are twenty. Among those nonvirgin adolescents, 71 percent of the boys and 46 percent of the girls had sexual intercourse by the age of fifteen. Only 5 percent of the boys and 17 percent of the girls in Sorensen's sample waited until they were eighteen or nineteen to have intercourse for the first time.[8]

This amount of adolescent sexual behavior would have been unheard of as recently as twenty years ago.

Sex is not the only thing today's teenagers know a great deal about. If you pick at random a family with a sixteen-year-old boy or girl, chances are that the teenager will have much more scientifically accurate information about drugs than his parents do. And of course the universal availability of drugs today is something that neither parents nor grandparents had to contend with a generation ago.

Today's teenagers have also picked up a good deal of popular psychology. You can hear them use this newfound knowledge to analyze their parents' actions, often with deadly accuracy. "The fact that you denounce sex so much to us, Dad, shows that subconsciously you must have some problems there yourself. Otherwise you wouldn't make such a big deal out of it." Such a statement comes as something of a bombshell to a parent, particularly if he *has* been having trouble with his sex life. Such a remark can be equally devastating to a grandparent.

One final point that deserves mention here is the influence of "how to parent" books on many parents today. These began with Dr. Benjamin Spock's *Baby and Child Care* in 1946, and are coming out in an ever-increasing flow. Many of these books are excellent; some are less so. The pertinent fact is that many parents read and follow these books. A generation or two ago, a woman could take it for granted that her children would raise the grandchildren more or less the way she had raised them. This is no longer the case. The books that her daughter or son swear by may advocate quite different methods than those a grandmother (or grandfather) believes in. This can create considerable tension between parents and grandparents.

What do all these facts mean to you as a grandparent in today's world?

I would say that the experience of many grandparents today can be summed up this way: It's as if you and your family have been living for many years as Hunzas in Tibet, isolated from the outside world. You are about to become a grandparent. Suddenly a huge jet airplane takes you, your husband, and your children to the United States, a strange and frightening country you have never seen in your life. You are confronted with television, drugs, transistor radios, bikinis, sexually advanced teenagers, and men and women who behave quite differently from the men and women in Tibet.

The old model you have in your mind of how a grandparent, parent, or child behaves simply does not fit this new country you are now living in.

You feel confused and uncomfortable much of the time. When you try to talk to people, you can't "connect," for you don't know the language. You want to fit into your new situation, but you just don't know how. And things never seem to get any better or easier for you.

Perhaps you are an exception to this. You're a "hip" grandparent, up on the latest ideas, mores, and styles, moving with the times. That's possible, of course. But most people as they mature feel less inclined to move ahead at the sometimes frantic pace of teenagers and young adults. It seems less necessary to follow fads or do what others expect of you. This is a very comfortable position to be in, and it is good to the extent that it gets you out of the daily rat race. But the danger, to which most people succumb at least in part, is that you tend to let more of the world go by than perhaps you should. Suddenly you find you're really out of the mainstream of daily life. This puts you at a kind of distance from younger people. And that's hard if those younger people are family members you care about and want to relate to.

If you are like many other grandparents, this is your situation to some degree. The old guidelines don't exist anymore. Telling you to "do what comes naturally" is about as foolish as telling a doctor who specializes in skin diseases to "do what comes naturally" in performing brain surgery.

Here are some random examples of the new kinds of situations that exist.

Here is a wedding, flower-decked, musical, and sedate, the kind of traditional scene that brings tears of joy to most women's eyes, and especially to a grandmother's. And here is the grandmother of the bride, tearful and smiling, as one would expect. And—surprise!—in her lap she has a baby, the bride's baby and her own great-grandchild.

Grandmother is holding the baby while its mother is getting married to its father.[9]

It's likely that there is nothing in your own upbringing that has prepared you for this new kind of role.

A daughter ran away with her lover, abandoning husband and children. This is a new pattern that we are seeing, of women taking their freedom as formerly only men used to do. The son-in-law in this instance was so undone, so helpless to care for his two young children, that the parents of his runaway wife took in the whole family, and grandmother became a mother to his children until he got his bearings. When he took an apartment of his own, he made sure it was near grandmother's, and she continued to watch over the children. When he married again, and settled his wife and the children in a new home, that too was near grandmother's, and the whole family, stepdaughter-in-law included, became regular visitors to grandma's house.[10]

Separation and divorce have always existed, but nowadays a grandparent is much more likely to have to care for grandchildren in a split-family situation.

For example, a grandmother ends up doing most of the parenting for her divorced twenty-two-year-old daughter, whose funds are scarce and who has to work.

Another grandparent takes over less of the parental function, but still delivers a grandchild to a day-care center each morning and picks her up every afternoon.

But awkward or demanding situations are not the only kind that arise today. Consider this one.

A newspaper clipping tells the story of a set of quadruplets who were born to a New Jersey couple not long ago, and how the babies' coming has changed everyone's life, especially the life of the grandparents. These grandparents live nearby, and they have been coming over every day to help. That's a routine task for a grandmother. But here is a grandfather also on the job, doing his share of bathing, diapering, feeding, cuddling the babies, and enjoying it so much that he is considering making an early retirement from his law practice to have more time for his grandchildren. He had never done any of these things before—as a young father he had never picked up his own daughter until she was a year old. Fathers of a generation ago were not expected to handle babies, and indeed they were afraid to try. But this grandfather quickly developed both expertise and confidence.[11]

Many problems can arise if grandparents fail to find creative ways of relating in their particular families. Some of these situations are old and familiar, and some are the results of recent rapid social change. All of them can cause pain and frustration.

A set of grandparents is at loggerheads with their children because of the sexual freedom the parents permit their teenagers.

Another pair of parents and grandparents get on reasonably well together, except for the fact that the grandparents feel imposed upon because they are called upon to act as baby-sitters often, at inconvenient times.

In another family, the grandparents constantly give advice on how to raise the grandchildren. The parents are afraid to object because it might hurt the grandparents' feelings. Their solution to the problem is to see the grandparents as little as possible, and the relationship has become strained.

With still another pair of parents and grandparents, bad feelings are not kept inside. Open hostility has erupted, with the result that the grandparents almost never see the grandchildren. Both parents and grandparents would like to resolve this ugly situation, but they do not know how to go about it.

When their divorced son marries a widow with three children, the grandparents find that they like two of the children just fine but that the third, a fourteen-year-old boy, is totally unacceptable. His presence spoils visits for the whole family, but they don't know what to do about it.

A grandmother has divorced her husband, which has created bad feelings in her daughter and, indeed, in the entire adult family. The divorce has not disturbed the woman's relationship with her two grandchildren, but it has certainly created difficulties in her relationship with their parents. She does not know how to handle the impasse.

You can see how each family situation is different. Perhaps you recognize some of these situations. Or perhaps your own situation is unlike any of these. There are ways of coping with every problem, no matter how big or small. There are also ways of making a reasonably good relationship even better. That's what this book is for: to help you find your own rewarding ways of grandparenting in *your own unique family.*

✎ 2 ✎

So You're Going to Be a Grandparent?

"A granny is jolly and when she laughs a warmness spreads over you."

J. Hawksley, age 11

The call came as she was cutting tomatoes for the salad.

"Mom, guess what?"

"Judy, you sound so excited! There's nothing wrong, is there?"

"No, nothing wrong. I've got good news. I'm pregnant. You're going to be a grandmother."

"You're pregnant? Wonderful!"

"Yes, isn't it marvelous? We didn't want to tell anyone until we were sure. And the doctor's office called just now."

"I'm so happy for you, darling." A note of anxiety crept into her voice. "You're feeling all right, aren't you?"

"I feel great, Mom. I'll probably keep on working right up until the baby comes."

"Well, not that long, I hope. You be sure and talk to your doctor about *that.*"

"Mom, I'm not a little girl anymore. I promise I'll take care of myself. Dad home?"

"Not yet. He had a late meeting."

"Well, I've got to go. Don't tell Dad. I want to tell him myself."

"Oh, Judy, I won't be able to keep it a secret. I'll just have to tell him."

"Well, all right. I've got to go now. I love you, Mom."

"I love you, too, Judy. Take care."

She held the phone in her hand for a full minute after the click told her that her daughter had hung up. Then, slowly, she replaced the receiver.

I wonder why I feel like crying, she thought. She remembered back— how long? it must be almost twenty-eight years—when she was pregnant for the first time herself. How happy she was. How she wanted to tell everyone, even strangers in the market!

She stood there, shaking her head, a slight smile on her face, remembering.

16

Then she caught sight of herself in the little mirror she kept over the sink.

A grandmother, she thought. But grandmothers are old. She remembered her own grandmothers. No, I don't look like them, she thought. Thank goodness for that. My friends Ellen and Lois have grandchildren—it won't be so bad.

She leaned over and looked closely at herself in the mirror, tracing wrinkles under her eyes, around her mouth. She started to cry. And she didn't know why she was crying.

*

I'm going to be a grandfather, he thought. When his wife had told him the news at dinner, his first reaction had been, My *baby* having a baby? It was foolish, of course. His "baby" hadn't been a baby for an awfully long time.

I hope it's a boy, he thought. I wish we'd had a son ourselves. I've never admitted it to anybody, not even to myself, until now. But it would have been nice to have had someone to go camping with, to go to football games with, maybe even to play football with. I wasn't so bad myself in college.

He picked up the paper and tried to concentrate on the news, but the thought of being a grandfather kept crowding all the printed words out of his mind. A grandson. Wouldn't that be something! He reached over and took his wife's hand and squeezed it.

"I kind of hope it'll be a boy," he said.

"As long as it's healthy, I don't mind," she said.

"Excited?" he asked.

"Yes," she said. But she didn't sound it. He looked at her closely. Just my imagination, he thought. He picked up the paper once more and started reading the sports page.

*

No matter what age you are when you become a grandparent, the arrival of your first grandchild forces you to confront the inescapable fact that you are getting older. To a person who has come to terms, psychologically, with the fact of aging, becoming a grandparent for the first time will probably be a fulfilling experience. But to a person who has avoided facing age, becoming a grandparent may provoke very defensive reactions.

Your reaction will be determined to some extent by where you are in relation to the normal "mid-life crisis" most of us go through. The mid-life crisis usually occurs for both sexes somewhere between the ages of forty and fifty. (In women, it usually coincides with the menopause.)

People tend to spend their early life looking forward, as if the future were endless. When the mid-life crisis hits, a person suddenly becomes aware that future time does not stretch out endlessly. No longer does he act, as Thomas Wolfe put it, "as if we were young and twenty and could never die." Intellectually, of course, the middle-aged person knows that everyone ages and finally dies. But now he suddenly realizes at a gut level that *he* is aging and will someday die.

All of his previous life, he has looked *outward:* working at his job, raising children, getting ahead in life, planning for the future. But now, perhaps for the first time in his life, he is forced to look *inward,* to raise questions he may never have faced before: What does my work mean to me? Is it really fulfilling? Is my marriage truly bringing me happiness? What do my children really mean to me? What is the meaning of life and all this striving and working? What's it all for?

All these questions, and more, must be faced and worked through until the answers have become a part of the individual's personality structure. It ordinarily takes at least a year for a person to do this.

There are many people who are not able to handle the mid-life crisis well. These are people like the New York stockbroker who, out of the clear blue sky, left his wife and job and children and fled to Guam to begin a new life as a beachcomber. People do quit their jobs, leave their spouses, flee to another country, take to heavy drinking, or do something else equally foolish in a desperate attempt to run away from the questions life is asking them.

If you happen to become a grandparent while you are going through your mid-life crisis, you may find it difficult to accept your new role gracefully and happily. The hope is, of course, that knowing you can be a loved and important part of your extended family will make grandparenthood exciting. But if the idea of becoming a grandparent disturbs you, one of the wisest things you can do is to make a few visits to a professional counselor—a psychiatrist, psychologist, or psychiatric social worker.

Let us assume, however, that you have already come to terms with the fact that you are growing older. Let's assume that you have looked forward to the day when you will become a grandparent. Then your initial reaction to the news of the pregnancy may still depend a lot on your daughter's (or daughter-in-law's) situation. For example, if you know your daughter has been trying very hard to conceive, you will probably shout with joy when you find out she's finally succeeded. If your daughter is fourteen years old and comes to you to say she is pregnant, you will probably groan in despair.

Obviously, if your child is a minor you are responsible for her. But if your daughter or daughter-in-law is of age and you are *not* responsible for her, you have to remember one very important thing: This is not your baby, and probably you will have very little to say in the matter of its fate. If you can relax and accept this, both you and your grown children will be better off.

When you learn you are going to be a grandparent, try not to blurt out such things as:

"Don't you think you're too young?"

"I think you should be more firmly established in your job."

"How can you afford a baby on your salary?"

Of course, if you are consulted before the fact (which is highly unlikely), by all means give your opinion—but try to do it as tactfully as possible. If you are presented with a *fait accompli,* then remember that your children are entitled to make their own mistakes. You can't write the script for other people, no matter how dearly you may love them and no matter how clearly you think you can see the dangers for which they are heading.

Being oversolicitous is a trap that many prospective grandparents are also likely to fall into:

"You're not planning on using *disposable* diapers?"

"You're going to work right up until *when?*"

"Do you really think an at-home birth is such a good idea?"

"You don't have your layette yet?"

"I know it's your baby, dear, but . . ."

"Now, when I had *my* first child . . ."

Give the prospective mother credit for being a responsible adult, capable of running her own family.

Also give the mother-to-be credit for knowing what's best for her body during her pregnancy. Many women today are more physically and psychologically attuned to childbearing than women were in the past. Many are also very health-conscious and aware of their bodies. As part of this awareness, they know that smoking and drinking are likely to damage the fetus. So if your daughter refuses a cocktail or asks you to stop smoking around her, try to respect her wishes. It's your relationship with your daughter and the health of your grandchild you are protecting.

After the baby is born, you will be even more tempted to offer advice. You may, in your desire to help, perhaps try to take over functions with your grandchild that are none of your business.

Control those impulses!

Here are some guidelines to help you become the kind of grandparent that your grown children will love to have around.

1. Remember that your grown children's children are extensions of their egos. This means that when you say something about the children, it's almost

as if you were saying it about the parents. For example, if you say, "Kim is such a smart baby!" Kim's parents feel complimented and pleased. But if you say something like, "Ricky has a terrible temper!" you are insulting Ricky's parents.

Although it may never enter your mind to criticize your grandchild, even an innocent suggestion about child-raising or discipline can be interpreted as a criticism. That is why you should never tell your grown children, or even remotely suggest to them, how to raise their children. They will always resent it, even if they appear not to.

Dr. Dodson's First Law of Grandparenting is *"Tace!"* (That's Latin for "Zip your lip!") Very rarely will you make a mistake by keeping quiet about something concerning your grandchildren. But very often you can make a mistake by voicing your opinion.

The corollary to this first law is: *Never* give advice to the parents of your grandchildren on *anything* unless you are asked. Many grandparents, seeing their grown children floundering around helplessly in handling an infant or young child, say to themselves, "They'll thank me for giving some good advice that'll help them see a better way to handle things." No, they won't! No matter how badly they are handling things, they'll resent your advice unless they've asked for it.

2. There are two more reasons why you should never tell your children how to raise their children: Either they think they know all about it, or they're afraid they don't.

Your children may have very definite ideas about how they want to raise their children. These ideas may have come from reading or from attending parenting classes, or they may be based on their childhood experience of being raised by you. But regardless of how they developed their ideas, your suggestions about raising the children will be seen as interference, especially if they're determined to raise their children differently from the way they were raised.

If your children feel insecure about raising their child, they will be enormously defensive about it. Your son (or son-in-law) may let some of his buddies give him advice on his golf game and take it calmly. Your daughter (or daughter-in-law) may let a friend give her advice on playing bridge and it'll be no big deal. But bringing up children? That's different. It's different especially if, way down deep, the parents feel terribly unsure of what they are doing. When we have an emotional need to do a particular thing right, our defensiveness about it is always proportionate to our unsureness about it.

3. Your children are bound to make mistakes in raising their children. Like all new parents, they are amateurs. But if you think back, perhaps you will remember how you, too, resented your own parents' telling you how to

raise your children. Accept the fact that your children are going to go ahead and make their own mistakes, just as you did.

In this respect, learning to raise children is no different from learning any other complex skill. When you learn to play tennis or golf or bridge or to be an auto mechanic or a lawyer or a doctor, you literally learn by making thousands of mistakes. So give your grown children the right to learn how to parent by making thousands of mistakes, just as other parents have from time immemorial.

4. There is always the outside chance that your children will ask for your advice on something regarding their children. In that case, you are entitled to say what you think, although you need to be tactful in what you say. But this occasion will seldom arise, and you must be careful not to imagine that it has just because you're itching to give your good advice.

5. As I pointed out in Chapter 1, there will probably be times when you are acting *in loco parentis*—in place of the parents—with your grandchildren. At those times, and *those times only,* you are being a parent to the youngsters. If your adult children criticize the way you handle your grandchildren when you are caring for them, point out that you are acting in place of them, you're doing the best you can, and after all you don't criticize *them.* It is psychologically impossible for you and the parents to handle the children in exactly the same way.

In practical terms, it's best to have a working agreement that when you are baby-sitting, especially at your own house, you will do what you think is best for both you and your grandchildren. Naturally you will avoid treating the children in any way that is likely to cause problems later for the parents.

6. There are bound to be conflicts between parents and grandparents. Conflicts are unavoidable in close relationships. But remember that the success of a relationship should not be judged by the amount of conflict or disagreement, but by the way you handle it.

If your relationship with your children is basically free and nondefensive, when a difficulty arises you can probably handle it by simply stating what you would like. Let's say that twice in the past week your daughter has come by unexpectedly to leave the baby with you while she runs errands. You might say, "I'd appreciate it if you'd give me a call ahead of time when you want me to keep Chuckie, so I can let you know whether I can do it."

But if there is real conflict over the problem—especially if it's something that has been going on for a while—you should express your feelings to your daughter, but *not* tell her what to do. Say, "It bothers me when you bring Chuckie by for me to baby-sit without checking first to see if I have other plans." Telling her how you feel is infinitely better than ordering her to do (or not to do) and the message is just as clear.

Your feelings are mental and emotional states pertaining to you and you alone. In your own individual way you feel joy, love, fear, hurt, anger, and a generalized state that covers several of these: "upset."

Usually when you tell someone else how *you* feel, it does not put that person on the defensive. Unfortunately, most people go immediately from telling other people how they feel to telling *them* what to do about it. In the case of your daughter and Chuckie, you might be tempted to say, "So, dear, please see to it that you call me first the next time." This sounds fairly harmless, but it is almost guaranteed to make Chuckie's mother feel defensive and say to herself, consciously or unconsciously, "I won't if I don't want to!" Any time we tell someone what to do, that other person is going to feel attacked and double his resistance to doing what we would like. Learn to tell other people *only* what your feelings are, and leave up to them what they will do about the situation.

This principle of telling other people how you feel but *not* telling them what to do about it is a very basic concept that makes for good human relationships. As a matter of fact, it's an excellent principle for you to teach your grandchildren when they are old enough to absorb it. But in order to teach it to them, you need to be able to use it effectively yourself. And using it with your grown children is an excellent way of making it a real part of your personality and of the way you deal with other people.

7. Don't sweep problems under the rug. The tendency of most people is not to speak up about their grievances. They try to ignore them. The catch is that the grievances don't go away. They just lie there fermenting in your unconscious mind. Sooner or later they explode, and the situation is much worse than it would have been if you had spoken up in the first place. It may be difficult or unpleasant to confront a problem situation when it first arises, but that's a thousand times easier than dealing with it six months later.

These are the central, basic guidelines for getting along well with the parents of your grandchildren. They are not the only things you need to know. But learning not to interfere, and knowing how to handle problem situations, will go a long way toward creating a healthy, warm psychological environment for you and your children.

✎§ 3 ƺ✑

Discipline as a Teaching Tool for Grandparents

"A grandmother corrects your grammar and wipes imaginary dirt from your cheeks."

Sara Spurrier, age 12

Probably the single most touchy subject between parents and grandparents is the issue of how to discipline. By "discipline" most people mean punishment, something unpleasant done to a child to make her straighten up and fly right. You hear this in comments such as "That kid sure needs some discipline," or "You can see that boy never got any discipline," or "If that were my child I'd discipline her all right—with a paddle!"

Small wonder that parents and grandparents often clash over such an emotion-laden issue!

Rather than use the word *discipline,* I prefer to say *teaching.* For I am talking about helping children to learn a broad range of behavior, much broader than "good" versus "bad." I am talking about teaching children ways of behaving that lead to their becoming happy, confident, productive, and mature adults. I am talking about teaching social and intellectual skills such as learning to love reading, to be self-assertive, to have good sportsmanship.

Even though you and your grown children will almost certainly agree that youngsters should learn such skills, I am not suggesting that you try to force my teaching methods on your grandchild's parents. My intent in this chapter is to help you teach your grandchild social and intellectual skills in ways that will enhance your relationship with him. It's between you and your grandchild, independent of the parents. Perhaps the parents will recognize the value of what you are doing and want to follow your example. That would be wonderful. But if not, don't worry about it. Just "do your own thing" and keep any opinions to yourself.

There have been thousands upon thousands of research studies on how to teach anything to anybody: children, adolescents, adults, chimpanzees, dolphins, guinea pigs, even flatworms! But when we ask ourselves how much

23

most parents and grandparents know about the scientifically researched methods of teaching children, the only honest answer is "Not much!" The average adult's discipline repertoire is something like this:

Parent/grandparent: "Stop doing that, Gloria."

Parent/grandparent: "Gloria, I said stop doing that. Now you pay attention to what I'm telling you."

Parent/grandparent: "Gloria, you stop it this instant or I'm gonna smack you!"

Parent/grandparent: "You want a smacking, don't you? All right, you're gonna get it!"

SMACK!

Parent/grandparent: "There! That'll teach you to mind me from now on." (If you really believe that, you're more naïve than anyone has a right to be who's involved with children!)

And that's typical of how many parents and grandparents try to guide the behavior of children. They threaten. They yell. They scold. They give little lectures. They spank. They take away privileges.

They use all of these inefficient and ineffective methods because nobody has ever taught them any better way. I am going to discuss some better ways.

In teaching or disciplining children, a parent or grandparent is trying to do two different things: First, teach the child desirable behavior, such as picking up his toys, doing schoolwork, loving to read books, or being self-assertive with other children. Second, teach the child to *avoid* undesirable behavior, such as being a bully, not doing schoolwork, being shy or withdrawn with other children, or lying or stealing.

Let's begin with the first category. How do we teach a child desirable behavior? The basic answer is simple, although the ways we work out that answer may sometimes get complex.

Here is the secret of teaching. Make sure you don't ever forget it! *Each action of a child that is followed by a payoff or a reward will be strengthened and will be more likely to occur in the future.*

Near my office in Redondo Beach, California, is Marineland of the Pacific, where different water shows using seals, whales, and dolphins are presented. The trainers teach these animals without using any of the standard methods most parents and grandparents use. They do not yell, scold, lecture, spank, or take away privileges. All of their training is based on the "positive reward system." In small successive steps, the trainer teaches the animal the trick she wants it to learn, rewarding it at the end of each step with a fish. After the animal has finally learned the entire trick, it is rewarded only once—at the end of the trick. The basic principle is simple. The trainer teaches the animal to perform the trick by selectively rewarding its actions and behavior.

Although animals and children are obviously different in many ways, the positive reward system works in much the same way with children. So, *when a child behaves in a desirable way, you follow the desirable behavior with a positive reward or payoff.*

There are two kinds of payoffs. I call the first "love payoffs." These consist of a hug or a kiss, praise such as "I like the way you picked up your toys, Mark," or those very basic words "I love you." Incidentally, it's important not to try to give a love payoff when you don't feel loving (for instance, if you're mad at your husband or someone else). Your irritable mood could poison your love payoff the way vinegar curdles milk.

If you start early in a child's life using love payoffs, they will carry you a long way. But sooner or later, you will need to use what I call "thing payoffs." Some people are under the impression that "thing" rewards are always either money or food. This is not true. There are a great number of possible thing payoffs that are neither food nor money. For example, here's one of the best kinds of payoffs you can use for a very young child (up to the age of two and a half). "If you do such and such, Grandmother will make a funny face for you (*or* dance the jig, *or* stand on her head)." Very young children find that type of performance hilarious and irresistible, so it makes an excellent payoff.

Middle childhood children (ages six to ten) will find other kinds of thing payoffs irresistible. For instance: "If you hang up your clothes, you can go to bed at your regular bedtime, but you can read as late as you want." This is also a delightfully sneaky way of getting the child to read more. What usually happens is that he will read a little and then fall asleep. Caution: Do *not* let the child go to bed and watch TV or listen to the radio or hi-fi. These are too stimulating, and will keep him awake too long.

Let me tell you how I taught some valuable behavior to my youngest child, this time using a financial payoff.

Rusty was ten at the time of this incident. He had always been an excellent reader, reading several grades ahead of his class. But he was not really *into* reading; he would read what was required for school and nothing more. I wanted to get him more involved with reading for the sheer joy of it.

This positive reward system was not something I planned out carefully, but something I more or less stumbled into. We were taking a family vacation in our camper, driving up the coast from California into Oregon with two of Rusty's friends accompanying us. From time to time we would stop at a bookstore and each of us would pick out some paperback books. I remember that Rusty picked out *Papillon, Jonathan Livingston Seagull,* and *Survive the Savage Sea,* the story of a family's shipwreck. I said to the three boys, "Guys, if you read a book and come to me and tell me the story of the book, I'll give you a dollar." I must have chosen a psychologically motivating amount of money, because each boy immediately grabbed a book and began reading.

That night we stopped at Cannon Beach, Oregon. Cannon Beach has no movie theater, but it does have a summer stock theater, and we planned to go to the play that night. We were eating dinner in the camper when Rusty surprised me by asking, "Dad, can I read *Jonathan Livingston Seagull* at the play tonight?"

I was somewhat taken aback and answered, "But, Rusty, how can you read at the theater? We'll be watching the play, and the place will be dark."

"I can read during intermission."

"Well, okay. I guess so."

At the play, Rusty grabbed his book as soon as the intermission lights went on. He read until the intermission was over. This is all the more remarkable because he knew that outside the auditorium was a booth where Cokes and candy bars were sold.

By the end of the trip, Rusty had read seven books and earned seven dollars. But the big behavior change didn't come until later. The trip was in early July. By the middle of November, Rusty had read approximately forty books. He could have come to me and told me the story of each one and earned forty dollars. He didn't bother to. His reading was no longer dependent on an external reward. Reading had become internalized for Rusty as a reward in itself. That camping trip marked a turning point in Rusty's whole attitude toward reading—the beginning of a love of reading for its own sake.

When I first describe a positive reward system for parents or grandparents, a certain percentage of them object to it on the grounds that this is bribing the child. So I'd better deal with that issue right away.

First, let's ask ourselves, "What exactly is a bribe?" A bribe can be defined as money or a gift given to someone to get him to perform an illegal or immoral activity. A contractor gives a building inspector a thousand dollars in cash so that he will overlook several violations of the building code. That is a bribe.

But a positive reward system that uses a chance to stay up later at night and read in bed, a trip to the movies, an ice cream cone, or a small sum of money could not remotely qualify as bribery. For parents or grandparents are not giving these rewards to get children to do anything illegal or immoral. No, they are giving these rewards to get the children to pick up their toys, hang up their clothes, make their beds, read books, become more assertive with other children, and develop other desirable habits that will stand them in good stead as adults.

So please do not think of rewards for positive behavior as bribes. I call them the "wages of childhood." We adults work for wages, and we wouldn't go on working long if we didn't receive them. Well, children also need wages to be stimulated to learn social and intellectual skills we consider beneficial.

Once you understand the system, it is really very simple to use positive rewards with your grandchildren.

Of course, the goals to be achieved need to be checked out with your grandchild's parent to make sure they have the parent's approval. Ordinarily this should be no problem.

First, you decide what social skills you want your grandchildren to learn. Let's suppose they are preschoolers and you want them to learn four basic habits: to hang up their clothes, to make their beds, to brush their teeth, and to pick up their toys at the end of the day. You begin by simply telling them that it's important to do these things. When they do them, you give them a love reward. You praise them for what they've done or give them a hug or a kiss. If the love reward proves not to be sufficiently motivating, you will then need to use something more tangible. A reward they can earn each day is more powerful than a reward they cannot get till the end of the week. Figure out something they like that can be their reward each day for hanging up their clothes, brushing their teeth, or whatever it is you want them to learn.

Remember the underlying idea of this system: *Whatever behavior you want your grandchild to learn, follow that behavior with a reward or pay-off.*

When your grandchild is just learning a new social skill, you need to reward every single desirable action. Then, after he has learned the new skill thoroughly, or the desired behavior has become a habit, you can begin to space out the rewards. You hope that ultimately the child stops needing the reward, just as my son Rusty stopped needing rewards for reading books.

There are other techniques you can use to teach your grandchildren desirable behavior, but the positive reward system is the most basic and the most powerful. If you wish to learn about these other techniques, you can consult my earlier book *How to Discipline with Love.*

It would be nice if the same techniques we use to teach children desirable behavior also worked to teach a child to avoid undesirable behavior. But, unfortunately, it's not that easy. We need an entirely different approach for that.

Probably the single most effective method for teaching children to avoid undesirable behavior is what I call the Time-Out. When a child is doing something that you find unacceptable—perhaps your grandson is whining, or teasing his sister, or throwing his toys across the room, or hitting his brother—here's what you do:

First, you tell the child what his unacceptable behavior is: "Tony, you're teasing your sister."

Second, you give the child a Time-Out. You say, "Tony, you need a Time-Out. Go to your room for a Time-Out. A Time-Out is five minutes long, and I'll tell you when the five minutes are up." (If he doesn't have a room of his own, a bathroom will do nicely.)

If he yells or complains loudly from his room, pay no attention to him. Paying attention to a child during a Time-Out constitutes a reward for complaining, and renders the Time-Out ineffective.

What does the Time-Out accomplish? First, it provides a *geographic* interruption of misbehavior. Tony cannot continue to tease his sister while he's in his room.

Second, it effects a *time* interruption of misbehavior. It provides five minutes during which Tony will not be teasing his sister, and can think of something else to do.

The idea behind this exercise, of course, is that Tony will not resume his misbehavior when he comes out of his room. But if he starts teasing his sister again at the end of the Time-Out, back he goes for another one.

The Time-Out is *not* a punishment, and it should never be administered as one. Give a child a Time-Out in as calm and collected a manner as you can manage. Try not to say something like, "All right for you! I've told you again and again not to tease your sister, and now you're gonna get a Time-Out. Go to your room!" When you give a Time-Out in this way, you are giving the child a reward—the reward of showing him that his actions have upset you. And this negates what you are trying to accomplish.

After you have used the Time-Out a number of times, the child will become accustomed to it. As you start to say, "Tony, you're teasing your sister," you may find him saying in a resigned tone, "I know, I need a Time-Out!" And that's good, for it means he has accepted the habit of the Time-Out.

The positive reward system and the Time-Out will work fine up until adolescence, and then they lose their effectiveness. The reward system, the Time-Out, and various other discipline techniques that are *unilateral* in nature do not work well in adolescence, because at this stage the child is beginning to rebel against the authority of parents and grandparents. The teenager wants to share in that authority, and in the decision-making that affects him or her.

A good approach to handling undesirable behavior in adolescence is the mutual problem-solving technique. This can be likened to the bargaining that goes on between labor and management, in which neither side expects to get all of its demands. Both are prepared to give a little, to negotiate a settlement that both can agree to.

In mutual problem-solving, you begin by defining the problem. "Kenny, now that your parents are off on vacation for two weeks and you're here with us, we're the ones responsible for the rules you need to observe. Well, I think we've got a problem. We said you had to get in by one o'clock on the weekends, and you said you would. But last Friday night it was around four o'clock, and Saturday it was five o'clock. So the problem is that you're not getting home by the time we agreed on."

Now that you have defined the problem and listened to Kenny's response, you tell him how the mutual problem-solving technique works.

"Here's a way we can solve this problem, Kenny. We can use the method of brainstorming, as they do in business. In brainstorming, we try to produce as many ideas as we can for solving the problem, and it doesn't matter how wild or far-out the ideas are. The basic rule of brainstorming is that nobody is allowed to criticize anybody else's ideas. We appoint one person to be secretary and take down and number all the ideas.

"After ten or fifteen minutes of thinking up ideas and jotting them down, we begin to analyze each idea and ask ourselves whether it will solve the problem, and whether we are willing to do it. All three of us—you, your grandmother, and I—have to agree on an idea or we throw it out. Because we know that if all three of us don't agree, the solution won't work out. That's why we don't vote; we have to have unanimous agreement."

So, the three of you produce ideas, and then you analyze them one by one. If some ideas get unanimous agreement, these are the ones you will use to solve the problem. If none of them gets unanimous agreement, you will need to start over with another brainstorming session the following day.

The mutual problem-solving technique is ideal for dealing with teenage misbehavior because it involves the teenager in the decision-making process. Since he is a part of the process, and a decision cannot be made without him, the teenager is much more likely to abide by any agreement that is made. Unfortunately, most adults make completely unilateral decisions about teenagers, with the result that the teenager usually sabotages the decision.

I hope you will seriously consider and try out the new techniques for disciplining and teaching that I've described in this chapter. After all, anybody can use the old "yell and swat" method that other parents and grandparents use, and be as unsuccessful as they often are!

If you do use these new methods, I think you will find your grandchildren an increasing source of pleasure. Instead of keeping a weather eye out for misbehavior, you will continually be on the outlook for things to praise. The more you praise and reward your grandchildren, the more praiseworthy things they will do. And then you and they will be spending more and more enjoyable times together. And that is one of our major objectives in the new extended family.

❧ 4 ❧

How to Talk with Children

"Grandmothers always come up with advice, which is given whether you need it or not."

Rita Bourke

Some of you may feel indignant at the title of this chapter. "What do you mean, how to talk with children? Any grandparent knows how to talk with children."

I disagree. I know that most grown-ups inhabit a world of their own—an entirely different world from the one in which children live. It is often as difficult for a grown-up to talk meaningfully with a child as it is for an American who does not speak Portuguese to talk with a street vendor in Brazil.

But most adults assume that since both they and their children speak the English language, all they need to do is speak and a child will understand. They do not know that children have a completely different set of rules for the English language. If adults don't use these rules, they won't be able to communicate with children.

Another problem is that many adults don't speak *with* children at all. They speak *at* them. They give unasked-for advice. They yell. They lecture. They command. They offer rational answers to children's emotional problems. And when they do all of these things, they fail to notice an interesting phenomenon: The child's ears fall off.

This "missing ear" phenomenon accounts for many of the difficulties between parents and grandparents on the one hand, and grandparents and children on the other.

Grandfather: "Jimmy, it's three o'clock and I told you to take the trash out two hours ago. What's the matter with you?"

Nothing's the matter with him, except that his ears fell off two hours ago when Grampa was talking to him. Grampa just wasn't observant enough to notice it.

If you truly want to learn how to talk with children, I suggest you try the following experiment for a week. Simply listen to other adults talking to children. You will discover that much of their talk is one-directional—from the adult to the child. Adults seem to assume that a child has a great deal to learn from them, but that they themselves cannot possibly learn anything from the child.

Making this scientific observation may increase your motivation to learn how to talk with children.

In learning to talk with children, the first rule is to stop talking so much and *listen.*

You can learn a great deal if you listen. The world of children deals with brute emotional realities that in our adult world are often covered up by rationalized packaging.

Children are really quite fascinating in their views of the world and of people. But adults often do not notice this because they do not take the trouble to listen to children. That's one of the reasons adults and children live in worlds that are isolated from each other.

Next, learn the art of asking questions of children. The secret here is to ask the right kind of questions. Not grown-up questions. Every day millions of school-age children are asked, "What did you learn in school today?" The same answer is given by millions of boys and girls: "Oh, nothing." The reason children give this answer is because it is a question they are not interested in. What you need to learn is to ask questions about things children *are* interested in. For example, "Did you notice that turtle over by the big tree?" or "Did you know that the Littles' dog had puppies yesterday?"

Learn to respond to children's little emotional problems on an *emotional* rather than a rational level. The following story will illustrate what I mean.

Little Jennifer, aged three, has just cut her finger with a kitchen knife, and it's bleeding. She runs to Grandmother.

"Grandma, Grandma, I just cut my finger and it's bleeding. I think I have to go to the hospital!"

"Now, child, that's foolish talk. You're not going to have to go to the hospital with a little cut like that."

"Yes I am, I know I am!" Jennifer begins sobbing. (Grandmother's explanation, while rationally correct, does little to help Jennifer's feelings of distress.)

"Come on, Jennifer. This is nothing to cry about. This is just a little thing. Here, let me put a Band-Aid on it."

"It may be a little thing to you, but it's a big thing to me! And I don't want a Band-Aid; I need to go to the hospital!"

At this point, Grandma throws up her hands in exasperation and thinks, I'll never understand children!

Let's try another version of the same scene, this time with a grandparent who knows that it is not wise to try to meet children's emotional needs with rational answers.

"Grandma, Grandma, I just cut my finger and it's bleeding. I think I have to go to the hospital!"

"Goodness, Jennifer, that's terrible. Let me see it."

Jennifer shows Grandma the bleeding finger.

"Yes, indeed, that certainly is bleeding! You probably will have to go to the hospital. But first let me put some Bactine on it."

Grandma takes Jennifer into the bathroom and puts Bactine on the cut, at the same time giving her some supportive hugs.

"The Bactine will make sure no infection gets in," says Grandma. "Now let's put a Band-Aid on it. That'll stop the bleeding."

Grandma puts on a Band-Aid, and gives Jennifer an encouraging squeeze.

"That feels better, Grandma. Maybe I won't have to go to the hospital after all."

In the first example, both Grandma and Jennifer were, theoretically, speaking the same language. But in reality Jennifer was speaking one kind of English and Grandma was speaking another.

When Jennifer says, "I think I have to go to the hospital," she is speaking children's English. Decoded, her statement means, "I'm very upset about this cut and bleeding finger." But Grandma No. 1 doesn't take it that way. She takes it literally and rationally, and explains to Jennifer that her injury isn't big enough to warrant her going to the hospital.

But Grandma No. 2 understands the code meaning of "I think I have to go to the hospital" and responds at the same emotional level: "You probably will have to go to the hospital." By this statement, she conveys her understanding of Jennifer's distress. (There is plenty of time later to decide whether Jennifer actually needs to go to a hospital.)

Grandma No. 2, whether she realizes it or not, is using the *feedback technique.*

The purpose of the feedback technique is to express to a child that you understand how she feels. Superficial responses such as "I know just how you feel" and "I felt the same when I was your age" will not do the trick. What you need to do to show your understanding can be summarized in the following two steps:

1. Listen carefully to what the child is telling you.

2. Put the child's feelings into your own words, and feed them back to her.

This procedure even has a corrective factor built into it. If you do not succeed in feeding back the child's feelings, she will usually say, "No, that's not how I feel," or other words to that effect.

Let's look at another example. The family has recently moved to a new neighborhood and a strange dog is outside the house, barking. The family's little five-year-old girl is afraid to go outside because of the dog.

First, here's how many parents and grandparents might handle the situation:

Melissa: "Grandpa, I don't want to go outside to play. There's a big dog there and he's barking and I'm scared."

Grandpa: "Nonsense, Melissa. That's just the Petersons' dog next door. He's nothing to be afraid of."

Melissa: "He is too something to be afraid of, Grandpa. He's big and fierce and he might bite me!"

Grandpa: "Melissa, he's not going to bite you at all. I was over at the Petersons' yesterday and I was petting him. And they say he likes children."

Melissa: "Well, he might not like *me*. I'm not going to take a chance on getting bitten. I'm going to stay right here in the house."

Grandpa: "Now, Melissa, this has gone far enough. There's absolutely nothing to be afraid of about that dog! And I'm going to show you how harmless he is. Because you and I are going outside to see that dog right now, young lady." (Grandpa grabs her by the arm.)

Melissa: "Grandpa, no, don't! I'm scared! Let me go! I don't want to get near that fierce dog!" (She begins to cry.)

Grandpa: "Oh, all right! Stay in the house then!" (He throws up his hands in exasperation.)

Notice how Grandpa judges the situation completely from *his* viewpoint— that there is nothing to be afraid of about the Petersons' dog. But Melissa is looking at things from a completely different viewpoint. What she sees is that the Petersons' dog is big, and he barks, and he might bite her. She has not had the experience her grandfather has of safely petting him. And Grandpa makes no effort to understand how Melissa feels. Rather, he tries to force her to accept his view, and is not successful.

Now let's see how the situation could have been handled using the feedback technique.

Melissa: "Grandpa, I don't want to go outside to play. There's a big dog out there and he's barking and I'm scared."

Grandpa: "I see. There's a big dog outside, and he's barking and that scares you."

Melissa: "Yes, and I want to stay inside."

Grandpa: "Can you tell me a little more about what scares you?"

Melissa: "Well, when I hear a dog barking that makes me think he's fierce and might bite me, and besides, this dog is a big one."

Grandpa: "So when a dog barks it makes you think he might bite you, and besides, this dog is big."

Melissa: "That's right. Aren't you scared, Grandpa?"

Grandpa: "No, I'm not scared. But then I know something about this dog that you don't know." (Notice how intriguingly Grandpa puts this.)

Melissa: "What's that?"

Grandpa: "Well, this dog belongs to the Peterson family next door. I was petting him yesterday and he didn't bite me. And the Petersons told me that he likes children."

Melissa: "The Petersons said he likes children?"

Grandpa: "That's right. I'll tell you what I'll do if you want me to. I'll go out and pet him and show you he doesn't bite. You can follow behind me so that if you get scared you can run back into the house. Would that be okay?"

Melissa: "I guess so."

Grandpa goes out of the house, with Melissa following timidly behind him. He goes up to the dog and pets him. He calls back to Melissa.

Grandpa: "See, honey, it's safe to pet him. Would you like to pet him with me?"

Melissa: "You sure it's safe?"

Grandpa: "I'm sure. But you can hold on to my hand if you want to."

Melissa timidly pets the dog, holding on to her grandfather with one hand. Soon she sees that he is a friendly dog and she feels secure enough to drop her grandfather's hand.

Notice that Melissa's grandfather respected her viewpoint that the dog was large and frightening. He accepted and fed back her frightened feelings to show her he understood them. He did not try to coerce her into pretending not to be scared. And he acknowledged her scared feelings by suggesting that she could run back into the house if she wanted to. Later, he told her she could hold on to his hand while she petted the dog—again recognizing that she might still have a residue of scared feelings.

This is merely one example of the way the feedback technique can be used in talking with children or teenagers. If you want further information, see the chapter on the feedback technique in my book *How to Discipline with Love,* or read the excellent book *Parent Effectiveness Training* by Dr. Thomas Gordon.

The world of children is fascinating and entrancing, and adults who go through life without ever entering it are missing a great deal. For when you really *talk* with a six-year-old, you temporarily become six again yourself. As you grow older, your grandchild will help you grow younger at the same time, by keeping you in touch with the delightful kingdom of the young.

Knowing how to talk together is essential in the new extended family. It is so important that I discuss it at some length in Chapter 19, "A Special Chapter for Parents." There I talk about how parents can learn to communicate better with their children and with you, the grandparents. I hope you will be curious enough to read this chapter yourself, for you can learn from it. In any case, be sure to offer it to your grown children to read.

Now that we have covered such basic techniques as discipline methods and how to talk with children, which can be used with grandchildren of any age, I'm going to discuss child development. In the next section of the book I'll start with infancy and outline the important ways in which you can relate to your grandchild through the seven main stages of development, up till the age of twenty-one.

Part Two

Ages and Stages

❦ 5 ❧

Gurgles and Goos: The Stage of Infancy

"Grandmothers are hardly ever cross with you. And without grandmothers, the world would be a different place."
                                                    Harry Bulley, age 11

No one is born knowing how to parent or how to grandparent.

This statement will surely come as a shock to anyone who has been brought up to believe that parenting consists of simply "doing what comes naturally," and that grandparenting works the same way, only more so. Nevertheless, it's true.

As I pointed out in Chapter 1, parents and grandparents need information about child psychology and teaching methods if they are to do a good job of parenting or grandparenting.

One of the most basic facts of child psychology is that children do not grow older and more mature in a smooth, untroubled way. They pass through seven different psychological stages, from birth through adolescence:

> Infancy (birth to approximately the
>   first birthday)
> Toddlerhood (approximately the first
>   to the second birthday)
> First adolescence (approximately the
>   second to the third birthday)
> The preschool stage (approximately the
>   third to the sixth birthday)
> Middle childhood (approximately the
>   sixth to the eleventh birthday)
> Preadolescence (approximately the
>   eleventh to the thirteenth birthday)
> Adolescence (approximately the thirteenth
>   to the twenty-first birthday)

In going from stage to stage, the child basically moves from a stage of equilibrium to a stage of disequilibrium, and then back again. This is something like marching from birth through late adolescence to the rhythm of three steps forward and two steps back. It is very important for parents and grandparents to be aware of this, or they will probably expect the child to be much more mature than he is capable of being at any given stage.

Let's say your first grandchild, a girl, has recently been born. What information do you need about child psychology to understand the first stage of her development, the stage of infancy?

In each stage of development, your granddaughter must face and master a particular developmental task if she is to proceed successfully to the next stage. The developmental task of infancy is to acquire her basic outlook on life. Your granddaughter will acquire a feeling of *basic trust* about life, or a feeling of *basic distrust,* or something in between.

Most parents do a pretty good job of helping their babies develop a happy and optimistic view of life. Your infant granddaughter will acquire such a viewpoint if her basic needs are met—that is, if she is fed when she is hungry and given cuddling, if she has a deep and fulfilling emotional relationship with her mother and father, and if she receives sensory and intellectual stimulation to aid in her general intellectual development.

What can you, as a grandparent, do to help the parents in this very important first stage of development?

As the time of the birth of a grandchild draws closer, you may wonder about helping when your daughter or daughter-in-law goes to the hospital to have the baby, and/or after she gets out. You may feel you should volunteer to help, or you may be asked to. Here are some factors to be considered before you reach any decision.

First, what kind of relationship do you have with the mother-to-be? Some men and women have warm and loving relationships with their grown children and children-in-law. For others, the relationship is far from ideal.

If for any reason you and your child (or you and your child's spouse) do not get along very well, consider carefully before you go to help. The birth of a new baby is a happy event, but, unfortunately, it brings with it a lot of tensions. New parents, especially new mothers, are often tired and insecure. Their lives are changing in complex and unsuspected ways. Both husband and wife are having to adjust not only to a new baby, but also to seeing each other in the new roles of father and mother. If you do not have a good relationship with both parents, you may only add to the tension.

Second, do you like babies? Show some people a baby and they immediately pick it up, put it on their knee, and start kitchy-cooing. Others give it a polite smile and keep their distance. Some grandparents aren't baby-oriented, not even toward their own grandchildren. So if babies don't appeal to you, don't pretend that they do. That's just the way you are. And don't let anybody make you feel guilty and "unnatural." Don't let outmoded stereotypes drive you into a situation you know is not right for you.

Third, is it convenient for everyone for you to help? If you are coming from out of town, is there room for you to stay, and will you be comfortable? It's one thing to sleep in a bed. It's still another to sleep on a couch. And it's another yet to sleep on the living room floor in a sleeping bag, with an air mattress, especially a leaky one. In other words, the situation may require that you rough it, but you may not be the roughing-it type. You may become grouchy if you can't get a good night's sleep. Or your back/arthritis/slipped disc/you-name-it may make it necessary for you to have a certain type of mattress. Remember, you can't help anybody else if you're going to need help yourself.

If such problems exist, then either don't go to help the new parents, or examine the possibility of staying with friends or relatives, or at a hotel. Don't forget to look into available transportation. If people have to drive you back and forth over long distances, you may not be so helpful after all.

If you do decide, for whatever reason, that you can't go to help the parents, please don't feel guilty. You've spent a good many years bringing up your own children. If they are old enough to have kids of their own, they should be able to manage without you, even if it causes them some inconvenience.

All right, let's say you feel you are capable of helping and want to do it. Now ask yourself: Are you *really* needed? Look carefully at the situation. Is there a sister, an aunt, a friend, or even another grandparent who could do the job as well as you? If so, volunteer to help but say you won't feel hurt if the parents turn you down. And when you say that, be sure you mean it!

If neither you nor anyone else can go to help out, you could consider the gift of household help—a live-in nurse when the new mother and baby come back from the hospital, or a cleaning person to come in on a regular basis.

Once the baby has arrived, if you are on the scene to help, what can you do?

What you can do will depend mainly upon the kind of relationship you have with the new parents. If it's one of free, open, nondefensive communication, then there is very little you *cannot* do if they request your help. And a mother with her first baby is, of course, inexperienced. This means she will often worry about things an experienced mother would hardly think about. She might, for instance, be afraid that some minor change in her baby's eating or sleeping patterns means that something is drastically wrong with the infant.

To put it in a nutshell, a new mother is usually an expert at making mountains out of molehills. A grandmother, who should be a seasoned hand at new babies, can usually help the mother reduce the mountains back to molehills.

On the other hand, the new mother may not allow you to play the role of older, more experienced comforter to her. Her attitude might be: "I may be scared to death of handling this new baby, *but it's mine,* and I'm not going to let anyone give me any advice!" If you sense that this is her feeling, then bite your tongue, bide your time, and wait until she decides to ask for help. Perhaps she never will! But you can only make matters worse by pushing her to hear advice she is determined not to listen to.

In this respect, the new mother may be relating to you the way a teenager relates to her parents. As I am writing these pages, my son Rusty is fourteen years old. I have had to learn to resist the temptation to give him advice about anything at this stage of his life. Advice from me, even if he obviously needs it, is almost sure to prompt a reaction something like this: "Dad, just keep out of this, will you? After all, you're old and senile now and can hardly be expected to keep up with modern developments." So I only offer my advice at times when *he* approaches *me* and says something like, "Hey, Dad, I'm kind of stuck on this. Would you give me a hand and help me figure it out?"

So the first role you can play—but *only* if your children will allow you to—is that of an older and more experienced basketball coach helping out a new coach in his first season.

A role that seems to come very naturally to grandparents is that of baby-sitter. Baby-sitting gives you a chance to enjoy the baby while being of real help to your grown children. It is psychologically very important for parents to have time away from their baby so that they can relate for a while as husband and wife, rather than as father and mother. Particularly with a first baby, the parents (especially the mother) can easily develop bad cases of parental cabin fever. A weekend off, or even an evening out, can do wonders to restore their morale.

But it is very important that you baby-sit *only* when you feel like it. If the parents ask you to baby-sit when you don't feel like it, or can't (you are going to a show that evening, you are down with a cold, you are cross or tired), tell them you're sorry, but you are not available at that time. Offer to pay for someone else to baby-sit instead, if you can afford it.

You may feel that if you don't have a "good reason" not to, you should baby-sit whether you feel like it or not. But if you do, deep down inside you will feel imposed upon and angry. And that is the recipe for a disastrous blowup between you and your children, sooner or later.

It is highly important for parents and grandparents to develop the habit of open and "up front" communication during the baby's infancy. It sets the pattern for your relationship as the child grows. If something is bothering you, speak up about it! It may make things bristly at times, but this is better by far in the long run than keeping grievances to yourself, which will silently sabotage the relationship.

Here are a few tips on baby-sitting. Some of these apply to older children as well as infants.

1. When the child is an infant and sleeps most of the time, it may be easier for the parents to bring the baby to you, rather than for you to go to their house, if transportation is a problem for you.

2. When the child is a toddler and gets into everything, it may be easier for you to sit at your grandchild's house, which should be fairly childproof. If there are several grandchildren involved, it's usually easier to sit at their home anyway.

3. Let's say you have several children and they all have children. There is no law written on stone tablets that requires you to give equal baby-sitting time to all of them. Life isn't always fair, and you can't be expected to divide your baby-sitting time the way you divided the last piece of cake when your children were young. You need time for yourself. Let your children sit for one another.

4. When you do sit, make sure you have the following telephone numbers handy:

> Child's doctor
> Nearest poison center
> Paramedics
> Fire department
> Police station

5. Always have a phone number where the parents can be reached. If they are on an extended trip, get an itinerary, and ask them to call home regularly.

Your relationship with your grandchild's parents is, of course, extremely important. But now let's go on to that other most important subject—your relationship with your grandchild herself.

Some of the things I'm going to suggest here are things you may not have done with your own children when they were babies. But try them out anyway and see if you enjoy them. Remember that being a grandparent is in some respects a chance to be a more relaxed parent than you were able to be years ago.

Whether you are aware of it or not, you probably have two great advantages in building a good relationship with your grandchild and exerting a positive, helpful influence on her life. One advantage I'm *sure* you have, and the other one I hope you have.

The first is leisure time. Whether they are still working or retired, grandparents nearly always have more leisure time than parents do. This means you probably have lots of time to do interesting things with your grandchildren. And even with an infant there are more interesting things to do than you perhaps realize.

The second advantage I hope you have is a relatively mellow attitude toward children. You will probably not be so uptight, finicky, and perfectionist with your grandchildren as you may have been with your children. Over the years as a parent you have learned what children are *really* like, as opposed to what you used to think they *ought* to be like. If you were overprotective as a parent, if you were critical, if you were domineering, you will probably be much less so as a grandparent.

Okay, you are a proud, mellow grandparent with a lot of time to spend with this terrific baby. You would treat a grandchild of either sex the same way at this age, but for the sake of our discussion let's say this one is a girl. Here's how you start building your relationship with her.

First of all, talk to your granddaughter from the very beginning. Maybe this is something you did as a parent, but, if not, it's time to start. Don't give her a bottle feeding or burp her or give her a bath or change her diaper in silence. Say things to her in your own unique way—for example, "Hey, kiddo, it's your wonderful grandmother again with a bottle for you," or "You lucky rascal, Grandpa's got a terrific bath for you. Now how do you like that?"

If you've never talked to a baby before, you may ask, "What's the sense of talking to the baby when she can't talk back?" The sense is this: Babies learn to talk by being talked to. Even though she is not able to talk back yet, every word, every sentence you say to her is being stored up in her computer brain in that lovely little head of hers. And when you are talking to her, you are helping her oral language development by feeding her with words.

Many people think children begin to learn to read when they are in the first grade and their teacher is working on their reading. Not so. Children begin to learn to read when they are young babies and somebody begins talking to them. Make no mistake about it, learning to read does not begin with learning the alphabet, phonics, and books. It begins with being talked to.

If you are a grandfather rather than a grandmother, I will bet my bottom dollar you didn't talk to your own children when they were babies. Typically, fathers are afraid they will seem silly or unmasculine if they spend time taking care of babies, because that just isn't a father's role.

Well, now's your chance to be different. And if you've never had the experience of bottle feeding a child, burping her, giving her a bath, or changing a diaper, why not try these things now and see if you like them?

And, while you're doing all of these things, talk or sing to the baby. I used to do this with my own children.

I happened to be a very unusual father with my babies, breaking away from the male stereotypes of that day. I bottle fed my children, changed their diapers, gave them baths, and talked and sang to them. My songs generally weren't traditional nursery-type songs. I leaned more toward "The Erie Canal," "The Eyes of Texas," and "Red River Valley." But the kids seemed to like them. I was doing something that both of us enjoyed, and stimulating the children's language development at the same time.

Talking to your grandchild, singing to her, and cuddling her are all expressions of love. In responding to you she is learning much more than just language. She is learning to be a loving human being.

When your grandchild gets to be about nine months old, you can begin to play a little game with her that will aid both her language development and the general growth of her intelligence. I call it the Label the Environment Game. You begin to teach her the names of everything in her environment.

When you feed her some banana, say "banana." When you give her the soap in the bathtub, say "soap." When you feed her with a spoon, say "spoon." And so on, naming everything she comes in contact with. This may seem like a relatively minor thing to you, but it will be doing great things for her rapidly developing little intellect.

Soon your grandchild will be ready to leave the stage of infancy. She will begin to walk and enter the stage of toddlerhood. Let's look back at what she should have learned in this first stage of development.

We hope she has learned a basic sense of trust and optimism about life.

If she has been fed when she is hungry, she has learned that the world is a friendly place, one in which her hunger is quickly satisfied.

If someone has always responded quickly to her crying, she has learned that people will come to her when she needs them.

If she has gotten a lot of cuddling, she has learned that she is loved in a way that is very meaningful to her: via physical contact.

If she has experienced close, warm, loving relationships with her parents and her grandparents, she has begun to learn how to establish satisfying emotional relationships with the other human beings she will come in contact with throughout her life.

And if she has received sensory and intellectual stimulation from toys and other objects, activities, and experiences such as the Label the Environment Game, she has found that the world is a fascinating and interesting place.

If your grandchild has experienced all of these things in her first year of life, you can be sure she has formed a good sense of basic trust about her world. And you can enjoy a sense of quiet satisfaction, knowing that this basic trust will give her the best possible preparation for all of her succeeding stages of psychological development.

≈§ 6 §≈

The Young Explorer: The Stage of Toddlerhood

"Grandparents do the same things as parents, only they're nicer."

Shelley Eastman, age 11

Grandparents and babies usually go together very well. There the baby is, the little darling, sleeping quietly in her crib or waking up to be fed and looking adorable. But toddlers are different. Toddlers have taken a giant step forward. They have learned to walk. And this gives them instant mobility around the house and yard. Often Grandma and Grandpa are two steps behind their toddler as she manages to get into things they didn't dream such a young child could get into. So grandparents and toddlers may often have a hard time with each other. (By toddlers, I mean children between the onset of walking and roughly the second birthday.)

But this problem exists only when there is a purely adult environment in your home. Toddlers can't get on very well in such an environment because they can only act like toddlers. To expect a toddler to act like an adult would be as foolish as putting an agile little monkey in your house and expecting *him* to behave like an adult.

The problem vanishes, however, if you change the environment to suit the toddler. Unless you plan to have a purely one-way schedule of visits— always going to visit your grandchild, but never having him visit you—you will need to do *something* about childproofing your house anyway.

I am going to talk about safety precautions to take in childproofing your house for children under the age of six, but particularly for children under the age of three. Obviously, the younger the child is the less judgment she has, and the greater the likelihood of accident or injury.

I hope the following pages don't frighten you, because that is certainly not what they're intended to do. What I want to do is simply increase your awareness of the possible dangers that lurk in your house (or anybody else's house) for an active, exploring child. Most people, because they look at a house from an adult perspective, are not aware of the various things toddlers can get into that can hurt them. This is no doubt the basic reason that, in the United States every year, approximately seventeen million children are injured accidentally. One child in three is injured severely enough to require medical attention, or to have his activities restricted for several days.

Many adults don't realize how easy it is for toddlers to get hold of liquids or other substances that could injure or kill them. Yet poisoning is one of the most common emergencies for pediatricians. Each year more than five hundred thousand children swallow household materials left within reach, and many die. The death rate from swallowing poisonous substances is higher for children under four than for any other age group.

Those of you who have had your grandchildren visiting constantly since they were infants already know how many precautions you need to take when there are children in the house. However, if your grandchildren's visits have been infrequent, you may have forgotten how much children—especially toddlers—can get into.

Toddlers combine great curiosity with mobility. Some of the things they do may merely annoy you—tearing up your favorite magazine, or scribbling on the wall. But other things may be downright dangerous—pulling down a pot from the stove, or sticking a finger in an electric socket. Here are some of the things you can do to make your home a safe environment for your grandchild's visit.

Remove breakables from tabletops and reachable shelves. Electric wall sockets not in use can be plugged with devices made just for this purpose—you'll find these at a hardware store. If you are celebrating Christmas, consider putting the tree with its enticing ornaments in a playpen. If you can't keep the child away from the tree, you can keep the tree away from the child.

When you cook, all pot handles should be turned in to the center of the stove. When something has to cook for a long time, make sure it simmers on the *back* burner. Don't leave anything cooking when a child is in the kitchen unattended. If anyone does get burned, remember that ice cubes are better for a burn than butter.

Never assume that something is safe just because you've put it up high. Toddlers are adept at dragging chairs over to use as ladders.

Toddlers love to taste everything. Household cleaning products, the kind you usually store under the sink, may contain caustic materials so swift-acting that the child can be hurt by taking just one taste. Find out which local hospital has a poison control center, and keep its phone number handy. Post the phone number of the nearest paramedics, too. Buy locks for cupboards, and use them.

Some children are cautious about tasting things in unfamiliar containers but will not hesitate to eat or drink from what looks like a familiar one. For this reason, never, *never,* NEVER NEVER store kerosene, cleaning solvent, or *anything* inedible in old soda pop bottles.

Grandparents who are gardeners need to realize that even a little taste of some fertilizers and insecticides can be fatal, and just touching them without gloves can cause skin irritations. Gardening tools have sharp edges, too. All these things must be kept out of your grandchild's reach.

No one would ever leave medications lying about where a child could get at them. But many women carry medications in their purses, which curious toddlers can get into. Brightly colored pills can be mistaken for candy. Store your purses well out of sight and reach, and ask any women guests to either let you put theirs away, or to keep them with them at all times.

It doesn't take much alcohol to make a child drunk. Many of us leave unfinished drinks around when we leave the room, especially when we are entertaining. When you or your guests are through drinking, clear away glasses and empty any remains into the sink.

Smokers should be careful not to leave cigarettes, pipe tobacco, or cigars around. Toddlers are mightily tempted to chew on these (and somehow, cigars are their favorites).

Tobacco may be intriguing, but the materials to light it with are even more so. Matches are an endless source of fascination to children, and a child can click on a lighter, without intending to, merely by handling it.

When a child accidentally starts a fire, he is often too frightened to tell anyone. If your little grandson starts a fire, he may first try to put it out himself—usually without success. Or he may run and hide in a closet. By the time he summons help—if he does—the room may be ablaze.

Do warn children about matches. Insist that they call you immediately if a fire should start. Have as many smoke alarms in your home as are necessary for its size. Keep a fire extinguisher handy.

One of the most important things you might ever do for your grandchildren is to have a fire drill to show them the escape routes to use in the event of a fire. You can do this without frightening them simply by "playing it cool" and being matter-of-fact about it. Children aren't frightened by fire drills at school, and there's no reason for them to be frightened by a fire drill at your house.

Always remember that in the event of a fire your best bet is to get out of the building *fast* and call the fire department from another building. Fire spreads with devastating swiftness.

What should you do if your grandchild gets hold of some medicine or substance he's not supposed to, and swallows it?

First, induce vomiting, unless the child is unconscious or having convulsions, or the poison he took is acid or lye.

The easiest way to induce vomiting is with syrup of ipecac. This is a nonprescription drug that you should keep on hand for a possible emergency. If your grandson is under a year of age, give him a teaspoon of syrup of ipecac and then a glass of water. If he is over a year old, give a tablespoonful, and then a glass of water. If no vomiting occurs within twenty minutes you can repeat the dose, *but only once.*

If the child has taken acid or lye, however, *do not* try to induce vomiting. Give him milk or water to dilute the poison.

Next, call your doctor or poison control center for advice. Describe the substance your grandchild swallowed as carefully as you can.

The reason toddlers are so vulnerable to poisons is that they put everything into their mouths. This is part of the toddler's exploring urge. Your young grandson is not being naughty—he just wants to see how everything tastes and feels to his tongue and mouth. You need to learn to be eagle-eyed as you scan the floor for buttons, beads, hairpins, small stones, or little pieces of broken objects, for you don't want your grandchild to swallow them.

For fairly obvious reasons, toys for children of this age should have no sharp edges, should be too large to swallow, and should be too tough to break. (For example, you should not buy toys made of tin for a toddler.) Also be sure the toy has no small removable parts the child can put in his mouth.

Even shallow water is dangerous for an unattended toddler. It takes only seconds for a child to drown. Never leave your grandchild alone in the bathtub or wading pool, or around open or frozen bodies of water.

Be sure that your grandchild cannot suddenly get out of a safe area of the house and into a dangerous one. Lock or otherwise secure doors that lead to stairways, driveways, and storage areas. If you use fasteners such as hooks, make sure they are out of reach of the toddler.

And finally, don't forget that your automobile is part of the environment of your home and that it, too, needs to be made safe for your grandchild. Travel beds are not usually safe in the car, and many children's seats provide inadequate protection. When shopping for a car seat, check the label to see that the seat complies with Federal Motor Vehicle Safety Standard 213. Look for the words "dynamically tested," which means that the car seat has been tested in a crash situation. Carefully follow the manufacturer's instructions for installing the seat and securing your grandchild in it.

At this point, you may be thinking, "It sounds as if you're asking me to make my house into a fortress! How can I enjoy my grandchild if I have to be on the lookout for a thousand dangers?"

The answer to this is "Think how bad you would feel if your grandchild got hurt because of your ignorance or carelessness." It does take some careful planning and a number of precautions to childproof your home. But a visit that is not a safe one can never be a happy one.

Besides, once you have taken the proper safety precautions, you can relax and enjoy watching your grandchild explore his environment. Toddlers are delightful to observe in action, because they are so absolutely charmed and fascinated with all of the world around them. For example: A toddler is sitting in his sandbox, happily gumming, one after the other, a bunch of plastic cowboys and Indians. Anyone who has not observed a scene like this has missed out on one of the keen delights of child-raising.

Another snapshot of a toddler in action: She has accidentally knocked over a glass of water on her lunch tray. The ecstatic expression on her face as she attempts to pick up the drops of water is indescribable.

There is a delightful innocence in a toddler that you will find in no other stage of childhood. Ordinarily, a toddler will not defy or deliberately oppose you. Your grandson may sometimes not pay attention to you—he is busy going about his self-appointed task of exploring the universe. But he will ordinarily not defy you the way a two-and-a-half-year-old will.

As a baby, your grandson could do little more than lie in his crib. But the toddler, with his gift of locomotion, has entered the Age of Exploration. He explores everything. He seems especially interested in obtaining his Ph.D. on the undersides of things. No one else in the family will be such an expert as he is on the underside of, say, the dining room table.

The developmental task of the infant was to build up a basic trust in the world. This is a passive kind of learning, because the baby is dependent upon others to minister to his needs: to provide food, cuddling, baths, diaper changes.

The toddler's learning is active, because the child explores his own world. The toddler's basic developmental task is *to learn self-confidence*.

Your toddler grandson will learn self-confidence if he is simply allowed to explore his world unhindered. But if he is hedged in with a thousand no-no's as he attempts to explore, he will learn *self-doubt* instead. And that (aside from safety considerations) is why you need to create a "toddler world" for him in at least part of your house and yard. If this special world is accident-proof and full of stimulating toys and play equipment, you will have little need for no-no's.

The toddler also needs an environment that gives him ample opportunity to work off the immense energy nature has endowed him with, and to develop both his large and small muscles. He needs an environment in which he can build his self-confidence in many different ways and with many different things. He needs to learn to feel confident of his growing abilities to walk and run and climb and jump. He needs to play with cars and trucks, to build with blocks, to play with sand and dirt and water, dolls and stuffed animals, rhythms and sounds. And he needs to socialize with his parents and grandparents, to babble and experiment with speech patterns as his language skills develop, to listen to nursery rhymes and learn them by heart, to play with books and have adults read to him.

Playing, in fact, is the toddler's main way of learning about life. And you, as a grandparent, can provide him with toys and other play equipment, and make yourself available as a playmate.

Let's start with the kind of play that helps toddlers develop their large muscles—running, jumping, climbing, crawling, pulling, and hauling.

If you have a yard the toddler can play in, that's great. If your yard is a beautifully manicured and landscaped thing with no room for a toddler, or if you live in an apartment, you may have to take your grandchild to a nearby playground for his large muscle development. But even if you do have a suitable yard, it's a good idea to take him to a playground sometimes, because the playground environment especially suits a toddler.

Your toddler needs some kind of climbing equipment in his play space. An ideal piece of outdoor climbing equipment is called the geodesic dome climber. It is built on the geodesic principles set forth by Buckminster Fuller. Because of the strength of the geodesic principle of construction, the dome climber will safely hold as many children as can climb onto it.

The dome climber will foster your toddler's climbing ability and increase his self-confidence in handling himself physically. It can also be covered with a piece of canvas, a tarp, an old sheet, or the like and used as an igloo, fort, tepee, tent, or any other dwelling your grandchild's dramatic play calls for. The dome climber is ideal for the toddler age, and it will be used enthusiastically up to age six. This type of outdoor play equipment may not be practical for all grandparents, but if you do have space for it in your yard, I heartily recommend it.

The problem with the dome climber is that it is hard to get; very few stores stock it. If you find that you aren't able to get it locally, you can order it by mail from Childcraft (see Appendix A). A jungle gym is a good second choice—not as versatile as a dome climber, but still a very good piece of climbing equipment for a toddler, and for preschoolers as well.

The next most important piece of outdoor play equipment is a sandbox.

You can buy one, but it's even better if you make your own, or have it made, because then you can make it large enough for several children to sit in. Along with the sandbox, your toddler will need such sand toys as cups, spoons, pie pans, sifters, and cans of various sizes. A used coffee percolator makes a fascinating toy in itself for a toddler, and also works as a good sand toy.

Sand is an endlessly fascinating material which does unpredictable things. A toddler delights in running it through his fingers, messing in it, building mounds and clumps out of it, and making designs in it. Sand play develops the child's imagination and encourages spontaneous curiosity about the nature of substances in the universe.

The sandbox is also a wonderful environment for playing with toy cars, trucks, buildings, cowboys and Indians, animals, dinosaurs, and armies. Toy people and animals made of plastic can be bought in any toy store, and one of their great advantages is that they can be left outside in the sandbox without being damaged.

A supply of large wooden or plastic hollow blocks, together with a few wide boards, will be used with delight by your toddler for all sorts of activities that develop his large muscles. If you can't find a place to buy large hollow blocks, you might make them yourself, or hire someone to make them.

Please don't let your toddler play outside by himself unless you have a sturdy, smooth fence too high for him to climb (that means six feet high). Otherwise the child may get outside the yard and into possible danger.

The most versatile piece of play equipment for your toddler's *indoor* environment is the indoor gym house, which, at this writing, is available through Childcraft (see Appendix A). Your toddler can do many things with this excellent toy. He can climb on it, slide down its slide, walk up both its steps as well as the slide, and climb on its rungs. Like the dome climber, the gym house can be draped with a piece of cloth or canvas and used as a fort, tepee, or what have you. And your grandchild will use it heavily for several years.

Please don't feel that you have to get every single piece of play equipment I have mentioned here. If you have space, and your grandchildren spend considerable time at your house, I do recommend all of it. But my main purpose here has been to open your eyes to play equipment you may not have been aware of, and to show you what it can do for your grandchild.

With all of the equipment I just have mentioned, you can play with your grandchild or just sit back contentedly and watch him play. But there are other kinds of play in which he needs you as an active participant. Language "play" is one of these.

What you do with your grandchild in these early toddler and preschool years can affect his future education and his success as an adult.

For your grandchild's early oral language development is the foundation for his later reading.

When it comes to reading, most adult Americans do not function on a very high level. The book-buying habits of adult Americans are an indication of how poorly they have been taught a love of books and of reading: The figures show that just 20 percent of adults account for more than 80 percent of all the books bought and read in the United States. So you can't expect your grandchild to automatically learn to love reading.

Chances are you have more leisure time than anyone else to spend helping your toddler develop a love of language and of books. All the other gifts you can give him will be as nothing compared to the gift of language development and a love of books.

During toddlerhood you can continue to play the Label the Environment Game I talked about in the last chapter. Your toddler will love to have you point out and name various things in his environment. He will also begin to be able to name them himself when you point to them.

Two books will particularly aid you in this language game: *Richard Scarry's Best Word Book Ever* and Dr. Seuss's *The Cat in the Hat Beginner Book Dictionary.* Each of them contains pictures of a myriad of things, together with their names. These are books your grandchild will love to use with you, and later by himself. Both of them will help to develop not only his oral language skills but his general intelligence as well. (Incidentally, Richard Scarry has written a large group of books that are particularly loved by toddlers. Consult Appendix B for the names of these.)

Toddlerhood is the time to begin reading nursery rhymes to your grandchild. Surprisingly enough, there are only two types of nursery rhymes available to English-speaking toddlers. There are the Mother Goose rhymes, available in a number of different editions, and there is my own book of modern nursery rhymes, *I Wish I Had a Computer That Makes Waffles.*

There are some Mother Goose rhymes that I think are fine for toddlers— for example, "Hickory, Dickory, Dock." But others contain outdated words that are confusing for today's children, or offer poor role models ("The Old Woman Who Lived in the Shoe") or are sexist ("Peter, Peter Pumpkin Eater").

I must confess I am biased in favor of *I Wish I Had a Computer That Makes Waffles* as a collection of rhymes that are both educational and up-to-date. By reading these rhymes to your grandchild, you will teach him some addition and subtraction, the concept of zero, counting, various "position" concepts such as up, down, behind, beside, safety lessons, and concepts of his feelings and his relationship to both parents and grandparents. It is a book you can begin reading to your grandchild at age one and a half and continue using till he is six.

I hope you have gotten my message about what is happening in the stage of toddlerhood. A great deal of learning is going on! And the learning that occurs in toddlerhood is of immense importance to the future success and happiness of your grandchild.

During this stage, your grandchild is learning or perfecting many large and small muscle skills. His imagination is being stretched. He is exploring his world tirelessly, examining everything he can get his hands (and mouth!) on. His oral language development can take giant strides if you help. He can begin to learn a love of books and reading that can be extremely important to him in the years ahead. But, above all, your toddler grandchild is learning *self-confidence.*

Toddlerhood can be a delightful stage for you as a grandparent. During this fascinating period you can participate in your grandchild's learning process and enjoy his wide-eyed romance with the universe.

❧ 7 ❧

Mr. Yes-and-No: The Stage of First Adolescence

"A grandmother is a mother who has a second chance."
Caroline Flitcroft, age 11

Toddlerhood begins when a child learns to walk and lasts till approximately the second birthday. First adolescence begins at approximately the second birthday and lasts till approximately the third. Notice the word *approximately.* These stages *do not* begin and end at fixed chronological moments. Some children go through them roughly "on time," but some go through them earlier, and others later. The important thing about every developmental stage is not the exact timing, but the progress toward psychological maturity as the child moves from stage to stage.

It would certainly be easier for parents and grandparents if a child moved smoothly and gently from stage to stage as she progressed toward maturity. But, as I said in Chapter 5, the reality is that Mother Nature has arranged for children to move from stages of equilibrium to stages of disequilibrium as they grow up. We can define *equilibrium* and *disequilibrium* very simply. Your grandchild is in a stage of equilibrium when she is a pleasure to have around. She is in a stage of disequilibrium when she is generally obnoxious.

Toddlerhood is a stage of equilibrium. But first adolescence is a stage of disequilibrium. At about the time the child turns three, she enters another stage of equilibrium, and so on. (An easy way to remember these ages and stages is to keep in mind that the even-numbered ages, two and four, are usually times of disequilibrium, and the odd-numbered ages, one, three, and five, are times of equilibrium.)

If you are not prepared for it and have no idea what is going on inside your grandchild's head, the stage of first adolescence may overwhelm you. There is no doubt that your two-year-old grandchild is in a state of disequilibrium! This stage is known to millions of parents as "the terrible twos," and with good reason.

56

The first adolescent can be very demanding. At this age your grand-daughter wants what she wants when she wants it. And she wants it right away! Everything has to be her way. It is difficult for her to compromise or adapt to others. She insists that things be done exactly the same way each time. Woe betide Grandfather if he leaves out a word of one of her favorite stories!

And, while she insists that things be done in a certain, precise way, she can also veer back and forth wildly in her own behavior.

My son Randy was two and a half and in the stage of first adolescence when his older sister, Robin, who was eight, had just completed a puppet-making class. After the performance which closed the class, the teacher invited Randy and other younger brothers and sisters to join the five older children in the class for an ice cream treat.

Randy climbed into the station wagon, but then got out again. "No, I dowanna go," he announced.

"Okay, Randy, you don't have to go," I said.

The group prepared to drive off without him.

"Wait!" he shouted. "I do want to go!"

He climbed back into the station wagon. As they prepared once more to drive off, once more he shouted, "No, I'm not gonna go!" He started to open the door and climb out of the station wagon again.

At this point I decided to intervene. I figured that, basically, he wanted to go, in spite of his vacillation. I knew he would be unhappy when the other children came back from the ice cream store and he hadn't gotten any ice cream.

So I said, "Randy, I know you'll be happier if you go," and shoved him gently back into the station wagon while he screamed, "No, no!"

That's what I mean by the kind of behavior that might get on the nerves of a parent or grandparent. But there's more. The first adolescent often acts like the Little Emperor of the house. In your grandson's mind, there are three ways of doing things: your way, the right way, and his way. And as he looks at it, the right way and his way are the same thing. He is domineering, and loves to issue orders.

First adolescence is an age of violent emotions, with frequent changes of mood, many outbursts of tears, and temper tantrums. At this stage your grandson can be Mr. Broken Record. He can go on, and on, and on, and on, and on, and on with one particular word or speech pattern until you are ready to climb the walls. It is often difficult to introduce new things to him, such as new foods or new clothes. He likes the security of the old, the tried and true. His ability to share, to wait, and to take turns is very limited. He can sorely try the patience of a parent or grandparent.

By this time you may be thinking, "Holy smoke, isn't there anything good about a child at this stage?"

Yes, there is, but it's not apparent on the surface. It's because the good is there that I vastly prefer the name "first adolescence" for this stage to the name "terrible twos." "Terrible twos" merely describes the child's outward obnoxious behavior. But "first adolescence" describes the positive growth forces that are operating in the child's mind, that are behind the trying surface behavior.

First adolescence is similar to the teenage years, or second adolescence. Both are transition stages. The latter is a transition from childhood to adulthood. The former is a transition from babyhood to childhood. Both are periods of growth, but also of considerable emotional upheaval.

Although your toddler grandson can walk and get around, he is still basically a baby in his mental outlook. The English call the toddler "a runabout baby," and he is exactly that. In order to enter true childhood, he must go through a period of transition, which is first adolescence.

Let me use this analogy: It's as if the toddler owns an old house on a nice lot. He wants to build a brand-new house, but first he has to tear down the old one. The old house is babyhood, with all of its mental mechanisms and ways of thinking. The new house he will build is childhood.

Now you can begin to see the reason for all your grandchild's irritating behavior in this stage. I often say it's a good thing for a parent or grandparent to remember that there is a "crazy center" in the brain of every teenager that causes him to behave crazily or obnoxiously. I'm convinced that the same thing is true of the first adolescent. Of course I'm not really serious about the existence of a "crazy center," but using that description may help you as a grandparent to keep your composure. You can get some emotional detachment from the difficult behavior of your grandchild at times by saying to yourself, "Oh, oh! There goes his crazy center again!"

The developmental task of first adolescence is to establish *self-identity.* To do this, the child must necessarily resist *social control.* The new house he is building on his lot is his self-identity and selfhood as a *child* rather than a baby.

It is important for you, as a grandparent, to recognize that negative self-identity precedes positive self-identity. Again, in this respect first adolescence resembles the teenage years. A young teenage boy (thirteen or fourteen) hasn't the faintest idea of what *he* wants. All he knows is what he *doesn't* want. And what he doesn't want is to be like his parents. He doesn't want to hear the same kind of music they hear, cut his hair the way they cut theirs, wear clothes that are like theirs, and so on. He has to rebel against his parents and what they stand for before he can find out who *he* is and what *he* stands for.

The first adolescent is going through a similar experience. It seems at times as if whatever your grandson's parents want him to do is precisely the thing he *doesn't* want to do. His favorite word is "NO!"

Not only is your grandchild rebellious at this age, but he is shuttling back and forth emotionally between his desire to forge ahead and become a full-fledged child, and the urge to retreat back to the safety of babyhood. At times he will indignantly spurn his parents' or grandparents' help in getting dressed, with a scornful, "I'll do it myself!" At other times he will suddenly go limp and proclaim that Grandma must do it all for him. The first adolescent swings back and forth from one day to the next, from one *hour* to the next, between his wish to be independent and his babyish desire to remain dependent on his parents and grandparents. He is Mr. Yes-and-No.

Because of this ambivalence, it is a mistake to insist on any absolute set of rules about dressing, bath time, bedtime, or anything else for a child of this age. It is wise to have firm and consistent rules beginning when the child is about three. But in first adolescence, it is well to remember Emerson's counsel: "A foolish consistency is the hobgoblin of little minds."

So how do you handle the child at this age?

I'd say that the most important thing is for you to keep firmly in your mind the *positive growth toward maturity* that is going on in your grandchild. Remember that as your granddaughter tears down her old house, she is also taking positive steps toward the building of a new house on the property. When the first adolescent is rebelling against you, defying you, and generally making a nuisance of herself, she is tearing down the old house of babyhood. Her rebellion may not seem positive to you at first glance, *but it is*. If you can keep your mind on this important point, it will help you to be less annoyed by your grandchild's behavior, for you will understand the reason for it.

It is also important to keep your requirements of the child to a minimum. This is not the time to be after her to pick up her toys, make her bed, or hang up her clothes. Please don't take this to mean that you should not expect her to do these things at a later stage of development, such as age three. But, for now, easy does it. When a child is experiencing the disequilibrium of first adolescence, we should not expect the same behavior as when she is in a stage of equilibrium.

When your granddaughter is in first adolescence, try to arrange to spend most of your time with her in things that are sheer fun for both of you and involve little risk of frustration or emotional upset. For example, an hour or two on the playground in the park should be full of fun and relatively frustration-free. On the other hand, fishing is full of potential frustration, for the child may not catch any fish (or as many as she wants). Miniature golf will also be very frustrating if the child can't hit the ball into the hole. So fill your time with activities like going to the playground and try to avoid activities requiring skill and patience.

You can try the positive reward system, the Time-Out, and other discipline techniques you have learned. But don't be surprised if they don't work at this stage! They will certainly work later (beginning at about age three), and they *may* work now, so they're worth trying. Do use the feedback technique of talking with your grandchild at this stage, because it should prove very helpful.

And now, a special word about how to handle tantrums, because this is usually the stage when they reach their peak. In the classic tantrum, the child rolls on the floor, kicking and screaming lustily. This is the ultimate in negativism, and many parents and grandparents have a great deal of trouble handling it.

First, what not to do: Many times a tantrum occurs when the child doesn't get his way. So, above all, don't give in to the tantrum and let your grandson have what he wants. If you do that, you are rewarding him for having the tantrum, and, of course, that will teach him to have more of them.

Don't try to talk to a child or reason with him when he is having a tantrum. You cannot get through to him then, for he is a boiling sea of emotions. Don't yell at him, for you will reinforce tantrum behavior by doing that. The child will realize that he can upset you any time he wants by having a tantrum.

Above all, don't try to get a child over a tantrum by threatening to spank him or by actually spanking him. We have all heard parents say to a child in the midst of a tantrum, "Stop that crying this instant, or I'll *really* give you something to cry about!" This is the equivalent of attempting to put out a fire by pouring gasoline on it.

What *should* you do about a tantrum? Convey to the child that you know he feels the need to have this tantrum, but that it will get him absolutely nowhere. How do you convey this? *You ignore the tantrum.* This means tantrum behavior gets absolutely no reward or reinforcement from you. And if you ignore your grandson each time he has a tantrum, the tantrums should grow weaker and weaker and finally disappear.

But what if your grandchild throws a tantrum not at home, but at the market or drugstore or shopping center? In a public place, your fear of "What will the neighbors think?" may get in the way of handling the tantrum wisely.

You are afraid other people are thinking, "What is the matter with that grandmother? She must be one of those wishy-washy types. Why doesn't she clamp down on that little boy and put a stop to that tantrum?" And if they are thinking such thoughts, so what? Are you raising your grandchild to be happy and psychologically healthy, or to please the neighbors? Handle the tantrum the same way in public as you do at home. Or if you can manage it, try not to let your fear of what the neighbors will think change what you know of how to handle the tantrum wisely.

It may seem to you that I've painted a rather dismal picture of first adolescence. But remember that among children there is a wide range of temperaments, so that while one child may go through an obnoxious first adolescence, another may have only a mildly difficult one.

I'd like to say just a few words on the subject of toilet training. This is something that parents, and especially mothers, often feel very strongly about. Each mother will have her own particular way of toilet training (even if she actually knows very little about how to go about it), and she usually doesn't want anybody else interfering.

In view of most mothers' defensiveness about this issue, it is wise for grandparents to go along with whatever method of toilet training the parents are using. Even if you feel strongly that their method is wrong, hold your peace. It is highly unlikely that voicing your disagreement over toilet training will change the parents' minds. All it will do is to drive a wedge between you and the parents. It's not worth it.

However, it may be that instead of being merely a part-time parent or a baby-sitter, you are doing the major share of raising your grandchild. Perhaps, for example, your daughter is divorced or widowed and working. In such a situation, it will be you, not she, who does the basic job of toilet training the child.

In this case, I suggest you refer to my earlier book *How to Parent* (pp. 139–43). There I give a simple, step-by-step approach to follow in toilet training a child.

Now, let's turn to a different aspect of first adolescence—learning through play.

Many of the toys and much of the play equipment from the stage of toddlerhood (such as the indoor gym house and the sandbox) will continue to be eagerly used by your granddaughter. But now she will be ready for new play equipment in keeping with her new level of maturity.

Since, during toilet training, she is being asked to give up any "messing" she may have done with the products of her own body, you should now offer her the opportunity to "mess" with sand, dirt, water, play-dough, clay, and paint.

Water play is very important to a child at this age. She will use the kitchen sink or bathtub. In fact, "taking a bath" is mainly a time of water play for a young child, rather than a time to scrub herself clean. A handful of soap flakes and some water toys will add variety and spice to water play.

A child at this age also loves to "paint" outside with water. This is something grandparents may not be familiar with. A large paintbrush and a pail of water are all she needs. She can "paint" the fence, her toys, or whatever she fancies.

Play-dough and clay are very relaxing for a first adolescent. She is not worried about creating any particular form. She just loves the material and delights in squeezing, folding, pounding, and shaping it.

Here is a very simple recipe for making your own dough. Mix two cups of flour with one cup of salt. Add just enough water to make it the consistency of bread dough. If it becomes too sticky, add more flour. By varying the recipe you can get dough of different textures. You can add a sprinkle of food coloring or dried tempera paint for color. You can also add a little bit of cinnamon or nutmeg (or any other sweet spice) to make it smell good. One or two drops of oil of cloves will preserve it for a long time. It can be stored in a plastic bag, and will keep for approximately a month.

Crayons, which are not recommended for use by toddlers (they will often eat them), can now make their appearance. Crayons for the first adolescent should be large and sturdy, not tiny things.

Your grandchild can also be introduced to painting at this age. You will need water-soluble paint, which comes in either liquid or powder form, and a liberal supply of paper. You can use newspaper and the child can paint over the print. Or you can use blank newsprint paper or wrapping paper. If you live anywhere near a newspaper printing plant, you can ask them for a "core" of unused newsprint left over from a printing run. Most newspapers have these cores standing around the room where the paper is run off, and will be glad to let you have one. Just one core will last a youngster a long, long time. Big sheets of paper are far better for your grandchild to use than the smaller sizes.

At this age your grandchild needs paintbrushes that are easy for her to handle. Instead of small brushes with tiny handles, give her big ones with long handles, with a bristle width of about three-quarters of an inch.

Most adults, when they see a young child's picture, make the mistake of asking, "What is it?" To a first adolescent, what she paints is not a "picture" in the usual sense of the word. To her, it is an experiment in color and line, and the *experience* of working on the painting is what counts. She is expressing important feelings through her painting, but she has no words for them yet. So don't ask, "What is it?" Instead, say, "Tell me about it."

This brings up a question you may have been wondering about. What is the value of all this messing about with play-dough or clay or crayons or paints? Is it really so important to go to all this trouble for a young child? Yes, it is! Your first adolescent has not yet learned to put into words all that she feels. Nonverbal activities such as working with clay or crayons or paints help her to express both the feelings for which she has no words as yet, and feelings for which she will never have words. These activities nourish and develop your grandchild's feeling life. They enrich her unconscious thinking, her creativity, her intuition.

In the stage of first adolescence your granddaughter is typically active and noisy. But even at this rambunctious age she can begin to learn to play quietly, if you teach her.

A particularly good quiet game is the Silence Game. Introduce it like this, being sure to call it a game, for young children like almost anything that is called a game. "Katie, I have a brand-new game you and I can play. It's called the Silence Game. Both of us will be just as quiet and silent as we can and listen to whatever we can hear. Shhh! Listen very silently and then tell me what you heard." Katie will then tell you whatever she can hear: the sound of birds, or a radio playing in the house next door, or a car down the street, or whatever.

The Silence Game is a very versatile one for a child of this age. It helps to train her to be quiet and listen. It can be used to calm her down when you are exhausted by her overactivity.

A variation of the Silence Game goes like this: "Now, Katie, listen just as quietly as you can and I'm going to whisper something in your ear very softly. See if you can hear it." Then whisper some simple direction for her to follow, such as, "Get up and walk over to the front door and touch it." After giving her several such directions, and having her give several to you, you can end the game by whispering to her where she can find some small surprise or treat you have hidden for her.

It's important to know something about the ability of a first adolescent to play with other children. Most parents and grandparents think their youngster is now old enough to play with several other children her age for an hour or so at a time. They believe she should be capable of taking her turn patiently, and of sharing with others. They don't know it, but they are expecting their two-year-old to be able to play with the maturity of a three-year-old.

And she can't. She can only play like a two-year-old.

One playmate at a time is a good rule for the first adolescent, because she is not yet ready to be a good member of any play group. She cannot as yet deal with the complexities of more than one personal relationship at a time. And you should not expect her to be able to share her toys or take her turn graciously with other children.

Interestingly enough, an older child, one of five or six, is often the best playmate for a first adolescent. But the older child must not be a brother or sister due to the factor of sibling jealousy.

During first adolescence, your granddaughter is not yet ready for truly cooperative play with another child. Rather, she engages in what is called *parallel play*. This means that two or more children may occupy the same play environment, and they may seem at a glance to be "playing together." They are not. The play of one will be completely unrelated to that of another, even though they may take pleasure in each other's proximity.

During first adolescence, your grandchild's language development takes a giant step forward. She shows a heightened sensitivity to words, the building blocks of language. To borrow an incisive phrase from Dr. Arnold Gesell, she is "word hungry." She loves to play with words, to imitate sounds, and to repeat familiar word rhymes. Her love for nursery rhymes in the toddler stage is nothing compared to what it is now, so you should continue to read to her during this period.

As you read nursery rhymes to your granddaughter, she learns many things besides the rhymes themselves. She learns to listen and to pay attention. (You can reflect on the importance of learning to listen carefully the next time you ask a clerk in a store to get you anything, or the next time you have to ask a telephone operator for assistance.)

She is also developing her memory, a very important asset in school and later life. She doesn't develop her memory by your drilling her on the rhymes, however. As you read them over and over to her, she will spontaneously remember them.

I want to conclude this chapter by calling your attention to the dynamic personality structure of a child in first adolescence.

It is rather ironic that while parents and grandparents want their youngsters to grow up to be forceful and dynamic adults, they often cannot accept these qualities of personality when a child is two years old. But a first adolescent is certainly nothing if not forceful and dynamic!

Your first adolescent's personality will never pass unnoticed. She is enthusiastically and totally committed to the world as she knows it. She protests lustily against restraints and rules. She has a hearty, rollicking, sensuous enjoyment of life, and demands that life be lived in the *now*.

All the things that make your grandchild a genuine person have come from this dynamism. Without her dynamic drive, she would not have learned to sit, to crawl, to walk, or to speak a language. This dynamic quality is a very important psychological resource. Do not be afraid of it, or try too quickly to "civilize" the child. Foster her dynamic life force and treat it as a valuable asset, not as something to be bleached out of her.

Think of your first adolescent as a proud, wild horse whose wildness needs to be respected, but who later on in life may become a Derby winner.

❧ 8 ❧

The Magic Years: The Preschool Stage

"A granddad is a person you never forget, never. I'm proud he's my granddad. And I'll never forget his hand in mine as we walk down the street together."

Suzanne Cairns, age 13

You will probably breathe a sigh of relief when your grandchild graduates from first adolescence and moves into the preschool stage, which goes from about age three to about age six.

This is a delightful stage. The three-year-old, as I have said, is in a state of equilibrium. At this age your grandson is a happy, cooperative, and delightful child. The four-year-old is feisty and difficult at times, but nowhere near as difficult as the two-year-old. And the five-year-old is in a wonderful stage, at peace with himself, his parents and grandparents, and the world around him.

Of all the stages children go through, this is probably my favorite. The children have a naïveté and innocence that are charming. The pseudosophistication of the school years has not yet set in. Preschool-age children are generally very interested in doing things with you, in contrast to school-age children, who would much rather spend time with their peers.

Now that your grandson is a preschooler, he is much more articulate. You can understand what he is asking for. You can hold a conversation with him. Preschoolers will generally speak their feelings and thoughts freely— again in contrast to the child of six to ten, who tends to reveal his feelings only to his peer group.

Many, many important things are going on in your grandchild's mind and body during this stage, and these three years are extremely vital for both his emotional and his intellectual development.

An indication of just how crucial this stage is can be seen in the fact that there has been only *one* developmental task for each of the three previous stages, but the preschooler faces no fewer than *nine* different developmental tasks. Some of them, of course, have begun in other stages, but they come to full flower in this one.

66

Here are the tasks:

1. To fulfill her biological needs for both large and small muscle development.
2. To develop a control system for her impulses.
3. To emotionally separate herself from her mother.
4. To learn the give-and-take of peer-group relationships.
5. To learn to express or repress her feelings.
6. To establish her gender identity.
7. To form her basic attitudes toward sexuality.
8. To work through the resolution of the "family romance."
9. To go through a period of development when she is particularly responsive to intellectual stimulation.

Let's take these developmental tasks one by one and see how you can help your grandchild to master each.

First, the child must fulfill her biological needs for both large and small muscle development. The practical meaning of this for you, as a grandparent, is that preschoolers are rarely still. They run. They jump. They climb. They ride all over the place on their trikes. They yell. They slam doors. When a three- or four- or five-year-old needs to exercise his muscles and work off the enormous energy Mother Nature gives him, he simply cannot do it in a calm and genteel manner.

If you take your three-year-old grandson to a movie, for example, he will probably go to the bathroom, get popcorn, slide his seat back and forth, and kick the seat in front of him—all during the first fifteen minutes of the show! It's important that you know this is normal three-year-old behavior. Your grandchild is not hyperactive. He's just a normal, active, boisterous, wiggly preschooler.

For the same reason that it is difficult to enjoy a movie with your preschooler (unless you go to a drive-in), it can be aggravating to take him out to dinner. A few preschoolers can be quiet and contain themselves well enough, but most cannot. I remember one scene I witnessed between a father and mother and their three-year-old:

"Sit down on that seat—you're going to behave yourself in this restaurant," said the father sternly.

The little boy continued to climb around on the sofa seat, and started to get down on the floor.

The mother took a hand. "Now, Jimmy, we all came out to dinner to have a nice time, so do as Daddy says and don't make him mad."

The boy paid no attention, and continued to explore the floor.

The father grabbed him and put him up on the seat. "Now you sit there! Can't you sit still?"

I wanted to say, "No, he can't sit still! He's only three years old. And you couldn't sit still either when you were three!"

The boy started to climb down to the floor again, and at this the father exploded. He grabbed the boy, held him up about an inch from his nose, and shouted, "Now you're going to sit still so we can all have a nice dinner or I'm going to give you the worst spanking you ever had in your life!"

At this the boy broke into a loud wail that could be heard all over the restaurant, and he sobbed fiercely for about ten minutes. Let us mercifully draw a curtain over this little drama, which started out as a pleasant dinner only to end up as a disaster for all concerned.

The simple fact is that a three-year-old is not able to be quiet and wait, without anything at all to occupy him, for more than a few minutes at a time. So if you are the kind of grandparent who expects young children to behave like little ladies and gentlemen, it will probably be best for you not to take your preschool-age grandson to places like restaurants and movie theaters. Instead, take him to a playground or a park. You can pack a picnic lunch. You won't have to worry about his manners or how loud he is. And he can climb on the playground equipment or play in the sand as long as he likes, whooping and hollering and saying, "Hey, Grampa, look at me!" If you're worried about what people think about the noise your preschooler makes, you can leave that worry behind at a playground or a park.

Some youngsters are quieter than others, and your preschool-age grandchild might not give you any trouble at all at the movies. In this book, I can only deal with preschoolers-in-general. And, of course, your grandchild is a unique little person. You need to ask yourself (and experiment to find out), "What kind of places can I take Allen where he will not cause a fuss, but can handle the situation adequately?"

But a preschooler is not a tornado on wheels. Indeed, this is the stage when most grandparents are delighted to find that their grandchildren are starting to turn into real people.

Preschoolers may appear to be perpetual-motion machines. But if you observe them carefully, you will notice that they are gradually getting their emotions and impulses under control. The two-year-old who howled in frustration because he couldn't tie his shoes is giving way to the three-year-old who is able to take it in stride if he can't immediately accomplish what he sets out to do. Not only does he have better muscular control, so that he really can do more things, but he is developing a sense of psychological maturity as well.

Three-year-olds are capable of playing with other children. If your grandson sees a toy in someone else's hands, he doesn't immediately rush over to grab it. Preschoolers are beginning to learn the rudiments of sharing.

Preschoolers are even starting to develop patience—a behavior change that you, as a grandparent, are bound to appreciate. When you are in the middle of doing something important and your grandchild wants your attention, you no longer risk a temper tantrum if you don't immediately pay attention to his demands. But learning to be patient does not happen overnight, so you will have to exercise some patience yourself. Imagine this situation:

You have promised your granddaughter a trip to the zoo. But the phone rings just as you are about to leave the house. It's a friend with some very interesting news, and you want to hear all of it. *You* know the zoo will still be there if you start fifteen minutes later.

But your granddaughter doesn't know it. Besides, your phone call isn't at all interesting to her. To her, it appears that you are not keeping your promise. By the time you finally get off the phone she is probably going to be whiny and sulky, and you are likely to become annoyed because, to your way of thinking, she is acting so unreasonably.

But time is not the same thing to preschoolers that it is to adults. Young children live in only one kind of time: *now-time.* And you need to take this into account when dealing with them. So don't spoil the whole zoo trip by trying to force your granddaughter's sense of time (which is really nonexistent) to conform with your adult sense of time.

Even though your granddaughter has probably made enormous progress since she was two, she is still only capable of acting like a preschooler. She is *not* a pint-sized adult.

Your grandchild's need to develop his muscles and work off his enormous energy means he needs play equipment that will allow him to do just that. This is where the dome climber I referred to in Chapter 6 comes into its own. I know of no outdoor toy that gives your grandchild a better opportunity for climbing and muscle development. If your yard will accommodate this sturdy piece of equipment you will find it an excellent investment (in spite of its purchase price) because of the years of use your grandchild will get out of it.

But don't neglect your grandson's *small* muscle development. Before he can learn the thumb-and-finger grasping of a pencil that is necessary for writing, he needs to have plenty of practice in scribbling. Where in his house can the average preschool child get practice in scribbling? Nowhere, except forbidden places such as walls.

If you have a separate room for your grandchild, where he can stay regularly overnight and which is used for nothing else, you can solve the scribbling problem with one simple, unorthodox solution. Go to a paint store and buy some blackboard paint. Cover every wall in your grandchild's room with blackboard paint. Then provide him with chalk and let him go to it! He can scribble to his heart's content, developing his thumb-finger small muscle coordination and having a wonderful time. Later he can print and draw pictures on those blackboard walls, and later still he can write on them. Those four blackboard walls will be invaluable to his intellectual development. (Incidentally, a huge blackboard has a fascination for a young child that a piece of paper does not.)

Of course I realize that this unorthodox use of an extra room will not be practical for many grandparents. But you can certainly provide your grandchild with a blackboard. Go to a toy store or educational supply store and get the biggest blackboard you can find and/or afford.

The second developmental task for the child at this stage is to develop a control system for impulses. The child began to learn self-control in toddlerhood. But even though the control system is developing nicely by the time the child is three, it is by no means *fully* developed. Learning to control his impulses is not easy for a child to do. A child's control system usually is not mature and fully developed until he is six years old.

I still remember vividly a scene that took place when my older son, Randy, was three. We had childproofed our house and reduced the no-no's to three, one of which was that Randy was not to play with the books in a floor-to-ceiling bookcase that extended the length of the hall. One day I spied him in front of the bookcase taking down one book after another. Each time he grabbed a book, he would mutter to himself, "No, no!"

An uninformed person might have looked at Randy and that scene and said, "What's the matter with him? Doesn't he know the meaning of no?" Certainly he knew the meaning of "no." That's why he said "No, no" to himself as he pulled the books out! But he had not fully developed the ability to control his impulses, and had given in to the temptation to play with those fascinating books.

Because it takes time for children to be able to say "no" to their impulses, you cannot rush them. But many grandparents do rush their grandchildren, expecting them to develop control systems overnight. They believe that for a young child to be able to control his impulses, all he needs is a system of STOP and GO lights in his head. When the child sees a red light in his head, he stops doing what he is doing; when he sees a green light, he goes ahead. But it isn't anywhere near as simple as that.

Here is a much better model of the process: Suppose that a young child is going to learn a complex sport, such as tennis. Only a very naïve tennis coach would say to the child, "Now toss the ball high in the air, hit it at this angle with your racket, be sure to follow through with your arm, and you will have a good serve." Ridiculous. The child must keep several things in his mind at once and practice them many times in order to develop a good serve. The same goes for a forehand, a backhand, a volley, and a lob, not to mention the total strategy of court play. And all these things must be practiced and mastered *together* if the child is to play a good game of tennis.

So forget about STOP and GO lights in the head. Instead, think of learning to play tennis and how complex it is and how long it takes. This will help you not to expect too much too soon of your grandchild when he is developing impulse control.

Above all, remember the positive reward system. Praise your grandson for what he has accomplished with regard to control of his impulses, and say nothing about what he has not yet accomplished.

The next two developmental tasks go together. The child must separate from his mother, and learn the give-and-take of relationships with his peers.

When your grandson is two years old, he is still very dependent on his mother. He circles around her the way a planet circles around the sun. But by the time he is three, that situation has changed. He is now ready to begin to separate from her and be off on his own.

This also means that he is ready to spend more time playing with other children and learning the give-and-take of peer relationships. He knows his mother accepts him just as he is, simply because he is her son. But he soon perceives that boys and girls he meets are a different story. They do not give him an unqualified stamp of approval. At times, they even reject him.

So the preschooler learns that the world of his peers is different from home. It is a new world, with new rules and new demands. In this new world, the child learns a whole new set of socialization skills that he could not possibly learn within the family circle. He learns how to wait his turn, how to stand up for his rights, how to share, how to put his feelings into words, how to develop self-confidence in handling other children. These are human relations skills he will use throughout life.

You are probably thinking, "But what on earth can I, as a grandparent, do to help my grandchild separate from his mother and learn to deal with other children?"

There is nothing you can do directly, but there is something you can do *indirectly* that can help your grandchild enormously in mastering these developmental tasks.

Grandparents often help out with the expenses of sending a grandchild to college, but very few of them think of helping to send a child to nursery school. Possibly this is because many adults, including grandparents, think that nothing very important of an educational nature goes on in nursery school. Adults often view nursery schools as large baby-sitting agencies. Nothing could be further from the truth. Actually, some of the best teaching in America goes on in nursery schools.

First of all, nursery school helps a child to separate psychologically from his mother. He is put in a room with fifteen other children and a new strange adult, the teacher. And his mother is not around. (By the way, I recommend that a three-year-old start out in nursery school for two days a week, then increase to three days a week, and finally work up to five days a week. This way, the trauma of separating from mother is kept to a minimum.)

As the child in nursery school learns to function without his mother, he also learns to relate to the fifteen other children, some of them more and some less assertive than he is. This is an extremely valuable experience for him. If he begins learning peer-relation skills at age three, he is going to be psychologically far ahead of the child who does not learn them until kindergarten.

But separating from his mother and learning to handle peer relationships are not the only important things your grandchild can get out of nursery school. At nursery school he will receive an enormous amount of intellectual stimulation, which will give him a good head start with the rest of his education. Depending on the curriculum of the nursery school he attends, he may learn printing, preparation for reading, preschool math, preschool science, and many other things. Books will be read to him, and he may also learn to dictate his own stories to his teacher, who will print them for him in the form of "his own book." He should thus develop a solid foundation for loving books and reading in later years.

I doubt that you could find a more meaningful gift for a grandchild than a three-year scholarship to nursery school. I am assuming that the child's parents will be delighted to have him attend. Let them pick out the school; you won't want to give the impression that you're running the whole show. Your job is simply to provide the money that makes nursery school possible.

The preschooler's fifth developmental task is to learn to express or repress his feelings.

I would guess that most of you grandparents were raised in the same way I was—that is, we definitely were *not* allowed to express our feelings to our parents or grandparents, or to any other adults. I was not even allowed to contradict my parents or grandparents. If my mother told me that Athens was the capital of Italy and I said, "No, mother, it's Rome," my mother would retort, "Don't you contradict me, young man!" Of course, telling your parents or grandparents that you were mad at them or hated them was *absolutely* forbidden. I remember that I had my mouth washed out with yellow soap four or five times for saying such awful things.

If you, too, were raised this way, you may believe that children should not be allowed to express any negative feelings to grown-ups. Even if you have become familiar enough with psychology to know that it's good to allow children to express their feelings, it may still be difficult for you to actually allow them to do it. Your own upbringing gets in the way. That's certainly the way it is with me.

I know from my scientific training that it's much better to allow children to express their feelings than to make them keep the feelings locked up inside. But sometimes when I am allowing one of my children to sound off at me, I hear a little voice inside my head saying, "Don't you dare talk that way to me; I'm your father!" That's not the voice of my scientific training. That's the voice of my own father, sounding forth from my childhood.

Just about every psychiatric syndrome that psychologists and psychiatrists encounter involves the inability of the person to express feelings, whether it's anxiety attacks, phobias, depressions, psychosomatic symptoms, or schizophrenia.

Let me cite just one case as an example. A young man of twenty-eight, married, worked in a factory where a train came into the work yard every day to deliver raw materials. The young man began to have this obsessive thought every time the train pulled in: "Throw yourself in front of the train and kill yourself." This persistent impulse to kill himself was very frightening to him, and he sought help through psychotherapy.

Through psychological tests and interviews, I determined what was going on in the young man's mind to cause this disturbing thought. From time to time, he would feel angry with his wife. But he had been taught as a child not to express negative feelings, so he couldn't express them to his wife now. Unfortunately, feelings don't just disappear when they are held back; they find someplace else to go. Since the young man couldn't release his feelings by putting them in words to the appropriate person, they became turned against himself. His anger became the impulse to hurt himself by casting himself in front of the train.

I invited the man's wife in for a special session and told her what was happening to her husband. I asked her to help me cure him by being a cotherapist. She was delighted to do whatever she could. I explained to her how he felt whenever he got mad at her. If he looked angry but said nothing, she was to help him by saying things like, "You look angry. I'll bet you're just hopping mad at what I said." Also, she was to give support to the idea that all married people get angry at each other from time to time and that it is normal for them to do so. (I made the same comments when he came in for his therapy sessions with me.)

I think it was mainly due to the influence of his wife that this young man made such rapid progress. Soon he was daring to speak up to her and tell her off. He found that, contrary to what he feared, this did not break up the marriage, but became an accepted part of the relationship.

When the young man was able to express his angry feelings to his wife, the voice telling him to throw himself under the train began to fade out of his life. In five months it was gone. He had been cured of that cruel, torturing voice by learning to reveal his negative feelings. But, of course, had he been allowed to voice his feelings as a child, he might never have developed any psychological symptoms at all.

So allowing your little granddaughter to express her feelings, both negative and positive, could be insurance against her having to spend time in a psychologist's or psychiatrist's office as an adult.

A person who can talk out her feelings will probably have a better marital relationship and more rewarding friendships than a person who keeps her feelings bottled up inside. Moreover, a person who can speak up to her boss and colleagues may be more successful in her work than a person who lets grievances fester. And, of course, a child who is allowed to speak her mind will be able to join in give-and-take with all the generations of her extended family.

The preschool stage is the right time to give your grandchild the precious gift of the right to express her feelings. I'm sure you're not going to have any trouble with positive feelings. I have yet to hear a grandparent object to hearing, "Oh, Grandma, you're wonderful—I just love you!" No, it's "Grandma, you're mean and I don't like you!" that gets put on the *verboten* list.

But think a bit. Does it really harm you for your granddaughter to say, "I'm mad at you," or "You're mean and I don't like you"? Whether you allow her to express these sentiments or not, she's going to think them. If you let her get the negative feelings off her chest, they will soon be replaced by positive feelings. But negative feelings that are not aired tend to hang around, blocking out positive ones.

By now you're probably thinking, "Yes, but what do I *do* when she says these negative things? How do I handle them?"

You handle them by using the feedback technique I discussed in Chapter 4. Let your grandchild express whatever feelings she has—love, warmth, hostility, joy, fear, sadness, etc.—and then put those feelings into your own words to show that you truly understand. Remember, the idea is to feed the child's feelings back to her, saying things like, "You're mad at me because I won't let you play outside in the rain," or "You're disappointed because it's Tommy's turn to lick the cake bowl, not yours."

You do *not* "correct" your granddaughter's feelings or moralize to her about them. You merely feed her feelings back to her. And nothing else. You are like a voice-activated tape recorder. When she has finished talking, you put her feelings in your own words and feed them back. Then you keep quiet until she expresses her feelings again. When you use this simple but powerful method of handling her communications, you show your grand-daughter that you truly understand how she feels.

Please don't jump to the conclusion that I am recommending that you let your grandchildren do whatever they want. Heaven forbid that I should recommend such a foolish and dangerous policy of child-raising. What I have been talking about is letting your grandchildren express their *feelings* freely. I am decidedly *not* recommending that you let them indulge in whatever *actions* they wish. Actions can get kids into a lot of trouble. But communications are merely the expression of feelings put into words.

The preschooler's sixth developmental task is to establish gender identity.

There is no such thing as a unisex child, any more than there is any such thing as a unisex adult. There are boys and girls. There are men and women. And though males and females have much in common as human beings, they are also different in many ways. It is the differences I'm talking about when I refer to gender identity. Obviously, it is important for a boy to be comfortable in his gender identity as a male, and for a girl to be comfortable in her gender identity as a female.

Unfortunately, up until relatively recent times male and female role models and identities have tended to be rather rigid and inflexible. Many of these models have had the effect of "putting down" girls, often in very subtle ways.

We first encounter this with picture books for the preschooler. Just at the stage when children are in the process of developing their own gender identities, and when they are very impressionable little people, they are presented with stereotypes.

The first thing you will notice if you look carefully at these books is that women are invisible. Most children's books are about boys, men, and male animals, and most of them deal exclusively with male adventure. Females are underrepresented in the central roles and stories of almost any picture book you can find. The conclusion most children draw from this is that boys and men are important, while girls and women are second-class citizens. How can girls be very important when nobody bothers to write books about them?

A close study of children's books will also show that, in general, boys are active and girls are passive. Boys are pictured in fairly independent and adventurous roles, and are often shown outdoors. Girls, however, are most often pictured indoors. There is little in this world of picture books to make you think that a woman could ever find fulfillment outside the home or through intellectual pursuits.

The first time I consciously examined the depiction of women in a representative sample of children's picture books, I was shocked to realize that when women were present at all, they were usually shown in subservient roles. In these books, very few mothers are pictured working outside the home. (It is really absurd that in children's stories almost 100 percent of the mothers work only in the home, whereas in reality almost 50 percent of all mothers work outside the home, too.) The women in picture books are passive, dependent creatures who look to men for guidance. Surely no one could seriously maintain that the girls and women of our country are as passive and lacking in initiative as the girls and women you find in these books!

Furthermore, the men and boys in these books, while dominant in number and in role, do not display a full range of psychological and emotional reactions. For example, boys and men rarely cry or show deep emotion. Fathers are practically never depicted as giving children baths, feeding them, or changing diapers. In fact, the fathers in these stories usually have only the most tenuous connections with their homes and families. Is it any wonder that, having grown up reading such books, so many men feel it is a sign of weakness to cry, or "unmanly" to pay attention to their small babies?

The rigid stereotyping of gender roles that we find in picture books is also found in most books for older children. Some children even grow up to write more of these books! This is a sad situation, for exposure to sexist literature helps to prevent both boys and girls from becoming full human beings.

I said a little while ago that it's important for boys and girls to be comfortable with their gender identities as males and females, respectively. You, as a grandparent, can help your grandchildren to become comfortable with their gender identities by exposing them to *nonsexist* literature and ideas. And you can start working on this during the preschool stage.

In Appendix B you will find lists of recommended children's books, both nonfiction and fiction. When you read these books to your preschool-age grandchildren, *point out* instances of sexism (women are invisible, quiet, and submissive; men are brave and adventurous) and talk about them.

Some feminists say we shouldn't read sexist books to our children at all, but I disagree. If you decide not to read sexist books, you may end up throwing out 80 percent of all of the children's books available! If a particular book is good in other ways, I think it's far better to read it to a child and point out the ways in which it is sexist.

Also in Appendix B is an annotated list of specifically nonsexist books for children. You can read those books to your grandchild knowing that there are no sexist distortions to mess up the other messages of the book.

Books for young children are very influential in ways that children don't even notice. It's important to do everything you can to help your grandchild grow up to be a free person in a free world, not someone who is limited by outmoded sexual stereotypes.

The seventh developmental task in the preschool stage is the formation of basic attitudes toward sexuality.

This is one area in which you probably won't be able to help your grandchild in any significant way. Chances are that the significant influence on the child's attitudes toward sexuality will come mainly from her parents. It will be her parents that your granddaughter asks those surprising questions about sex. But, who knows? She may surprise you and ask you one of them. You can never be sure just what kinds of questions preschoolers will ask, or when.

Keep your answers to all questions on sex simple and to the point. Perhaps your grandchild sees a TV program on homosexuality and asks you, "Grandpa, what's a homosexual?" Say, "Peggy, a homosexual is a woman who likes other women instead of men, or a man who likes other men instead of women." If the child wants to ask you further questions, she will.

In other words, try to answer a preschooler's questions about sex just as you would answer her questions on any subject.

There is an excellent book on love and sexuality and the family called *The Wonderful Story of How You Were Born* by Sidonie Gruenberg (Doubleday). The late Mrs. Gruenberg made many wonderful contributions to the mental health movement in the United States, and this is one of her finest works. It is a splendid book, with excellent text and wonderful illustrations. You can read it to your grandchild a number of times.

The preschooler's eighth developmental task is to work through the resolution of the "family romance."

You are probably wondering what on earth I mean.

The phrase "resolving the family romance" is a fancy term for a very ordinary but important psychological task. At about age three, a little boy falls romantically in love with his mother. He continues to be in love with her till roughly his sixth birthday. During this time, the child begins to create a mental model of the woman he will one day marry. A little girl goes through the same thing with her father.

Some little boys and girls do this quietly and unobtrusively. Others are very bold and obvious in their statements: "When I grow up, I'm going to marry Mommy," or "Daddy and I are special to each other. We may get married soon." Sometimes parents or grandparents make the mistake of poking fun at such statements. Don't do that. This whole "falling in love" phenomenon has very important ramifications in a child's later life, for, as I have said, it basically determines the choice of a life mate.

What has all of this to do with you as a grandparent? Probably nothing at all, if your grandchild's parents have a stable, healthy marriage. But if death or divorce should deprive a little girl of a father, then you, as grandfather, may find yourself elected to be the father surrogate. Especially if you live close by and see your granddaughter often. Then *you* may be the one she thinks she is going to grow up and marry. And, of course, a grandmother may find herself playing mother surrogate to a little boy.

Please don't flee from this role your granddaughter or grandson may cast you in. Feel complimented that you have been selected to be father or mother surrogate. You are being of enormous emotional help to your grandchild by playing this role. After a couple of years, the child will have worked through the romance, and will not need to romanticize you anymore.

The final developmental task of the preschool stage is to go through a particularly sensitive period of development in which your grandchild is very responsive to intellectual stimulation.

You can help your grandchild enormously with this task and, incidentally, have a terrific time yourself. A child who receives a great deal of intellectual stimulation during the preschool period will have a gigantic head start when she enters school. And you are probably in an excellent position to give your grandchild this stimulation, because you probably have more leisure time than her parents.

Let's start with the easiest thing you can do. You can read books, both nonfiction and fiction, to your grandchild. Refer to Appendix B, which lists hundreds of good books to read to preschoolers. You can get these books in the library; if your library doesn't have one of them, the librarian can get it for you on interlibrary loan. You can buy any books you especially like from a bookstore.

There is one guideline I always used in choosing books to read to my children when they were preschoolers. I had to like the book myself. If I didn't like it, I knew it wouldn't be fun for me to read it to my children.

If you did *nothing else* except read books to your granddaughter regularly, you would be doing enormous things for her. You would be stimulating her intelligence. You would be teaching her to love books and reading. You would be building a solid foundation for the reading skills she will start to acquire in first grade or kindergarten.

You can also begin to teach the preschooler arithmetic through a series of games played with something called the Cuisenaire rods. You start with very simple games and gradually move on to more complex ones. The equipment consists of a series of wooden rods of different lengths and colors, representing the numbers one to ten.

Playing Cuisenaire rods games with your granddaughter is the single best thing you can do to teach her math at a preschool level. George Cuisenaire, a Belgian, saw that the teaching of arithmetic in schools was far too abstract— it was over the heads of many children. He invented a system that used rods of different lengths and colors so that children could learn arithmetic not by memorizing an abstract equation on a blackboard $(2 + 3 = 5)$, but by actual physical manipulation and matching up of the rods.

For example, you say to your grandchild, "I'm going to make a train here" (a 2 rod and a 3 rod). Then you say, "Now let's see how many trains you can make that will match mine." The child discovers, after some trial and error, that a 5 rod will match the 2 and 3 rod; so will a 4 rod and a 1 rod; so will five 1 rods. One of the beauties of this system is that the child can check her own answers very easily, which she cannot do in the same easy, physical way with arithmetic as it is conventionally taught.

Sets of Cuisenaire rods come complete with step-by-step instructions in the form of easy-to-use games printed on cards. If you can read, you can teach your grandchild arithmetic with the Cuisenaire rods games. You can order the Cuisenaire rods by mail. Write to: Learning Games, Inc., Box 820-C, North White Plains, New York 10603. Ask for the Cuisenaire Home Mathematics Kit.

And what a great thing you will be doing for your granddaughter by playing these Cuisenaire rods games with her! When other kids enter first grade, they will probably have had zero experience of learning arithmetic with concrete materials. They are likely to be bothered and bewildered by the typical, abstract approach to arithmetic. But your grandchild will be different. She will have had three years of learning to derive abstract arithmetic principles through the use of concrete materials. This will give her a solid foundation in math, no matter how arithmetic is taught in the school she attends.

I think every elementary school in the United States should teach arithmetic and math by using the Cuisenaire rods. But, unfortunately, far too many schools in the United States are still firmly committed to nineteenth-century methods of teaching arithmetic.

Here are two more games you can use to teach thinking and to have fun with your grandchild at the same time. You don't even need to buy these games, because they are in your head! The first is an adaptation of Animal, Vegetable, and Mineral for preschoolers. Simply eliminate the Vegetable and

Mineral part—that's ordinarily too confusing for a child of this age. Here's how you play Animal:

You say, "I'm thinking of an animal, and you try to see if you can guess it. You can ask me as many questions as you want, but you have to ask the question so it can be answered 'yes' or 'no.' The animal I'm thinking of can be an 'animal animal' or a 'human animal.'"

At first you will need to help the child learn to narrow down the possibilities. Teach her to explore, through questions, how large the animal is, whether it is tame or wild, what part of the world it is found in, whether you can usually find it in a zoo, whether it is a mammal, and so on. If you don't teach this, your grandchild will probably just burst out abruptly with questions like "Is it a kangaroo?" or "Is it a lion?"

If you pick a human animal, you will need to show your grandchild how to narrow down the possibilities in a similar way: Is it a man or woman? A child or a grown-up? What field is he famous in? What country does he come from? Is he living or dead?

Start with animals or humans that are relatively easy to guess, to build up your grandchild's self-confidence. Once she has gotten the hang of it, this is a terrific game for training her in logical thinking. And, by the way, this is a good game to play while driving in a car.

Here's another game a preschooler usually finds quite interesting. Say, "I've got another game for you, Jennifer. Here's how we play it. If cars ran on water instead of gasoline, what would happen?" (There would be water stations with water pumps. The price of water for the car would be a lot lower than the price of gasoline. There wouldn't be any cars waiting in water lines because water is so easy to get.)

Here's another one: "What would happen if the grown-ups had to obey the children?"

And so on. This game stretches the imagination of a child, teaches logical thinking, and is fun for both of you.

Up till now, I have talked about three- and four- and five-year-olds as if they were all pretty much alike. It might be helpful to close this chapter by talking about how three- and four- and five-year-olds *differ* from one another.

Three-year-olds are absolutely delightful. They can usually speak plainly enough to make their wants known to you. They are usually toilet trained. They have better motor control than toddlers and first adolescents. They can dress themselves and sit for longer than two minutes without becoming unbearably fidgety. They interact with people, including children their own age. They will share their toys to a certain extent. They are much more cooperative in every way imaginable than two-year-olds. When asked to do something, they do not automatically say, "No." Often, they will do what you ask at once, amiably. Enjoy your three-year-old grandchild because, unfortunately, the pendulum swings once more at four.

Some three-year-olds are so quiet you hardly know they are around. This is seldom the case with four-year-olds. This is not to say they are the holy terrors they were in first adolescence. But they make their presence felt by their loud voices and their constant inclination to talk. Bathroom humor is the "in" thing at this age—as are silly jokes that you may not see the point of, but which will cause your grandchild to laugh uproariously.

When you are with a four-year-old in public, you can count on unpredictable behavior. However, in his own life, your four-year-old grandson is very routine-oriented. He may eat only certain foods, for example. Peanut butter may be a great favorite at this time. However, the child's food whims are subject to change without notice, and they usually change right after you have stocked up on what he particularly likes! Once his whim changes, it is almost impossible to get him to eat his old favorite until he is good and ready.

It takes considerable patience to watch a child play with a dinner that you have gone to a good deal of time and effort to prepare. If your four-year-old grandchild does this, I think the best thing to do is to take the food away. Refrigerate or freeze it for another time.

Ritualistic behavior often occurs at bedtime. If stories are read to the four-year-old, they must be the same ones in the same order every time. The same toys go to bed, and are put in the same place on the bed. If you are baby-sitting with your four-year-old grandchild at your house, try to remind his parents to bring along the toys and books you will require to get the child to sleep, and ask them to tell you as much as possible about his routine.

Four-year-olds usually have a high energy level. They always ask, "Why?" Sometimes when you answer these endless questions, you get another "Why?" in response. When you have had enough, you can say, "I have answered all the questions that I can right now." And when the child asks "Why?" to that, you can repeat, "I am through answering questions." And say no more. Sometimes it's hard to keep cool. But if your grandchild sees the "Why?" game as an endurance contest and you lose your temper, you reinforce him for pestering you, and you're in for a lot more of the same.

Four-year-olds *are* exasperating. They take things. They have no sense of other people's property. They "borrow" their friends' toys. If you have things that are very special to you, lock them up as inconspicuously as possible. Children don't consider themselves thieves for pocketing collectibles, and it may cause feelings of suspicion on both sides if you make a big issue of this. Just remember, four-year-olds are very much like two-year-olds in some ways—and you have already survived that.

You will be pleased to know that after the turbulence of four, you will have the joy of a pleasant and placid five. Five-year-olds are sociable. They want to please you. They will do what you ask. Their worlds are expanding, and they are interested in learning new things. They have a much longer attention span than younger children. They are physically adept. They know their limitations and try to achieve only what they know they can accomplish. You don't find the frustrations that you found in the four-year-old when he was unable to succeed in a physical or mental task he had set out to do.

Five-year-olds are communicative. They have sizable vocabularies. When they draw, they draw recognizable pictures. Many can print their names. Although some are starting to read, they still love to be read to. A trip to the library is a treat for a five-year-old. And unlike the four-year-old, who wants the same few books read over and over, the five-year-old wants to hear as many different books as possible.

If you like to travel, you can probably take a five-year-old with you nearly anywhere. And it is possible to have a five-year-old grandchild visit you for an extended period of time. Children this age are often quite capable of entertaining themselves for fairly long periods. They also generally behave well and obey without stirring up a fuss.

Preschoolers, even four-year-olds, are usually a delight to have around. But remember that until a child is about seven years old, the odd-numbered years are easier than the even-numbered ones.

If you do not see your preschool-age grandchild on a regular basis, you will be surprised at how much he changes from visit to visit. The preschool years are a period of great growth, physical as well as emotional. When grandparents see these changes, it is sometimes hard for them to remember that preschoolers are young children. They often think that preschoolers are capable of more mature behavior than they actually are.

But preschoolers are not even close to being young adults yet.

Preschoolers generate a good deal of energy and need a means of releasing it. They say what they think, and it's better to let them. (In the short run, your feelings may be hurt. But in the long run, you are helping them to grow up to be happy and healthy adults.)

If you have preschool-age grandchildren, learn to enjoy them. To be around them and watch them grow, and to be able to participate in that growth, can help you to feel young again yourself.

❦ 9 ❧

The Three Worlds of Middle Childhood

"My granddad can fix nearly everything."

Helen Wilton, age 9

Now that your grandchild is about six, he has moved out of the preschool stage and into middle childhood. You may feel the child has gained certain things or lost certain things, or done a little of both, as he moved up the psychological ladder into this new stage.

When your grandson was a preschooler, he was basically focused on the family (including you). The family was his world and his only world. Even though he might have gone to nursery school and then kindergarten, the family remained the extent of his world and his vision.

All that is changed in this new stage, which lasts roughly from the sixth to the eleventh birthday. Although there is obviously considerable difference between a six-year-old and a ten-year-old, in general the personality of the child is fairly stabilized in the middle childhood years. There are few, if any, of the startling ups and downs of the preschool period.

In this new stage, your grandson must simultaneously live in three different worlds: the world of school, the world of his "gang," and the world of his family. It's very important for you to understand the meaning of these three worlds to your grandchild, and the psychological adjustments he must make to each one.

First, there is the world of school. In the preschool stage, which is dominated by the family, your grandchild is accepted for what he is by his parents. But in school, he encounters a new situation. For the first time in his life, his acceptance is truly conditional. Whether he gets good grades or not is conditional on how he performs on tests and reports, in classroom discussions, in answering questions. Students are roughly sorted out by the students themselves into the categories average, below average, and above average. Below-average children may be mercilessly labeled "retards" by their peers. Students who are above average or extraordinarily bright learn to keep a low profile, for they find out that other kids don't like them if they flaunt their academic superiority.

83

Kids are quickly sorted out according to sports ability, too, when games are played during physical education classes and recess. No matter how nice your grandchild is, if he can't hit a baseball, nobody wants him on their team.

Children are also classified "desirable" or "undesirable" according to their diverse personalities. Much teasing goes on, and if a child can't handle teasing well, that's considered a black mark against him. Children can be vicious as they choose the people they let into their cliques and the people they reject.

All this is a far cry from the automatic acceptance and love your grandchild found within his family circle. He may have been a winner when he was in the preschool stage. He may continue to be a winner in middle childhood. But if he turns out to be below average in his studies, or is poor in sports, or has a personality problem, he may now be rejected by his peers.

You can be important to your grandson in these situations. If he's not liked by other kids, he will certainly be unhappy about it. He will need somebody to pour out his feelings to, and that somebody could be you. Use the feedback technique, give him your earnest attention, and you may do great things for him just by listening and giving him the opportunity to talk.

What is your grandchild's developmental task during the five years of this stage? It is to learn *mastery* and thereby avoid *inadequacy*. This is the first time the child has had to do this. In the earlier stages of his life, he was, as I have said, loved and accepted for simply being himself. But now he must master his schoolwork. He must master sports. He must master other extracurricular activities. He must master interpersonal relationships. If he does not, he feels inadequate and inferior to his peers. And that is a miserable way to feel.

There are some things you and your grandson's parents can do to help him in school. For example, if he is academically weak in one subject, such as math or English, you can arrange tutoring for him, or tutor him yourself. Tutoring will not make an A student out of an average student, but it may help your grandchild enough to enable him to make acceptable grades instead of poor ones. A little later on I will discuss some other things you can do.

If the child is awkward or inexperienced in sports, you can help by teaching him how to hit or throw a ball, toss a pass, kick or pass a soccer ball.

If your grandchild is not physically skillful or agile, you can do your best to keep him out of such adult-run sports as Little League baseball, Pop Warner football, and soccer. First of all, these sports can be physically bad for him—pediatricians are now quite familiar with injuries known as "Little League elbow" and "Little League shoulder," and with other, similar problems. (The trouble is that the musculature of a child of this age is not sturdy enough to handle too much adult-type sports activity.) But I think that even worse than the physical strain is the emotional strain involved in performing not only before your own team and another team, but before a whole crowd of ego-involved, emotionally pressuring adults. The pressure on some kids in such situations is incredible.

Imagine the devastating psychological effect on a not-too-agile child of six who has trouble catching or fielding a ball, and who goes up to bat only to strike out again and again. If you actually wanted to lower this child's self-esteem, what better way could you devise to do it?

As I think back over my own childhood, I am very glad that adult-run sports did not exist then. We organized our own baseball and touch football games. And in all my years of playing those games, from the time I was six till I was twelve, I do not remember a single boy crying because he was upset by striking out or missing a fly ball.

If your grandchild is a terrific star on the team and gives an outstanding performance game after game, then obviously he's going to love it, and his self-esteem will be enhanced. But he may still be subject to the sports injuries of this age, which might prevent him from playing sports later in high school or college. (Because of the danger of injuries, I thoroughly agree with the American Academy of Pediatrics that the beginning age for competitive sports should be twelve or older.)

One thing you can do at this stage, if it fits in with your way of life, is to take your grandchild camping or backpacking. This has many advantages. Both boys and girls usually love camping and learn the needed skills quickly. It helps a child's self-esteem greatly to know that he is skilled as a camper or backpacker—that he can pack his backpack well, hike a trail while carrying a pack on his back, set up a tent, build a fire, and cook meals. You may be a camper and backpacker yourself and already know how to do these things. Or you may know nothing about it but feel like trying it, in which case you can go to any library or bookstore and find numerous books on camping and backpacking.

If your grandchild does not have any special skills that make points with her peer group, you may be able to help in finding one.

When I was in middle childhood, my role in basketball, football, and baseball teams was strictly that of substitute, Grand Exalted Keeper of the Bench. So my excellence in sports was not winning me any plaudits from my peer group. And there was nothing else I could do—except for one thing, and it proved to be my salvation.

I discovered that I could draw, and my parents and grandparents staked me to two different mail-order courses in cartooning. I worked hard at them and became a pretty good cartoonist. So I ended up drawing all the posters for the school plays and sports events. I made sure my name was down at the bottom of each poster in big bold capital letters, and I got to be famous at school—everybody knew me as the school cartoonist. Later, I often wondered how I would have gotten along in middle childhood if I hadn't cultivated that one special ability. Maybe you can help your grandchild unearth and cultivate a similar type of special ability.

To help your grandchild in the world of school, you must first learn what goes on in school. Most parents and grandparents haven't the faintest idea what school is all about, though they hold the pious belief that school is good for the child and piously hope that the child will do well there.

There is a way you can find out what is being taught in elementary school. Buy a paperback book by Dr. Nancy Larrick called *A Parent's Guide to Children's Education*. I think that every parent and grandparent should own this book. For Dr. Larrick not only tells you what a child will be taught in school and why, but she tells you things you can do at home to enhance your grandchild's education.

The most important skill your grandchild will use in school is reading. Therefore, anything you can do to help him in his reading skills will help him in every subject.

Unfortunately, many schools do a poor job of teaching reading. In spite of the research evidence showing the clear superiority of phonics to look-and-say as a method of teaching beginning reading, many schools use a high proportion of look-and-say in their beginning reading instruction. Your grandchild may be one of the victims of this kind of inferior instruction. If so, help the parents to find a competent reading tutor, and hire the tutor to diagnose your grandchild's reading problems and teach the child to read. Then reading will become a pleasure rather than drudgery for the child.

Once a child has learned to read, in the first and second grades, the school usually proceeds systematically to teach him to dislike reading. One of the ways this is done is by insisting that all children in a particular class, regardless of their individual tastes, read the same book and write a report on it.

When my son Randy was eleven, he was attending a school that required its students to read three books over the summer and take an exam on them when they came back to school in September. One of the books Randy selected was Jack London's *The Call of the Wild*. This was a perfect book for him, and he really enjoyed reading it. I can't remember the names of the other two books, but he just hated them and had to force himself to read them.

When a child has to *force* himself to read two out of three books because he hates them, his school is clearly teaching him to hate reading. If you don't want your grandchild to end up as a nonreader, you and his parents are going to have to figure out a way to show him that reading is pleasurable.

At this stage, one of the best things you and his parents can do for the child is to create a personal reading program for him and arrange to give him some reward for each book he reads. (I suggest that you refer to Chapter 3 and reread the section on the positive reinforcement program I set up with my ten-year-old son Rusty.) You can begin such a program at eight, or nine, or ten. It doesn't make any difference what the reward is, as long as the program meets two conditions: (1) the child can choose each book himself, and (2) the reward is powerful enough to induce him to read it.

Take your grandchild to a bookstore once a week and let him pick out any paperback he wants. This way, he will develop a small but growing library of his own. You may also want to take him to the public library once a week to pick out whatever books he would like.

The ultimate aim, of course, is for reading to become so pleasurable that the child will read for the sake of reading, without any external reward. But you may need to reward him for a couple of years to get him to that point.

When it comes to reading, most parents and grandparents overlook the powerful influence of TV programs. When *Roots* was on TV, children's librarians reported that an unusually large number of children wanted to read the book. So when your grandchild sees a TV show, movie, or play he likes that is connected with a book, whether it is *Tom Sawyer* or *Jaws,* offer to take him to a library or bookstore to get that book.

With younger children (six, seven, and eight), you can revive the practically extinct art of reading aloud. If you do this interestingly, the child will love it. But if it becomes clear that he is bored, drop the reading.

You can also stimulate your grandchild to read by offering him comic books. That's right—I said comic books! Most boys and girls in middle childhood love them. Remember that as long as your grandchild is reading something, regardless of what it is, he is improving his reading skills.

When your grandchild reaches the later grades of middle childhood (fourth, fifth, and sixth), it's a good idea to find out what subjects he is especially interested in and then give him a subscription *not* to a child's magazine, but to his first adult magazine—for example, *National Geographic, Sports Illustrated, Popular Mechanics,* or *Natural History.*

In the middle childhood years you can continue to play the same educational games with your grandchild that you began to play back in the preschool period. You can play Animal through age seven. Then, at age eight, you can introduce the greater complexities of Vegetable and Mineral. Explain that in the game, "vegetable" is anything that grows in the ground, and does not have to be like a vegetable that you eat. Also explain that something "vegetable" can be in its natural state (for example, a tree), or in its manufactured form (for example, a newspaper). Likewise, something "mineral" can be in its original state (for example, iron in the ground), or in its manufactured state (for example, a steel car).

I stress this game because when your grandchild is playing it, he is learning a great deal about how to analyze, classify, and organize data, and about how to *think,* while at the same time having a walloping good time. I am sure you could take almost any class hour in the average school and have the teacher and students play Animal, Vegetable, and Mineral instead of holding regular class, and the children would learn more.

There are also store-bought games that are educational in nature, such as Scrabble and Facts in Five. If you are lucky enough to live close to an educational supply store that sells to both teachers and parents, you will probably discover a bonanza of educational games that aren't in the average toy store or toy section of your department store.

Now let's talk about the world of the gang. The word "gang" may have bad connotations for some readers, but I don't know any other word to take its place. For a child of this age, it certainly doesn't mean a scruffy bunch of kids on motorcycles with switchblade knives and tire chains. Far from it! It means four eight- or nine-year-old boys in a tree house or a handmade fort. They have formed a highly secret club called The Dreadful Assassins, and the club's chief rule is "No girls!" Overall, the club's most important feature is its secrecy. I remember that when my son Randy was nine, I overheard him and a friend talking, and his friend used the term "Cow Society." I asked Randy what it meant. He was very sheepfaced because his friend had unwittingly revealed one of the key secrets of their club—its name. "Aw, it's nothing," he said. "It's just a little secret club we've got."

"Gang," as it relates to children of both sexes at this stage of development, simply means "the peer group outside of school." Usually the gang will be neighborhood children.

The members of his peer group are terribly important to your grandchild. As I have said, in the preschool stage your grandchild lived only in the world of his immediate family or extended family. Now he has left this emotionally secure nest and ventured out into the larger universe. This is a frightening thing to do.

Imagine a child who has lived the first years of his life in a town of five thousand people. Then, at the age of six, he and his family move to a huge city with a population of six million. Is the child afraid as he sees that man-swarm stride and push and scurry around him? You bet he is! Well, that's what the middle childhood youngster feels like as he begins to cut himself away from the moorings of home and family. As he does this, he needs to find new sources of emotional support. These he finds in his peer group.

Your grandchild used to be dependent on parental authority. But now he is less and less concerned about what his parents expect of him, and more and more concerned about what his peer group expects. And he tries to conform in the minutest detail to their expectations. This way, he wins the emotional security of their loyalty and support.

Your grandson can no longer give unquestioning belief or loyalty to you or his parents. He is learning that other adults—family friends, teachers, Boy Scout leaders, and church school teachers, for example—have different values and ideas. He is beginning to compare and test these ideas against the ideas of his family. He is able to do this challenging and testing because of the emotional strength he gets from his gang.

His gang is the one thing in your grandson's life that is not organized by adults. School is organized by adults. So is home life. Many groups, such as Indian Guides and Little League, are organized by adults. But the gang stands alone. It is organized solely by children, and they want no adults within sniffing distance of what they are doing. Hence the secrecy that is so characteristic of clubs (and many activities) at this stage.

The subculture of the gang becomes a special little society within the neighborhood. It has unwritten rules, traditions, games, and values all its own. This subculture is very important to the psychological development of your grandchild. Connected by strong emotional ties to the gang, he will learn many valuable socialization skills. And he will learn them independent of adult direction or evaluation. Many of the most important activities of the gang are not organized, in any real sense of the word, but could best be described as "hanging around" or "doing nothing."

You, as a grandparent, must try to understand and accept the psychological importance of a gang that is free of adult influence. Don't take it as a personal rejection if your grandchild prefers the company of his gang to your company. There will be other times when he would rather be with you.

Is there anything you, as a grandparent, can do to help your grandchild succeed with his peers? Yes, there is.

If possible, help your grandchild to learn physical skills that will help him win the esteem of his peers and will also be a source of healthy exercise and fun. (I am speaking of such sports as swimming, tennis, and skiing.) And help him practice fundamental skills (throwing, kicking, batting, etc.) if you can. Chances are he won't practice these skills when he is with his gang, because they will be playing, not working on the fundamentals.

You can also try to help your grandchild with the kinds of socialization skills he needs to succeed with his peers. Sometimes, for example, a child is not able to handle insults or teasing. You can teach him how. Here is one good way:

Choose three or four words in a foreign language—for instance, the Greek words (spelled phonetically) *Hey gay melaina pinei,* which mean "The black earth drinks." Teach them to your grandchild. When he has them down well, tell him that when another kid insults him, he is to look the other kid straight in the eye and say, *"Hey gay melaina pinei,"* and nothing else. Under no circumstances is he to reveal what the words mean or what language they are. It will be difficult for the other kid to keep up the insults or the teasing when all he gets in return is a monotonous repetition of *"Hey gay melaina pinei."*

Or perhaps your grandchild is timid and fearful of body contact. You can help by providing him with a class in karate or self-defense, which can give him some real confidence in handling himself.

Can you teach your grandchild how to use tools—a hammer, saw, plane, pliers, and wrench? This can be of real help in giving him status in the eyes of his gang. Or if you are good with automobiles, you can pass auto repairing skills on to your grandchild.

Don't forget about inviting your grandchild to go camping, backpacking, or fishing with you. Tell him to bring a friend, if he wants to. Going on an outing with you and one of his friends expands your grandchild's socialization skills.

And if you can afford it, help your grandchild's parents send him to summer camp. But don't rush this. Send him to day camp at ages seven and eight and then, at age nine, to a one-week session at a sleep-away camp. By ten and eleven, he will be ready for a two-week session at sleep-away camp. The YMCA and YWCA generally run very good, relatively inexpensive summer camps. And I'm sure there are good private camps near where you live.

Even though I have been emphasizing the importance of the world of school and the world of the gang, it would be a huge mistake to conclude that the world of the family is of no importance to your grandchild at this stage. Dr. Barbara Biber has summed up the psychological situation of the middle childhood child and his family better than anyone else I know: "The child is looking for ways to belong to his family and feel free of them at the same time."[1]

If you conclude that your middle childhood grandchild wants little to do with his family or you, and that he uses his home or your home only as a place to eat and sleep, then you have sadly misjudged the situation.

At this stage your grandson is still being quite powerfully influenced by his parents and by you, but he doesn't want you to know it! Adolescence is a time of *real* struggle for independence from the family. But in middle childhood, your grandson is putting up only a pseudo-struggle for independence.

You may continue to be an influence on your grandchild much longer than you think—possibly for the rest of his life. I once met a young man, a CPA at the youthful age of twenty-seven, who had taken a year off between graduating from college and getting a master's degree to travel and work around the world. I asked him where he got the idea of doing that. "I got it from my grandfather," he said. "He used to tell me stories when I was a little kid about all kinds of exciting places he'd been, and all sorts of things he'd done. He had one whole wall of his room covered with maps, and he'd point out all the places I could travel to. I thought a lot about Grandpa and where he'd traveled, and when I graduated from college, I decided to do it, too."

In middle childhood, a girl is in the paradoxical process of identifying with her parents and grandparents, and at the same time growing away from them emotionally. Children of this age often disobey parental commands *in their actions*. That's why it's crucial to recognize that underneath the actions of your grandchild, parental *feelings* and *attitudes* are still being absorbed. If more parents and grandparents realized this important psychological fact, they would breathe a huge sigh of relief.

What all this boils down to is that your grandchild's parents, and you, are still his most important role models. But there are a lot of other influences in your grandchild's life now. If you are to get through to him, you'll need to cultivate a one-to-one relationship with him.

If you have several grandchildren, try to be with them one at a time. When you're with two or more, you will probably just be presiding over a sibling rivalry squabble. But if you can spend time with just one, he will not need to fight with any other child to have your full attention.

I can't tell you exactly what things to do with your middle childhood grandchild because I don't know what activities you enjoy. I can tell you *not* to do something with your grandchild that he enjoys if you *don't* enjoy it. He will quickly sense that you are doing it out of a sense of obligation, and that will spoil the fun.

Both of my sons love to fish; my daughter does not. I never took either of my sons fishing, because I am not a fisherman and to me fishing is boring. If I had overriden my feelings and taken them anyway, I'm sure a bad time would have been had by all. However, luckily for me, their grandfather is a fisherman and loves it, and he is the person who has taken them fishing.

When you are doing something one-on-one with your grandchild, be true to yourself and what you really enjoy.

Here are some things you could do with a middle childhood youngster if you enjoy them: going to spectator sports events; going hiking, camping, fishing, or backpacking; making visits to libraries or bookstores; taking weekend trips to explore the countryside; going to movies or eating at restaurants you both like; playing indoor games such as checkers, chess, backgammon, or Monopoly. This list, of course, is only a starter.

When you are with your grandchild on a one-to-one basis, no bells will ring or trumpets blow. But each time, you are influencing him with your character, your value system, and your ways of doing things. All of this will be very valuable to him as an adult, and as a member of his extended family.

❧ 10 ❧

The Blitzkrieg Kid: The Stage of Preadolescence

"Every time I went over to her apartment, I got twenty or twenty-five cents. As I liked my grandmother, I went over to her apartment about five times a week."

Andrew Austin, age 10

I remember vividly how my daughter Robin announced, through the language of her behavior, that she had moved into the stage of preadolescence. From the time she was six through the age of ten, her personality was stable and easygoing. She was a delightful child to have around.

Then at dinner one night, it happened. Robin was about two months shy of becoming eleven. When we had finished dinner, I asked her to take out the trash, as I had asked her countless times for the past five years. But this time, her response was definitely different. "ALL RIGHT," she yelled. "IN THIS FASCIST TOTALITARIAN SOCIETY THAT POSES AS A DEMOCRACY, THIS FAMILY IN WHICH ADULTS HAVE ALL THE RIGHTS AND CHILDREN HAVE NONE, IF THAT'S WHAT YOU WANT, I'LL TAKE OUT YOUR LOUSY TRASH!"

My wife and I were stunned. I asked myself, "Where has my sweet little ten-year-old gone?" But, unlike many parents in similar circumstances, I knew the answer to that question: "She has gone into the stage of preadolescence."

Typically the ten-year-old, who is at the top age of middle childhood, gets along reasonably well with everybody. This is a stage of equilibrium and the child is at peace with herself. But underneath the placid exterior of the ten-year-old's personality structure, the growth forces of adolescence are at work. These forces suddenly erupt during the eleventh year, and usher in the stage of preadolescence.

For parents and grandparents alike, preadolescence is a zinger. The preadolescent usually becomes quite obnoxious to live with. In the stage of middle childhood, there is no particular problem getting her to do her household chores. But, now, motivating her to cooperate on household chores becomes equivalent to trying to tip over a pyramid with one finger. In school, she is

93

talkative and restless. She loves to play jokes and tricks on her classmates. She is quite critical of adults, and is keenly aware of all their shortcomings. For this reason, sixth grade is not an easy one to teach.

The preadolescent stage covers the years from approximately the eleventh birthday to the thirteenth birthday. Most parents and grandparents, when confronted with the sudden difficulty of handling their preadolescent, are likely to be very upset. "I just can't understand what's gotten into her!" a parent or grandparent will moan helplessly.

To understand what has gotten into her, you first need to understand the developmental task of preadolescence. You will remember that the developmental tasks of all the other stages—infancy, toddlerhood, first adolescence, the preschool years, and middle childhood—were all positive. But this one is different. The developmental task of this stage is *disorganization*. No, your eyes did not deceive you. That's what I said: *disorganization*. I don't mean by this a *permanent* disorganization of the child's personality. Actually, it is the prelude to a new organization of her personality on a higher plane.

Remember that in discussing first adolescence, I used the analogy of the toddler owning a house called babyhood? It's a similar situation with the preadolescent. Since she was six years old, she has been living in a house called childhood. In order to build the new house of adolescence, she has to demolish the old house of childhood. This means she has to disorganize the childish ways by which she has been living.

She has been used to living by her parents' rules and regulations. Now she begins to challenge and criticize them, to comment on all of the defects in her parents' personalities that she had noticed before but not mentioned. You can easily see why this is not a pleasant stage for the two older generations.

Several major changes occur as part of the process of disorganizing and breaking up the psychological equilibrium of middle childhood. One change is the evaporation of the child's previous cooperation with her parents. This is gone, gone, gone. The parent will make a reasonable request that the child wear a coat if it is cold outside, or that she go to bed at a sensible hour. In middle childhood, these requests were accepted in a reasonable spirit and complied with. Now the child reacts with ill-concealed disgust, as if she were being ordered around by power-hungry dictators disguised as parents. Parents are often at their wits' end because even simple, everyday life with their preadolescent is a never-ending round of mind-rasping irritations over even the most minor or inconsequential things.

The standards of morals and behavior that the parents thought they had instilled in their child now seem to have vanished. She suddenly begins to lie about everything, from important matters to trivial ones. She may steal at school or at home, or from stores. Her conscience seems weakened, and her control of her antisocial impulses has slipped.

As if that weren't enough, the preadolescent begins to step on parental toes exactly where she knows it will hurt the most. For a number of years she has been making a careful study of her parents and grandparents, though they were not aware of this. Now she puts this espionage to work. When she wants to prove how emancipated she is, she will choose just those actions and attitudes that she knows will irritate her parents or grandparents the most.

If school grades are important to her parents, she will suddenly, for no apparent reason, begin to bring home a series of D's and F's. If her parents are very moralistic and anti-sex, she will suddenly begin telling jokes at the dinner table that would make a longshoreman blush. And then she will wonder innocently why her parents are shocked!

I recall all too vividly that when my son Randy was in this stage he began to do imitations of me (driving, lecturing to the family, etc.). I must admit that the imitations were accurate, but somehow I did not find them very funny.

Our preadolescents are not merely stepping on *our* toes. They are stepping on the toes of the whole adult society that their parents and grandparents represent. For parents are not merely themselves. They are representatives of the value system of the whole adult society, which the preadolescent must rid herself of in order to progress toward her own individual adulthood. It is important for parents and grandparents to realize that many of the rebellious actions of preadolescents are not aimed at them at all. They are aimed at the total adult society. Although it is difficult for parents and grandparents to fully appreciate this emotionally, they are really just innocent bystanders.

I have spoken so far as if all the changes taking place in your preadolescent are psychological. This is not true, for the changes are also biological and physiological. Because, for the first time in her life, your grandchild has run head on into *puberty*. Or puberty has run head on into her, if you prefer that way of phrasing it.

One of our greatest experts on the growth and development of children, the late Dr. Arnold Gesell, described the way parents feel about eleven-year-olds:

> There may be an odd, vague, uncomfortable feeling in the minds of the parents of eleven-year-olds. It is as though some force of nature were grabbing hold of their offspring—as though he were acting under some influence quite apart from those of the tangible environment in which he lives.[1]

So it is not merely psychological change that is causing parents to feel this way about their preadolescents. It is puberty as well.

Obviously, parents cannot *see* puberty taking place in their youngster, particularly at age eleven, when it is just beginning. All they can see are the outward manifestations of the sexual and hormonal changes taking place inside.

Throughout the stage of middle childhood, your grandchild's biological system was more or less in equilibrium. But with the coming of preadolescence, vast biological and hormonal upheavals play havoc with this equilibrium.

In this stage your granddaughter shows a marked increase in activity level, as well as an enormous increase in one particular activity: eating. When your grandchild invites two friends to come in for a "little snack," by the time they depart the kitchen is likely to look as if it had been raped, looted, and pillaged by Attila the Hun.

All in all, it seems to parents as if some mysterious and evil supernatural force has gotten inside the skin of their child. She looks just the same, but she is a different person.

This new child is a perpetual-motion machine, always on the go. She never sits; rather, she squirms her way over chairs and couches. She will argue about anything with anybody at the drop of a hat. Above all, she is subject to emotional changes and shifts of mood she has never before experienced in the entire ten years of her life. This stranger in the midst of the family is argumentative, disagreeable, rude, resentful, fidgety, and sulky. Anger in its various forms colors much of her conduct during the day. Disappointment and hurt feelings are also important.

It is important to keep in mind that these emotional changes are symptoms of growth. The whole biological and psychological organism of your grandchild is going through profound changes at this time. The changes in her emotions and behavior are part of an all-pervasive process of developmental reorganization that is taking place silently within her body.

The preadolescent often throws up her newfound sense of self against the selves of others in order to help her define who she is and who the others are. She does this through confrontation with others, particularly her parents. She criticizes and accuses her parents in order to get a response. She will often lash out at her parents without really understanding why she is acting this way.

Grandparents need to realize that the unpleasant qualities of the preadolescent—her defensiveness, her belligerence, her argumentativeness—are all expressions of her search for selfhood. And this new self she is groping for is radically different from the self she has had for many years as a child.

It is important, too, for parents and grandparents to understand that the positive growth forces underlying the negativism and rebelliousness of their preadolescent will eventually help to create a positive, warm, loving, and well-adjusted person. But the preadolescent must react negatively to what her parents want before she can find out, in a positive fashion, what she herself truly wants. If adults don't understand this, they will merely throw up their hands in disgust at the behavior of their preadolescent and conclude that she is a spoiled, selfish, angry brat.

And now we come to the crux of this chapter. How can you handle your grandchild intelligently during the very difficult stage?

First, remember that she's not rebelling against *you*. She's rebelling against all of adult society. If you can avoid taking her rebellion personally, you can more or less sit back and act as a sounding board, using the feedback technique to help your grandchild cope with her problems and difficulties. If you take her rebellion personally, you will react very defensively, which will throw sand into the gears of your communication. This, unfortunately, is just what many parents and grandparents do. They feel angry and hurt at the snotty behavior of their preadolescent; they feel that this behavior is aimed at them. It is not. Try not to make this mistake, and your family will be miles ahead in dealing sensibly with your preadolescent.

Second, keep in mind that the obnoxious behavior of this age is *normal*. If a preadolescent is too sweet and loving, that is something to be concerned about, because it isn't normal! Naturally, we would prefer that children always be sweet and easy to get along with. That would certainly be more comfortable for us. But that isn't possible. Before a child can create a new self-identity as an adolescent, she must destroy her childhood identity. So, preadolescence may be a bitter pill to swallow, but it is a *normal* bitter pill.

Third, remember that the preadolescent's difficult behavior is *temporary!* So many parents and grandparents react as if this obnoxious behavior would continue year after year unless they did something immediately to stop it. You'll hear parents say, "I'm sick and tired of this defiance of me. I'm going to let him know once and for all who's boss in this house!" And then the parent lands on his preadolescent like a ton of bricks. The result is what a person with even the faintest knowledge of psychology could predict. The child's behavior gets worse. He may become more defiant and more difficult to control, using new commando tactics to strike out at his parents. Or he may put on a show of outward compliance, but engage in forbidden activities behind his parents' back.

Realizing that a preadolescent's behavior is temporary should help parents and grandparents to "cool it" and avoid the use of parental overkill.

Fourth, in dealing with your grandchild's behavior, please try to distinguish between important situations that call for your firm intervention, and unimportant ones that can be left alone.

Preadolescent behavior is difficult enough to cope with without fighting on all fronts at once. Emulate the late President Franklin Roosevelt, who always concentrated on the most important measures he wanted Congress to deal with, and ignored the other things.

Fifth, think of the unpleasant behavior of your preadolescent grandchild as a message in code to his parents and you and the other significant adults in his life. Try to look beneath his distressing behavior to the feelings and attitudes he is expressing. Say something like this to yourself: "This outward behavior of my grandchild—his failing grades, his smoking, his attitudes toward authority—all of this is a message in code. Let's see if I can learn to read the code and understand what he's saying." If you are able to take this kind of an attitude, you will certainly be way ahead of the average grandparent.

One of the best things you can do for yourself and your grandchild at this stage is to learn the one-day delay system.

When you hear that your grandchild has been caught smoking at school and suspended, or has been found stealing and the police have been called in, or has done something else that raises your hackles, your natural response may be to get on the phone and read him the riot act: "Now listen here, young man, don't you know what your behavior is doing to your parents? Your father doesn't work hard to make money so he can send you to that private school so you can get suspended for smoking!"

This may be a very spontaneous and natural reaction, but it certainly will not motivate your grandchild to improve his behavior. And it is not going to encourage him to turn to you for advice the next time he gets in trouble. The only effect it will have on him is to make him think (and possibly even say aloud), "I wish Grandpa would mind his own business and keep his big mouth shut!"

Instead, when you hear some distressing news about your grandchild, use the one-day delay. Don't react to the news that same day. Sleep on it. Talk it over with your spouse, or perhaps a friend or a business associate. Let a day go by before you contact your grandchild. And instead of phoning, see him in person if that is possible.

When you see him, don't present him with a packaged solution to his problem, or lecture him in holier-than-thou tones. Instead, explore with him why he was smoking or what happened to get him into trouble with the police. It's certain that he will be upset by what he's done and will want to talk to somebody. Be sure to use the feedback approach—your grandchild won't want to talk to somebody who will scold him or give him a hard time. He will want to talk to somebody who will be unusual enough to give him a chance to air his feelings. And you just might be that unusual someone.

As a grandparent, you are really in a very fortunate position with your preadolescent, compared with other adults. You are probably not the one who has to get him to do chores around the house. You probably are not the one who monitors how he is doing his schoolwork. In fact, you probably don't need to monitor him at all.

So where does that leave you? In the same type of relationship you have with an adult friend, only this friend is younger. You don't monitor an adult friend's finances, or his work, or his relationships with others. *You merely enjoy him.* Why not do this with your preadolescent?

Find things that you and your grandchild mutually enjoy—going to movies or sports events, camping out, or whatever—and then do these things with him. Your only "obligation" during the time you spend with your grandchild is to enjoy the movie or the basketball game or the camp-out. You do not have to straighten your grandchild out, improve his behavior, or reform him in any way. What a relief for him to be with an adult who is not trying to improve him!

I am not saying that the preadolescent will be a perfect companion. He may start giving you some typical preadolescent flak: "Gramp, why'd you get us awful seats like this for the baseball game? I can hardly see anything! And the hot dogs taste cruddy, too!" In a case like this, I'm sure you will feel like saying, "Listen, I paid six bucks for these seats, and if you don't like the hot dogs, that's too darn bad!" But if you restrain your first impulses and keep silent, his complaints will probably die down, and soon you will find the two of you enjoying the game together.

So try to ignore your grandchild's "bristle-talk" and surly behavior. Concentrate on the areas where you can have fun together. Let somebody else have the job of reforming him!

Finally, learn to respect your preadolescent's newfound independence. Over the last ten years you have become accustomed to talking to him and treating him like a child. Now he is no longer a child. Actually, he is in a kind of psychological twilight zone. He is not a child any longer, but he is not yet an adolescent.

Just as your grandchild has moved up to a new developmental stage, so you as a grandparent must move up to a new *adult* developmental stage in order to handle him wisely. You need to mentally promote him to a new level, put him more on an equal footing with yourself. Sooner or later he *will* be on basically the same footing with you, when he is twenty-one or twenty-two and a young adult. You need to be breaking him into adulthood when he is eleven!

It will be hard for you to change ten years of habits overnight and stop treating your grandson as a child. But now you need to learn how to respect his new, clumsy ventures at independence, and accord him a more adult status. His new, shaky independence is not easy or comfortable for you to live with. But it represents his first big step on the road to adulthood. Treat it with respect!

❧ 11 ❧

Where Bras and Funny Papers Meet: Adolescence

"She's the person who tells me all the things about my parents they would rather not have me know."

Sarah Scott, age 15

Of all the developmental stages your grandchild passes through in his journey from birth to adulthood, there is no doubt that adolescence is the most bewildering, the most complex, and the most difficult. And not just for the parents and grandparents, but particularly for the adolescent.

There are many reasons why this stage is such a difficult one, but I suspect that the basic one is this: All the other stages merely lead up to the all-important breakaway from childhood and entrance into adulthood. In adolescence, that breakaway and that entrance actually take place.

The developmental task of this stage is *to form a new ego identity,* separate from that of the parents. The adolescent is silently but urgently asking himself for the first time in his life: "Who am I?" And by the time he has passed successfully through the stage of adolescence, he will have answered that question. He will finally have an ego identity, because he will have become independent of his parents and family. He will be an adult.

But who can define "adulthood"? All of us know very adult nineteen-year-olds and very childish, even infantile twenty-six-year-olds. I will take an arbitrary stand and define twenty-one as the age at which adulthood begins. So, for the purposes of this discussion, adolescence lasts eight years, roughly from ages thirteen to twenty-one.

There are vast psychological differences between younger adolescents and older ones. For that reason, it helps to divide this period into two substages. Again somewhat arbitrarily, I will call the years from thirteen to sixteen "early adolescence," and lump together the years from sixteen to twenty-one as "late adolescence."

In early adolescence the teenager is trying to answer the question of who he is *within* his family, and at the same time he is probably expressing this

101

search in rebellious terms. In late adolescence he is wrestling with this question in the larger arena of his society. During this second period, he is also having to make two very important choices: a choice of a vocation, and a choice of sexual and affectional relationships.

Even though you didn't exactly grow up in the Dark Ages, you've experienced an enormous change in society in your lifetime. You've lived through an incredible amount of scientific and social advancement. But the realization that times have changed will never come to you more forcefully than when you have to deal with your teenage grandchildren.

As you well know, moral standards have changed as much as technology. Today's teenagers are very different from your own children when they were growing up. They demand freedom from parental restraints. But because it takes more education to get good jobs now than it used to, young people may want to stay in school longer. So they may end up being dependent on their parents for a longer time. Teenagers must make decisions about things like drugs and sex, and deal with other large issues, without very much maturity. It's not easy for them, and it's certainly not easy on their parents and grandparents. If you are not involved with your teenage grandchildren on a day-to-day basis, you may be only peripherally aware of some of the problems they face. In that case, a sudden confrontation with your adolescent's problems could come as a shock.

Before discussing how to deal with teenagers in general, I'm going to give you a thumbnail sketch of the adolescent at each age.

Thirteen: Depending on the local school system, most thirteen-year-olds are in their first or second year of junior high, intermediate, or middle school. This first year of the teens is not a particularly good one. Thirteen-year-olds are very inner-directed and egocentric. They think everybody is prying into their personal lives, their schoolwork, their friendships, everything. So they have invisible PRIVATE! KEEP OUT! signs hanging around their necks at all times. They are also full of self-doubts. That's one reason they may stay locked in the bathroom for so long, studying their faces zit by zit. Molehills truly do become mountains in their eyes.

Much of this is understandable. The bodies of thirteen-year-olds are undergoing significant changes. Girls think their breasts are either too large or too small. Boys' voices squeak in mid-sentence. Thirteen-year-olds of both sexes feel ugly and unloved. Most thirteen-year-olds have fewer friends than they did a year earlier. Girls use their friends as confidantes; boys use theirs as people to do things with. But even though the thirteen-year-old may have fewer friends, he is under more pressure than ever to conform to the norms of the peer group. The group has become a reflection of the teenager's own image, and gives him a strength he cannot yet find within himself.

At this age, relationships with parents are stormy. Criticism is not taken lightly, although there is much to be critical of. You'll find a lot of shouting by parents and a great deal of withdrawal by teenagers. What can you do, as a grandparent, in this situation?

First, try to be warm and understanding and as uncritical as possible. Brush up on the feedback technique and make liberal use of it. Don't try to talk your thirteen-year-old grandson out of his negative feelings, either about himself or others. Just accept them, feed them back to him, and let it go at that. Strangely enough, the only way to change a teenager's feelings from negative to positive is to accept them.

Second, see if you can share a skill or hobby with your grandchild. In spite of being group-oriented, thirteen-year-olds are starting to develop specialized interests. In sharing your knowledge, you and your grandchild get to know each other by doing something side by side. Many junior high schools today not only allow but encourage boys to take cooking and girls to take shop. So don't think that just because your grandchild is a different sex than you he won't be interested in learning your specialty.

Fourteen: Fourteen-year-olds in general are much more pleasant than thirteen-year-olds. They are more sociable with their parents and friends— so sociable, in fact, that they always seem to be talking on the telephone. If you want to give a fourteen-year-old a special gift, give him his own telephone. (But remember that the cost of installation is only the beginning, and make sure that the parents don't get stuck with the monthly payments; either you or the teenager should pay the bills.)

This is the age when dating starts in earnest. (Girls usually are more mature physically and emotionally than boys, so they often date boys who are a year or two older than they are.) It is an age of sexual awareness for both sexes. Junior high school teachers have often remarked that intensely romantic feelings bloom in their classrooms as predictably as new leaves each spring.

Sexual awakening breeds confusion for both fourteen-year-olds and their parents. The teenagers are looking for information on sex; but unfortunately, many parents are too embarrassed to give it. Schools are beginning to provide more and more courses to fill this need, but these often do not devote enough attention to the emotional commitments involved in sexual relationships.

Probably the most important thing for you, as a grandparent, to recognize at this age is the importance of peer socialization. The withdrawn and introspective thirteen-year-old has blossomed into a group-conscious extrovert. Fourteen-year-olds want to be with their own friends, and they no longer need you as much. In this emotional climate, it's hard for a grandparent not to feel neglected. Unfortunately, many young people are callous in the way they let you know they are too busy to get together with you.

At this stage your grandchildren may sometimes act as though you are an old fuddy-duddy and they're secretly ashamed of you. It can be a heart-wrenching time for you, and I would be callous myself if I told you to merely shrug it off. However, if you try to make your grandchild feel guilty about his neglect, you will certainly lose his affection. The best advice I can give is this: Try to continue to share hobbies and skills with your grandchild. If he isn't interested, offer to share them with people in hospitals or convalescent homes.

Fifteen: The benign neglect that you suffered at the hands of your fourteen-year-old grandchild may be nothing compared to the outright rejection you may get when he turns fifteen. Your grandchild is now in the stage of transition to late adolescence, and he is likely to be going through a full-fledged identity crisis. This is a time for introspection. But the adolescent is no longer concerned mainly with appearance and peer group acceptance. The fifteen-year-old is contemplating his real future for the first time.

Very often this is the year when an adolescent must make a choice between an academic and a vocational course of study for the last two years of high school. A boy may be pressured by his parents to plan to go on to college when he would actually feel more comfortable in a trade. A girl may be pressured by her parents *not* to plan to go into a traditionally "nonfeminine" field.

Suppose you agree with the parents that your grandchild's choices are not the best ones? The best thing to do is to say as little as possible after voicing your opinion *once.* Your grandchild's choices are not irrevocable. The decisions made at fifteen can easily be changed. At the worst, the teenager will lose a few years of education and may have to retrace some steps.

Another dilemma facing your grandchild at fifteen may be whether he even wants to continue with high school. Many children are bored in high school, and these days more school districts are allowing them to drop out and find jobs. (Educators find that if such teenagers are forced to stay in school, they are simply disruptive.) However, the problem is finding a job at this age; youngsters usually have to be fifteen and a half to get a work permit. And young workers are often exploited, being expected to work long hours with no overtime pay. If your grandchild is determined to drop out of school there is very little you can do about it. Just don't adopt a harsh I-told-you-so attitude; that could make it difficult for him to go back to school if he finds that he made a mistake.

A possible alternative to dropping out is a change of schools. If you live in a different school district than your grandchild, perhaps arrangements can be made for him to live with you during the school year. However, bringing a teenager into your home, even temporarily, is not a step to be taken lightly. It requires a long, unemotional look at all facets of the plan.

Besides themselves, fifteen-year-olds are interested in sex and sports. Many teenagers are also very interested in cars and learn how to take a car engine apart and put it back together long before they are old enough to get a driver's license. This applies to girls as well as boys, so don't discourage your granddaughter if she starts messing around with cars. Knowing how to fix your own car is a definite asset, regardless of your sex.

Because the fifteen-year-old spends so much time thinking about himself in relation to the world around him and the people who inhabit it, he is apt to consider himself an amateur psychologist. But unlike the professional psychologist, who does not try to thrust his views on everyone, the fifteen-year-old often feels bound to pontificate on what everyone else is doing wrong. Schoolteachers, administrators, law enforcement officers, siblings, parents— these are rarely spared an iota of criticism. You will probably not be immune, either.

If there ever was a time when you needed a sense of humor, this is it. The kindest thing you can do for your grandchild now is to listen and not be judgmental. There *are* a lot of bad teachers, cops who hassle, and unfair employers out there. Just by listening to what your grandchild has to say and not automatically defending the Establishment, you will be doing him a great favor.

Sixteen to Twenty-One: Take heart! Just when you think your fifteen-year-old is going to make you lose your mind, sixteen, an age of equilibrium, arrives. By now, your grandchild is probably able to drive (at least in many states) and to work, and these things can help her feel good about herself.

Seventeen: The seventeen-year-old is on the threshold of adulthood. The maturing process is becoming more evident. Your grandchild is starting to be seriously concerned about career choices. Now is the time to make the decision about going to college, and choosing a college. Seventeen is an age when adolescents are finding themselves, and they are not always easy to live with.

Eighteen: Some experts place the end of late adolescence at age eighteen. I believe this is a mistake, because I think that at this age there are still symptoms of the subterranean struggle to break away from the parents. In other words, the young person is still an adolescent. These symptoms can be of various sorts. The eighteen-year-old may be overly dependent on her parents, excessively aggressive toward her parents, or otherwise give evidence that a back-and-forth struggle with the parents is still going on.

Nineteen and Up: Even beyond the age of eighteen most late adolescents are still caught up in the struggle to release themselves from dependence on their parents. The signal that this psychological struggle is over is that the adolescent begins to assume the role of younger adult relating to older adults when she deals with her parents. In my experience, this new relationship usually does not develop until the young person is twenty-one or twenty-two.

By the time your grandchild has reached the later teen years, she is less likely to fall into behavior patterns that can be categorized by age. And by the later teens, your relationship with your grandchild has pretty well been formed.

Many grandparents who were fond of their grandchildren when they were young (and pliable) become disenchanted with their teenage grandchildren's life-styles. They may alienate their grandchild with criticism, or they may themselves withdraw from the relationship. Some grandparents forget that disliking their grandchild's *actions* doesn't mean they have to dislike the grandchild as well. If your relationship with your grandchild has become lukewarm and you would like to reestablish contact while she is still on the verge of adulthood, there are several things you can do.

Listen to her with an open mind, and don't be too quick to criticize. It's harder to be a teenager today than it was when your children were that age. There are many more temptations and fewer emotional supports in this generation. Instead of noticing how difficult your grandchildren have become, why not notice how well they manage—in spite of all the obstacles they face?

Roles are not as rigid as they once were. There's no longer such a stigma attached to boys' helping with housework, washing their own clothes, or cooking meals for the family. Girls are becoming auto mechanics, steelworkers, and truck drivers, as well as doctors, lawyers, and ministers, without losing their femininity. If your grandchild wants to enter a career that seems unsuitable to you, don't try to discourage her unless you know *exactly* what you're talking about. Otherwise, you'll lose your credibility and hurt your own cause.

Your relationship with your grandchild throughout the whole teenage period can be very difficult at times. Teenagers are mercurial. Their actions toward others, particularly family members, reflect their own inner doubts about themselves.

Having a grandchild at any age represents a learning experience, and at no time is this more true than when you have teenage grandchildren. You may be tempted to condemn all teenagers out of hand. And some of their habits *are* pretty bizarre. However, if you are willing to look under the surface, you will be pleased to find many bright, inquiring minds. It often takes patience to develop good feelings about a teenage grandchild. But the rewards are well worth it.

When your teenage grandchildren do something you approve of, let them know it. Warm, sincere praise is a wonderful soothing balm for teenagers' troubles. They usually hear about messy rooms, staying out too late, poor grades, unsuitable friends, and so on and on and on. When you have some good feelings toward your teenagers, sing them out loud and clear. And thank teenage grandchildren for any courtesies they show you.

Now let's move on to discuss in detail three very important areas in the total experience of adolescence: sex, drugs, and the choice of a vocation.

You and your grown children may have similar expectations and attitudes about your teenagers' sex life. But it is more likely that your views will differ, which means that you and your grandchildren's parents probably disagree on such issues as: Should you give an adolescent birth-control information, and, if so, at what age? At what age should an adolescent be allowed to single date? Is premarital sex permissible? Should a college-age girl be allowed to live with a boy in a coed college dorm or an apartment? If a girl gets pregnant, should she marry the boy; have the child and then give it up for adoption; have the child and keep it; or get an abortion?

My advice to you here is short and sweet: Keep your opinions to yourself! You are in a no-win situation, whether you speak to the grandchild or the parents or both. You may have very strong beliefs on any or all of these subjects and want to make them known. But the parents and the grandchildren undoubtedly have equally strong views. Sex is a very delicate issue. And if there is a conflict between your grandchildren and their parents, chances are your interference will only make things worse. You may think the parents are handling the situation all wrong. Perhaps they are, but it's very unlikely that you can do anything constructive about it except continue to be a friend to both parents and grandchildren.

The same goes for the issue of drugs. You may think that the parents are entirely too lenient or entirely too strict. You may think their approach is going to drive your grandchildren into drugs as a way of hitting back at a harsh and punitive parental attitude. Or you may think that your grandchildren are going to go hog-wild on drugs because their parents have been afraid to be firm with them. But whatever the parents' attitude, it is *their* attitude, and they have their egos invested in it, just as they do in their attitudes toward teenage sex. The last thing the parents want is anybody (including you) coming in and telling them there's anything wrong with the way they're handling things.

Let me use this as an analogy. Suppose your grandson is now twenty-two. He is head over heels in love with a woman of thirty-one and wants to marry her. She first got married at age sixteen and has had three divorces. She is known as a woman who is rather free and easy with her favors. Furthermore, she has a habit of belting the booze every night. You add up all these factors in your mind and you doubt that the marriage could last a year. In short, you are aghast at your grandson's choice of such a marriage partner.

Now for the crucial question: Do you think you should have a heart-to-heart talk with your grandson, pointing out his beloved's shortcomings, showing him how the marriage is doomed from the start? Will your grandson thank you for your enlightening him and saving him from a fate worse than death? He will not! He will have an answer for every argument you give him, and by the time you are through talking to him he will be seething with anger at you.

We usually say that "Love is blind." Your grandson's love for this girl is certainly blind to your arguments. And the ego-involvement of parents in their chosen method of handling sex and drugs with their teenagers is also blind.

On only *one* condition can you safely speak up on these ticklish issues. That is *if you are asked.* And you aren't likely to be asked unless the situation becomes desperate. What do you say then? I'd suggest something along the lines of the following:

"You've tried to solve this problem yourselves and it hasn't worked. I think it's time to get professional help—a psychologist, a psychiatrist, or a psychiatric social worker."

Some people assume mistakenly that a professional should be consulted only when the teenager needs extensive treatment. But just as you can consult a doctor for a virus as well as cancer, so you can consult a therapist for a relatively minor problem as well as for a major one—for a few visits as well as for a year (or more) of treatment. If your grandchild's parents can't afford professional help and you can, this could be an extremely important gift for you to give your family. If money is a problem for all of you, there are always agencies that offer professional help at rates based on the family's ability to pay. There are also help groups that cost nothing, such as Families Anonymous for families of teenage drug users. Your family doctor or pastor should know how to get in touch with these service groups.

At this point I'd like to say just a few words about discipline. Many parents are afraid to discipline their teenager for fear they won't be loved if they are too strict. Other parents adopt a hands-off policy because they have faith in their child's judgment and self-discipline. It's a shame that parents don't realize how badly rules are needed during this period. Rules do more than just control a child; they are guidelines that help him control himself. Rules and limits also let a child know that his parents are taking a sincere interest in him; lack of parental discipline is often interpreted as indifference by the adolescent.

However, you, as a grandparent, usually cannot set limits on your grandchildren's lives unless you are responsible for their upbringing. And you should not try to. This is the parents' province; *don't* try to butt in. As I've said before, your grown children have a right to make their own mistakes in raising their children.

Now let's turn to that very important step that is usually taken in adolescence—choosing a vocation.

This is one of the two most important choices that we make in our lives (the other, obviously, is the choice of a mate). And yet our society provides very little help to adolescents who are trying to pick a vocation. There is seldom any meaningful talk between adolescents and their parents on the subject, and, anyway, parents are often ill-equipped to give the kind of advice teenagers need. For example, could parents be of help if their daughter was trying to decide between being a nurse and being an occupational therapist? Of course teenagers frequently discuss such problems with their peers, but this is a process remarkably similar to that of the blind leading the blind.

What most parents and grandparents are completely unaware of is that scientific help is available to their teenager. Colleges, universities, and psychologists in private practice can give your adolescent grandchild a battery of tests to determine the types of jobs he or she is best suited for. I think that such vocational testing is a very good investment for young people fifteen and older. (If the child is tested before she is fifteen, the test results will not be valid.)

Vocational testing should cover the following areas: intelligence, evaluated by an individual intelligence test; interests; aptitudes; and personality, evaluated by such tests as the Rorschach inkblot test, the Thematic Apperception Test, and the Sentence Completion Test.

Vocational testing will not magically end all of your grandchild's difficulties and ambivalences in the choice of an occupation. Nor will it announce that a specific field (law, architecture, medicine, teaching) is *the* one the teenager should choose. Rather, the testing will reveal, through the interpretations of a skilled psychologist, the teenager's areas of vocational strength and the occupations in which he is most likely to be both happy and successful.

In the vocational testing I do, I ask teenagers to do considerable research on the vocations that interest them. I encourage them to learn such things as future demand for the vocation; potential salary or economic compensation; working hours; vacations and fringe benefits; education or training required; and the length of time this training will take. With all these factors laid out on the table, and the test results in hand, I then help the teenager to see where his areas of vocational strength are, and in what fields of work he will be most likely to succeed as an adult.

I want to emphasize that vocational testing and guidance should be done *only* by a person professionally trained for it. This means your grandchild should be tested by the counseling or guidance center of a college or university, or by a Ph.D. psychologist in private practice. There may be no person or institution near you qualified to do this testing. But, believe me, it is worth the time and money involved to drive to the nearest place where your adolescent can get quality professional vocational testing and guidance. If you succeed in interesting your adolescent grandchild in such testing and guidance, and underwrite the cost of it, you may be giving her the most important personal gift imaginable.

Well, there it is—adolescence. It's not an easy time for either parents or grandparents to live through. I've tried to cover the various substages of adolescence comprehensively so that you can be fully prepared to deal with them.

Perhaps it might be best to end this chapter on an upbeat note with a word from someone who is not a psychologist, psychiatrist, sociologist, or anthropologist, but who is nevertheless an acute observer of the genus *Adolescentus.* He is a poet, and his name is Ogden Nash. Here is a spoonful of his humor to help make the medicine of this chapter go down more easily.

> O Adolescence, O Adolescence,
> I wince before thine incandescence.
> Thy constitution young and hearty
> Is too much for this aged party.
> Thou standest with loafer-flattened feet
> Where bras and funny papers meet.
> When anxious elders swarm about
> Crying "Where are you going?", thou answerest "Out,"
> Leaving thy parents swamped in debts
> For bubble gum and cigarettes.

. . . .

Ah well, I must not carp and cavil,
I'll chew the spinach, spit out the gravel,
Remembering how my heart has leapt
At times when me thou didst accept.
Still, I'd like to be present, I must confess,
When thine own adolescents adolesce.[1]

Part Three

Special Aspects of Grandparenting

～§ 12 §～

Long-Distance Grandparents

*"The nice thing about her is that she says I've got two homes,
my home and their home."*

Julia Gambold, age 9

We've come a long way since your grandchild was born in Chapter 2!
I've covered all the stages of development from birth through late adolescence.
I've sketched in the unique features of the child at each stage of development
and suggested the best ways of relating to your grandchild during each one.
Without this basic knowledge of child development, a grandparent is like a
Boy Scout lost in the forest without a compass.

Now that we have surveyed all these ages and stages, it's time to discuss
some special aspects of grandparenting. First, I want to talk about a special
kind of grandparents: long-distance grandparents.

You may live in the same city as your grandchildren or a half hour's
drive from them, or you may live hundreds or even thousands of miles away.
Throughout most of the discussion so far, I have dealt with grandparents
who live fairly close to their grandchildren. These I call *constant* grandparents,
because their proximity should enable them to see their grandchildren quite
frequently.

Those of you who live farther than a convenient drive from your grandchildren I call *occasional* or *long-distance* grandparents. Handicaps of distance
make it likely you will see your grandchildren only occasionally. But that
needn't mean you cannot become an important person in your extended family
and in your grandchildren's lives, and enjoy the children immensely. Let's
see what the long-distance grandparent can do.

Suppose you have not had the opportunity to be with your grandchildren
for a year, or have had no contact at all with them. When you and your
spouse finally show up for a visit, the grandchildren may well wonder, "Who
are these two old people?" You will mean nothing to them because they will
have the words "grandmother" and "grandfather" in their minds, but only
a big blank space to go with them. So, first, let's talk about how to fill that
big blank space, perhaps before your grandchildren ever meet you.

115

Children get few letters. Whether they are three or six or eleven, they are all in the same position with respect to the U.S. Postal System: Hardly anyone writes to them. That's where you can come in. Write to them! Write them postcards. Write them letters. Send them "grandparent newspapers." Send them gifts through the mail.

Postcards are the easiest. Collect colorful picture postcards and print some brief message on each. Especially if your grandchildren are young, they will love your cards and probably save them. To adults, a letter is much more important than a postcard, but children do not feel this way. The important fact to them is that they're receiving mail. If you write them letters, be sure to include snapshots of yourselves, your pets, scenes from your trips, or anything else you think they might like. Children, especially young children, love to look at pictures of any kind.

You can write more or less conventional letters to your grandchildren, or you can occasionally try to do something different. One possibility is to take a large sheet of paper and paste pictures and words cut from magazines on it, supplementing them if necessary with words printed with a felt-tip pen. Another thing you can do to enliven your postcards and letters is to sprinkle them with odd facts—for example, "Did you know that Reading, Pennsylvania, is called Pretzel City?"—gleaned from books like *The Super Trivia Encyclopedia* by Fred Worth, and *Fascinating Facts: Weird Bits of Information on Practically Everything* by David Carroll. One reason that children (especially those aged eight to fourteen) love these odd facts is that they can quote them to their peers.

You can write postcards and letters to your grandchildren from about age three on. But you can begin communicating with them in another way at the age of one or two. Make sure that the children's parents have your picture. Then, from time to time, send little inexpensive gifts, and each time you do, ask the children's parents to show them your picture and explain that you sent the present. You can also write and send presents (at all ages) from your grandchild's "secret pal." Children love this kind of game. Even after they guess who you are, they will continue to delight in it.

For children three and older, you can send a "grandparent newspaper," which can consist of stories (true or imaginary) about your grandchildren, about yourself, and about anything else you want to put in it. Type up the newspaper, paste on any pictures you want, and have the whole thing Xeroxed. Here's a sample newspaper to show how you do it.

George Pierson Named Top Soccer Player

George Pierson has been named top soccer player of all the United States children under eleven by J. W. Chilton, captain of the U.S. Olympic Soccer Team. "I'm very proud of George," said Mr. Chilton. "He's absolutely incredible for a soccer player, when you consider he's only eight years old. Mark my words: He'll be another Pele someday!"

George will receive a silver medal, a lifelong free ticket to Disneyland, and a free ten-gallon keg of popcorn every month.

Katie Beats Computer

FLASH! Katie Pierson, ten-year-old daughter of Mr. and Mrs. Thomas Pierson, was the only student in the annual Computer Olympics to beat UNIFAX, the chess-playing computer, in the finals held at the Montebello Science Fair.

For her achievement, Katie was awarded a scholarship to the college of her choice.

Katie is at present working on a book entitled *How to Beat a Computer at Chess.*

Katie and George Will Go by Jet To Visit Grandma and Grandpa in Michigan

FLASH! Katie and George Pierson will take a two-week summer vacation at the home of their grandparents, Walter and Harriet Pierson, in Dearborn, Michigan.

The Pierson children will be making their first trip by jet airplane to see their grandparents.

Their grandparents have many exciting events planned for Katie and George when they arrive. They will see Greenfield Village, a reconstruction of an early American town. Here they can ride a paddle-wheel boat like those that formerly operated on the Mississippi River.

They will see many horse-drawn carriages, as well as early automobiles. They will see demonstrations of candle-making, weaving, and soap-making.

They will go to Camp Dearborn, a man-made lake with a beach that has many activities for children.

Grandpa has promised to take both children fishing during their visit. In addition, Grandpa and Grandma will take the children to a secret, absolutely TOP-SECRET SURPRISE!

The children will leave Sacramento, California, on July 8 and return home on July 24.

Tape cassettes can add another dimension to long-distance communication with your grandchildren. Tapes have several advantages: They are more personal than a written letter and your grandchildren can play them over and over as many times as they wish. Younger children, aged one to three, can understand a cassette "letter" more easily than a written one. And the children can return your communications by making cassettes of their own. If you want to exchange tapes with your grandchildren, you might suggest that their parents help the children make tapes by interviewing them. Answering questions is much easier for children than simply talking at length into the tape recorder.

Then, of course, there are phone calls. For some grandparents, the cost of long-distance calls is within their means, and phoning is a simple and effective way of maintaining constant contact. For others, such calls need to be reserved for special occasions in order to keep the family budget in line.

You constant grandparents can also write your grandchildren postcards or letters, make a "grandparent newspaper," send "secret pal" letters and gifts, and use tape cassettes to send special messages. Though you might not think of doing these things because you live near the children, they can be worthwhile and lots of fun for both you and the youngsters.

For both constant and long-distance grandparents, visiting is the chief means of getting together with the grandchildren. I'll have more to say about visits of all kinds in the next chapter. Here, a few words about the long-distance grandparent's particular situation.

When it comes to visits, long-distance grandparents are obviously at something of a disadvantage. But perhaps it's possible for you to arrange to have your grandchildren visit you more often than you had imagined. These visits can generally start when the child is about five.

Some parents might be hesitant, but I feel it is perfectly safe to put a five-year-old on a plane as long as she is picked up at the other end. (However, I do not recommend this if the child has particular problems, psychological or otherwise.) Most airlines will give an unaccompanied youngster special attention, take care of any special needs that might arise, and make sure she is delivered to the proper person at the end of the journey.

Of course, the airplane is not your only option for travel. A bus trip could work out fine if the child is nine or ten or older and the trip is no longer than a single day. Again, some parents may be nervous about allowing their nine-year-old to take a day-long bus ride alone, and their decision should of course be final. (But how is the child going to learn to do things of this nature alone, unless a parent gives him the chance?) A good book or an electronic game can be taken along as an antidote to boredom.

If you have several grandchildren, it is generally better to arrange for them to visit you just one at a time. Otherwise, you are almost sure to run into sibling rivalry, and nothing is more of a detriment to a happy visit than that. When you just have one child visiting, and she knows she does not have to share you with a brother or sister (or cousin), she can relax and enjoy you and her visit.

If you can, set aside a special room for your granddaughter, or at least a special corner of a room that is "her" corner. If you cannot, then camping out in a tent in the yard is always a thrilling adventure. (I am assuming that, ordinarily, your grandchild will come to visit you during summer vacation.) Even if you live in an apartment rather than a house, you should be able to set aside a corner of the apartment as your grandchild's "special corner."

A child's first visit to his grandparents should be no more than a week long. The reason for this is that the first time a child is away from home, whether he is at his grandparents' house or at camp, he may become homesick or bored (or both) by the end of a week. Even if this doesn't happen, it is still better to limit the first visit so the child will be eager for more the next year. The second visit can be for two weeks (or even longer if the child and his parents agree).

You, your grandchild, and your grandchild's parents all benefit when the child spends time away from home with you. You and your grandchild will enjoy seeing each other and doing things together, of course. And the parents will enjoy a respite from riding herd on the child. (This is especially good if it's a single-parent situation, because single parents have a deeper psychological need for vacations from their children than parents in intact families.)

Remember to prepare for the possibility that the child may be homesick. If she is, use the feedback technique (see Chapter 4) to let her know you understand how she feels. Then try to plan something especially interesting to do either that day or the next. Distracting activities will usually help the child get over her homesickness quickly.

Perhaps the most important thing you can do to ensure that your grandchild has a happy visit is to plan it carefully. Don't just wait until the day your grandson arrives, and then decide what to do each day on the principle of "doing what comes naturally." Your program doesn't need to be rigid and inflexible; in fact, it should be open to change at any point. But if you and your grandchild talk over and plan the visit several weeks in advance, the two of you will be able to sort through the various possibilities and select activities that you both like and are comfortable with.

Particularly if your grandchild has not visited you before, it's psychologically important to start off with something especially interesting planned for the first or second day. (I say "first or second" because if the child is arriving late in the day, it's a bad idea to rush him off for some excitement right away. He may be tired and need to rest.) If you live in the Los Angeles area, a visit to Disneyland will be sure to make a hit. Or if you live in a city with an amusement park, a visit there is certain to please. Use your imagination. If you live just a short drive from a good fishing spot and you and your grandchild like to fish, that would be a great way to begin.

If possible, give your visiting grandchild the opportunity to meet some other children his age. It makes a nice psychological mix for him to be able to play and go places with you, and also play with his peers part of the time. Or you may want to take a few other kids with you on some interesting day trips.

Don't think that you have to keep your grandchild occupied 100 percent of the time. That can become wearing for both of you. Give the child and yourself some "psychological space" during the visit. If you feel tired and want to take a nap, do it. Your grandchild can have some free time to watch TV or read a book or play with toys. Among the most engrossing toys for children between six and fourteen are the various electronic games such as baseball, football, basketball, and space. (Such games are also excellent for a youngster to play with on a long airplane or bus trip.)

So far, I have talked about your grandchild visiting you. Is the situation psychologically different if you go to visit him? It definitely is. You have him all to yourself when he visits you. He is on unfamiliar turf and usually has no one but you to play with and to turn to. He does the things you have planned to do with him. But when you visit his house he is on his home turf. He has his friends and his parents, not to mention all of his own toys, his own room, his own familiar bed, and so on. He may very well want to do something with his friends on a day that you had planned to do something special with him. If this happens, try not to feel rejected, for it is a very normal thing. Just be prepared to have him run off and leave you part of the time, and enjoy the time you do spend with him.

Grandparents and grandchildren can also visit each other by taking a trip together. You might drive and stay at hotels or motels, or you might camp in a camper or a motor home, or you might travel by train, plane, or bus. Two retired grandparents I know who live in Rochester, New York, drove at a leisurely pace across the United States to Modesto, California, and picked up their nine-year-old grandson. Then they drove him back across the country in their camper, showing him things he had never seen before, including Prehistoric Gardens in southern Oregon, where there are wonderful replicas of dinosaurs in a "prehistoric" setting; various national parks, including Yellowstone; a number of excellent fishing spots; and Niagara Falls. When they got back to Rochester the grandson stayed a few days, getting acquainted with his grandparents' house and hometown and way of life, and then they put him on a plane back to California.

Of course, not every grandparent has the time or money for such a fabulous trip. But you can take your grandchild on little trips that will be quite enjoyable. Do not judge by adult standards. Going, say, from Los Angeles to San Diego may not appear to be a big deal to you, but a child's view is different. Driving, flying, or taking the train from one town to another, visiting the zoo, staying at a motel with a swimming pool, going to a movie, and eating a big Sunday buffet dinner can all add up to a very exciting weekend for a child.

While writing this book, I interviewed a number of boys and girls from six to fourteen and asked them a simple question: "What things have your grandmother and grandfather taught you?" Unfortunately, the overwhelming majority of the children said that they had not learned anything in particular from their grandparents. But the answer of one twelve-year-old boy stands out in sharp contrast to the others. He answered, "Jeez, my grandfather taught me a lot of things. He taught me how to fish and shoot a .22, and he taught me all about tools and how to make things, and he even taught me how to weld." Clearly he and his grandfather had a close and fond relationship.

You do not have to live in the same city as your grandchild in order to have this kind of warm, influential relationship. Building such a relationship is a matter of making the time you spend with your grandchild special for the two of you. These special times need not involve exotic or spectacular activities. You can develop an important relationship in the course of doing ordinary things together.

I have a very fond memory of something I used to do with my grandfather. I would get my little red metal wagon and go with him to the store about six blocks from our house, where we'd do our marketing. I remember holding his hand when we crossed the street, and how strong I felt he was. (It is the only memory I have of any physical touching between us.) I think we must have started this custom when I was three or four and continued it until I was nine or ten and had outgrown it. I felt thrilled and very grown-up to be taken shopping with him. Somehow, shopping with my mother did not seem as special as shopping with my grandfather.

Yet I think of ways my grandfather could have had a greater influence on me, taught me many things, and built up a closer relationship, just based on those shopping expeditions alone. For instance, he could have explained where the food we bought came from: "Look, Fitz, this can of mackerel comes from Japan. I'll show you where that is on the map in our atlas when we get home. And these sardines come from Portugal. I'll show you where that is, too."

He could have explained that there was a big produce market in downtown Baltimore and that early in the morning the storekeeper or his employees went down to that market and bought the fruit and vegetables for the day. He could have told me how the farmers for miles around brought their vegetables and fruit to sell in the produce market. He could even have gotten me up at four A.M. one day in the summer or on a weekend and taken me down to see that market. I am sure that as a young boy I would have been thrilled, particularly if he had finished the trip by stopping for an ice cream cone or one of my beloved Baltimore snow cones.

These are some of the many ways in which my grandfather could have taught me about the world, developed a closer relationship with me, and learned to enjoy me more as a person.

As I have said, my grandparents lived in the same house with us, so it was natural for me to spend time with them. But even if you are a long-distance grandparent rather than a constant one, you can do some of the same kinds of everyday things with your grandchild when the two of you are together. It is the *way* you are together—the sharing of experiences, knowledge, and skills—that becomes important and special.

I think of my grandparents who lived with us in Baltimore, and of my Uncle North and Aunt Maryon who lived outside of Wilmington, Delaware. I saw my grandfather and grandmother every day of the year. Even though I saw Uncle North only on holidays and about two or three times the rest of the year, he had a great influence on me—a greater influence than Grandma and Grandpa. He was a commanding figure of a man, and I remember being very impressed by him as he swept into the house. His *joie de vivre* and good sense of humor certainly left a lasting impression on me. I still remember his incisive dinner-table discussions of how to make smart business decisions and sell people on your ideas. Even the way I mark my books and write comments or questions in the margins I got from him. The point is that he left his mark on my life, despite the fact that I saw him infrequently.

You, as a long-distance grandparent, can certainly enjoy your grandchild and become an influential person in his life. In fact, armed with the knowledge in this book, you may end up being closer and more important to your grandchild than grandparents who live three blocks away from him!

᨞ 13 ᨞

Visits, Long and Short

"One of a grandmother's most prized privileges is to spoil her grandchildren. She arrives armed with pockets of candy and special pocket money to buy the child things denied it by its parents for numerous good reasons."

Tessa Ing

Whether you are a constant or a long-distance grandparent, visits are probably your principal means of getting together with your grandchildren. For those of you who live too far away to visit your grandchildren very often, your visits are bound to be a big event for the whole family, and it's very important to try to get the most out of them. Let's define these visits as the kind that occur less often than twice a month, require a journey of more than three hours, and involve at least an overnight stay.

Unfortunately, for many grandparents the anticipation of a visit with the grandchildren is more pleasant than the visit itself. By the time you get to the farewell kisses, your feelings are often a mixture of relief at finally saying good-bye, and guilt at feeling so good about saying it. This is the kind of visit I would like to help you avoid.

Many problems could be avoided if both guests and hosts would take a little more time to prepare before the visit.

Sometimes family members don't take the trouble to prepare for one another because they think, "They're just family, not company. They won't mind." Sorry, but this usually isn't so. Family members do mind if the house isn't clean, the guest bed and bathroom towels aren't ready, and the meals are catch-as-catch-can instead of planned, with at least one company-style dinner. In other words, they will mind if there are no signs that you have been looking forward to their visit and have done some planning for it. They will not only mind, they may very well say they mind. As guests, they feel insulted. Then the host(ess) may become defensive. This is *not* a good atmosphere for a visit.

So I offer some advice: Parents, when you're expecting *your* parents, go to as much trouble as you would if your boss were coming to dinner. Perhaps you really can't get your house in perfect order and gourmet meals prepared, but at least take special care with the space the guests will use, so that they will feel expected and welcomed.

Grandparents, if you are doing the visiting, try to be good guests. Don't be hypercritical if things aren't exactly the way you hoped they would be. And for heaven's sake, plan the details of your arrival and your stay so that they cause minimal disruption to the household.

Grandparents are more likely to be the visitors, for several reasons. It's expensive for a whole family to travel. Many grandparents have moved from larger homes to small apartments, so there is often more room for all at the grandchild's home. Many families have children in school and can only travel at certain times of the year, while many grandparents have flexible schedules and can travel when they like.

If you are one of those lucky grandparents with enough money to travel and enough freedom to choose your time, try to make sure that the time you choose is convenient for your grown children. Think about the last time you visited your grandchildren. Was the visit for a specific occasion? Were you invited? Or did you just say you were coming? Did you ask if it was convenient for you to visit?

If you're not going for a special event, try *not* to visit your grandchildren when the other set of grandparents will be there, unless none of you is staying at the house, or you know one another very well and get along fine. Two sets of grandparents can cause trouble. They tend to engage in competition for the grandchildren's affections, creating a situation that smart children can exploit.

If you have a choice, plan your arrival time so no one will have to leave work or other duties in the middle of the day to pick you up. Pretend that your grown children are friends you are going to visit, and ask only as much of them as you would of a friend.

As for the length of your visit, it's always better for it to be too short than too long. Far better for everyone to feel, "I wish it could have lasted longer," instead of, "Thank goodness it's over!" It's true that travel is expensive, and maybe you feel that to have a short visit means you're not getting your money's worth. But think in terms of quality, not quantity. A really good week-long visit is far better than four weeks that just drag on.

You should be aware that many grown children are afraid to speak out and tell their parents their real feelings—and vice versa. I know a mother here in California whose mother has been retired for six years. Every one of those six years she has come to visit her granddaughter, and because she lives in Minnesota, she has timed her visits to spend January and February in California so that she can avoid the grim Minnesota winter.

I know how the mother really feels about those visits, because she tells me even though she keeps her feelings hidden from her mother. Along about December, her complaining begins. "Oh, Lord, Eunice will be here soon on her annual pilgrimage." Once I inquired exactly what was wrong with Eunice and her visits. "Well, if she would just come out and visit for two weeks, I think it would be fine. But two months—holy cow!" I said, "Well, why don't you tell her how you feel about the ideal length of a visit?" "Oh, I could never do that; her feelings would be terribly hurt."

When the grandchildren visit you in the summer, a stay of one or two months may be fine. But it's highly unlikely that a month or so is an ideal length of time for you to spend at the grandchildren's house. Remember that the whole family has to live differently and adjust their schedule in various ways when you're there—and that puts a strain on them.

So let your family know when you're coming, and also let them know when you're planning to leave. I know one grandfather who felt insulted if his children asked him how long he expected to stay. "I think you just want to get rid of me," he'd answer in an aggrieved tone of voice.

But look at it from your children's point of view. Maybe they have other people they'd like to invite to visit them. Maybe they'd like to take a trip themselves. Maybe there are things they want to do that are difficult to do with you there. And remember, no matter how loved you are, and no matter how helpful you may be, having more people in the house is still having more people in the house. Unless the house is large and/or there is a lot of help, your visit can be a burden if it continues indefinitely.

Very few homes today have the luxury of a full-time guest room. When you come to visit, you are usually displacing someone. Being displaced is something we willingly endure for someone we love. But one's patience can wear pretty thin after a while, especially if the visitor is not considerate.

Let's imagine, for example, that you are coming for your granddaughter's high school graduation and you will have to share her bedroom. If possible, plan to arrive after she's through with her final exams and to stay longer *after* graduation.

Try to travel light. It's all right to wear the same clothes several times. You don't want to take up all of someone's precious closet space. If you're coming for a special event, find out as much about it in advance as you can so you can bring the right clothes. This makes much more sense than bringing three outfits and deciding what to wear once you get there.

If you don't know what kind of weather to expect, check your local newspaper. It probably has a weather map of the whole country. You can also check with the local weather bureau, your library, a travel agent, or your children. Of course, weather can be notoriously unpredictable. But instead of carrying lots of extras, invest in a small folding umbrella and a reversible coat, or one with a zip-in lining.

Make sure your clothes are comfortable, especially your shoes. Nobody wants to hear Grandma complain about her blisters because her new shoes don't fit right. Nobody wants to have to cut an outing short because Grandpa's feet hurt.

What else do you have to pack? Gifts? That's a hard one to answer. It's no fun to have a grandchild run up, hug you ecstatically, and say, "Hi, Grandma, what did you bring me?" Unfortunately, many grandparents bring this on themselves by announcing the gift within moments of their arrival, almost as if it were their ticket for entry. If you feel you must play Santa Claus, perhaps you can bring just a small token gift, and/or buy something more substantial while you're there. You also might consider a family gift, such as an outing for the whole family, rather than individual presents.

If you're visiting and bring a special gift for one grandchild, be sure to bring token gifts for the others in the same household, including any step-grandchildren. The exception is at birthday time, when the birthday child is the one honored.

However, beware of surprises. Don't make an announcement that you're taking everyone to Hawaii, Disneyland, or even out to dinner without first consulting your grown children. They may have other plans, or they may have strong feelings against your idea, for whatever reason. If you announce your treat without their prior knowledge, you may be putting them on the spot. They may be pressured by their children into agreeing to the treat, or they may be put in the position of being "bad guys" if they say no to it.

Surprises of all kinds are usually a bad idea. If your doctor has put you on a special diet, write to your children and let them know about it in advance. It's unfair to say, "I can't eat that," when someone has gone to a lot of trouble to prepare a special meal.

"Why didn't you tell me what your doctor said?" asked one daughter when her visiting mother announced the rigorous diet her doctor had prescribed.

"I didn't want to worry you," said her mother.

Her working daughter gritted her teeth and remained silent. She had spent the entire weekend cooking a freezer full of food for her mother's stay!

There are a lot of things you can do to prepare yourself for your visit. Are you familiar with the city you'll be going to? Do you have friends you'd like to see? If it's an unfamiliar place, perhaps you could read up on it before your arrival. If there's an attraction that you'd particularly like to see, tell your family in advance. If both parents work and you'll be on your own all day without a car, find out what kind of public transportation is available. The more planning of this kind you do before your visit, the more likely it is to be a successful one.

Once you've arrived, what then? Well, the most important rule to remember is that it's your children's house, so you go by their rules. It doesn't matter that you once changed their diapers and fed them their pabulum. That was a long time ago. Your children are now parents themselves, responsible adults, I hope.

Please think before you speak. Don't remind your grown children to wear sweaters or carry umbrellas. It will drive them mad if you treat them as if they are still little children. And it damages their credibility with their own children (or damages *your* credibility) if you find fault with them.

Remember that grandchildren have ears. They may be young, but that doesn't mean they're deaf. Don't talk about them if they might be listening—unless it's to praise them.

You no doubt remember that back when you were a child, you listened as hard as you could when there was company, hoping you wouldn't be discovered before you heard all the fascinating grown-up talk and gossip. Kids may have changed in a lot of ways, but not in that way. So be careful what you say if your grandchildren are anywhere in the house.

Be resourceful. Look after yourself. Don't expect to be entertained or to be waited on constantly. And, once in a while, get out of the house by yourself. It will give everyone, especially you, a rest and a change of pace.

Money, for some reason, is a taboo topic in many families. Suppose you are staying at your grandchildren's home and realize that you are an extra expense for them. You want to help out. But who pays for what—and how?

If you suggest an evening out, with or without the grandchildren, you can make it plain that you intend to pay by simply telling the parents that you'd like them to be your guests. If you feel that even the cost of a baby-sitter might keep them from going, tell them you'll take care of that as well.

What if you are a very traditional grandmother who believes that when there's a man present, he is the one who should pay the check? Of course if your husband is on hand, this presents no problem. But what if he's not? Customs have changed, and today it's hardly necessary that the man pay, but if it makes you feel more comfortable, you can slip your son (or son-in-law) the money. (It's preferable to do this before you leave the house, rather than in the restaurant.)

How about everyday things, like helping out with the groceries? This, of course, depends to some extent on the family's financial situation—and your own. If they are obviously struggling to make ends meet and you are well off, you can help. But try to be diplomatic.

If you do suspect your visit will impose a financial burden on your children, write in advance that you don't want to wreak havoc with their budget, enclose a check, and then *don't mention it again.* Don't play Lady Bountiful at the checkout counter, either. Don't insist in public, "I know you can't afford this; let me pay." Don't make your children look or feel like charity cases.

If you discreetly offer financial aid and it's refused, then drop the subject. Your children may have saved for your visit. They may have made sacrifices to have you there. They may even have an overwhelming sense of false pride. So don't insist once they have refused.

Suppose you're going to stay at a hotel or motel when you go to visit your grandchildren. If you'll be doing this at your own request, then of course you should pay for it. If you know the area, make your own reservations. If not, when you tell your children about your plans, ask them to make reservations, being sure to give them your price range. If you have made your own arrangements to stay at a hotel or motel, tell your children in advance, *not* on your arrival.

Suppose that midway through a visit you decide you'd be happier at a hotel or motel. Can you move out without hurting feelings? Probably not. Everyone is bound to feel at least a little bit hurt and guilty. But if things would just get worse if you continued to stay at your grandchildren's house, then the sensible thing would be to go ahead and move to a motel. You could always go home earlier than you intended. But if you've come for a graduation, wedding, confirmation, birthday, or any special event, leaving before it takes place will be bound to leave very bad feelings. So make every effort to stay.

So far we've been talking about visiting your grandchild at home. There are occasions when you may visit the child when she is away from home— at camp, in college, or setting up her own living arrangements. When you're visiting grandchildren away from your home and theirs, it's usually best to act more like a friend than a grandparent. Keep in mind that the more independent your grandchild is, the more you should treat her like an adult. This may sound obvious, but it's easy to forget.

For example, suppose your grandson is living with someone of the opposite sex and you don't approve. When you visit him, concentrate on thinking about how you'd act if it were a friend's grandchild instead of your own. You'd probably keep your feelings to yourself, wouldn't you?

Sometimes you may visit your grandchildren in their homes when one (or both) of the parents is away—for example, when the parents are going away on a trip, when there is a new baby, or when someone is hospitalized. Then you are usually more baby-sitter than visitor.

In discussing the stage of infancy (Chapter 5), I gave you some guidelines for deciding whether to volunteer to help out with your newborn grandchild. If you're *asked* to help, think the situation through carefully before making a decision about what's best. If you do go, be sure to do everything you can to make the visit a success.

Maybe you've been asked to baby-sit with your grandchildren while their mother is in the hospital having another baby. And maybe the children are very young and very energetic. If you enjoy the children and feel you can cope with them, by all means stay with them. But if you're afraid they will worry you and get on your nerves, and you sense that you will not be able to handle the situation very well, it's better to say no. If you and your grandchildren just can't get along, you will only be adding to the mother's tension, because she'll be worrying about how you and her children are making out. It will be far better for you, for the mother, and for your grandchildren if you hire someone else to stay with the children.

Suppose you are baby-sitting with your little granddaughter while one of her parents is sick in the hospital. If she asks, "Why is Mommy in the hospital?" be truthful with her. Say something like this: "Because she's very sick, and when you are very sick they can cure you better in the hospital." Do not give false reassurance to try to cheer her up if you know that false reassurance may boomerang. If her mother has a very serious illness, you can say something like this: "Mommy is very, very sick, and sometimes it takes a long time for the doctor to help her get well." If the child asks, "Is Mommy going to die?" *don't* say things like, "I'm sure she won't," when you're not sure at all.

Facing death with a youngster is very difficult. Let her work out her grief and share your own. Don't be stoical. Don't tell her the person who died is on a trip. She will keep wanting to know when she will return. She will be even more upset if she feels you've lied to her.

Suppose you are going to have responsibility for your grandchildren for a long period of time, and you won't be able to get in touch with their parents (for example, the parents are going off on a trip to a foreign country). You will find life considerably easier if you can get lists, lists, and more lists made up.

Try to get on paper a daily schedule for each child, especially for younger children, who appreciate a fixed routine. Try to write up a list of such information as the children's favorite foods, the foods they hate (and do they have to eat them?), the TV programs they aren't allowed to watch. When are the children allowed to visit friends? When can they have friends over? What are the children's outside activities (sports, music lessons, etc.)? Are there any car pools you might have to drive? What are curfew hours, bedtimes? Are these different on weekends? What are the rules about talking on the telephone, using the car, chores, homework, and who takes care of the pets?

Have a list of the names of each child's friends, and the telephone numbers of those she is likely to visit.

On a separate list, to be kept by the telephone, you'll need the numbers of the police, fire department, children's doctor; of the nearest paramedics, ambulance service, hospital, and poison control center; of the family dentist and lawyer. You should also have the names of any health plans the children may be insured under. You will want the names of the house insurance and car insurance companies, and the names of their agents.

Even though you are the grandparents, it helps to have a signed letter of parental consent so that you can easily get medical treatment for your grandchildren if necessary.

Why do you need so darn much information? Obviously, you need to know things like the name of the children's doctor in case of illness or emergency. The information on the children's daily lives is valuable because:

1. The children will be less affected by their parents' absence if their own lives are disrupted as little as possible.

2. The more you know, the easier it is for you to take charge. You won't be put in the position of having to decide whether your grandchild is stretching the truth when she says, "But my mother always lets me do that."

3. Having this information allows you to relax the rules when you want to. Tune in to your grandchildren. If they miss their parents badly, be flexible. Loosen up. You can say, "I know your mother doesn't allow you to stay up past nine on school nights, but just this once you can stay up fifteen minutes later. I'll read you a story."

The more stress children feel because their parents are away, the more flexible you should be. In any case, don't be so rigid that the children regard you as a jailer. On the other hand, don't be so lenient that your grandchildren turn into spoiled brats. With lists you've prepared with the parents' help, you'll have a pretty good idea of what's allowed and how far you can go.

When you're faced with the options, it's probably better to be a little on the indulgent side.

Things are different when your grandchildren visit you. Then *your* home rules apply. You can set limits for the children that you feel comfortable with. If the parents are visiting, too, try to reach a reasonable compromise between your rules and theirs. But remember, it's *your* home.

Young people are flexible. They can sleep on couches, floors, wherever. The question is: Are you as flexible as they are? Are you prepared for toddlers? Maybe you've finally fixed up your house just the way you want it. Can you bear the thought of jam-smudged fingers all over your beige couch? Or maybe you're just a very tidy person. Does the idea of shoes and sneakers strewn around your study make you shudder? Do you want to scream at the sight of nail polish, lipstick, a hair dryer, and four bottles of perfume sitting on the edge of your bathroom sink?

Think twice before you invite your grandchildren to visit you. If you are afraid that you are going to have to spend their whole visit trying to guard your possessions, or being driven crazy by their sloppy habits, it's better that they don't come at all.

It's difficult if your grandchildren come with their parents and the parents then expect you to baby-sit, if this was not at all what you had in mind when you invited them. It's better to have these things worked out before the visit. If you are a working grandparent, or if you don't work but have a busy schedule that you don't want to interrupt, it's better to forewarn your would-be visitors.

If you agree to baby-sit with the children while their parents are off doing other things on their visit, plan for it just as if the children were visiting by themselves. Remember what I said in the last chapter about making your time together special.

Some museums have special classes for young people. Local factories and newspapers often give guided tours. Racetracks sometimes open their early morning workouts to the public. Parks offer recreational programs. You can consider sending, or taking, your visiting grandchildren to any of these. If your grandchildren are old enough to enjoy going to the park or zoo or planetarium, but you don't have the time and/or stamina to take them, consider hiring a college student to go exploring with them. You can usually find someone through college employment offices. Nursing students often make excellent baby-sitters. (Remember that it's best to ask for references whenever possible.)

You should not invite your grandchild to visit you without his parents until the child is really old enough for this experience—and this means at least three years old. Sometimes having the parents leave and being in strange surroundings is too much for a very young child.

Even the best-adjusted visitor can become homesick, and it's hard for a grandparent to cope with this kind of misery. One of the most effective "cures" I know is when-I-was-your-age stories. Most grandchildren are intrigued by tales of what life was like in the Dark Ages when you were young.

Whenever grandchildren visit, keep on hand the names of a local pediatrician and the children's own pediatrician, a list of the children's current shots, and so forth. In fact, it wouldn't be a bad idea for you to have the same kind of lists that you'd have if you were sitting for them at their house, for the same reasons.

Visits can be a delight or a horror. The more carefully you plan ahead, the more they are likely to be delights.

14

Gifts

"I think my granddad is fantastic—most granddads are. If you are saving up for something they are like walking piggy banks and give you money."

Jeremy Shilling

My parents and grandparents, uncles and aunts, and assorted other relatives regularly gave me presents on my birthday and Christmas. But if I had to grade them on their gifts, I'm afraid they would not rate very highly. Because, with the exception of an Erector Set my parents gave me when I was eight or nine, I cannot recall a single one of the gifts these adults gave me during my entire childhood!

My Cousin Emma, however, was a different matter. Every birthday and every Christmas she gave me a book, because she knew how I loved to read. (Nobody else ever gave me a book.) I have no way of knowing how she did it, but every book fitted in perfectly with my age and my stage of development and what I was interested in.

The two I loved best were *Robin Hood* and *Treasure Island.* Among my other favorites were *Tales of King Arthur* and *Robinson Crusoe,* and John Steinbeck's *Tortilla Flat,* which she gave me when I was in high school.

Reading Cousin Emma's book was the highlight of Christmas for me. I opened all my other presents and saved hers for last. I would play with some of my toys, and then I was ready for the Main Event of Christmas Day. I'd take Cousin Emma's new book, along with a tall glass of milk and some Christmas cookies, and retire upstairs to my room, where I would read the book straight through (with a break for dinner) until I had finished it. What bliss and contentment!

Cousin Emma was good at gift-giving because she put care and thought into her gifts. She was interested enough in me to know not only that I loved reading, but also what kind of books I would like. She never selected a book that was too babyish for me or too adult and over my head.

You can give your grandchildren gifts that will be as special to them as Cousin Emma's books were to me. The children's parents may give them more gifts than you, and even more expensive ones. But parents usually give presents that they think the children need, or that they want the children to have. Or they give an item because the child has asked for it, and they are afraid to turn the child down. You, as a grandparent, can concentrate on selecting a gift that has no other purpose except to delight the child.

Unfortunately, grandparents are often far from the mark when they pick a birthday gift, Christmas gift, or any other type of gift for their grandchild. This is because they do not know the three basic rules of gift selection:

1. You need to know what types of toys, books, records, etc., a child of your grandchild's age and stage of development is ordinarily interested in.

2. Then you need to consider what particular things *your unique grandchild* will enjoy as a gift. Your grandchild is not eight years old in general, or eleven years old in general.

3. You need to know what gifts have the greatest play value or interest for the child over the long haul.

Parents and grandparents often give in to the hard sell of TV advertisements for toys. A child may make urgent and even tearful requests for the toys he sees continually on TV between the first of November and Christmas. What happens when he gets them?

This is what happened once to a family I was counseling. The grandparents had bought Gaylord, a battery-operated dog that walked across the room and wagged his tail. Their four-year-old grandson played with the dog enthusiastically for about forty-five minutes and then lost interest. He took the dog to his room, and about half an hour later, the parents and grandparents were horrified to discover that he had taken the dog completely apart.

"Why would he do an awful thing like that?" his grandfather asked me. "That damn dog cost us twelve dollars and fifty cents!"

I explained to the grandparents that Gaylord had very little lasting play value for their grandson. Once the child had finished marching the dog around the room, there was nothing left for him to be interested in except taking the toy apart to see how it worked. And in taking the toy dog apart, he had demonstrated an interest and capability that all young children have for investigating mechanical things. A more appropriate gift, and one with longer-lasting value for their grandson, would have been something like a Lego construction set or a good set of blocks.

The appendixes in the back of this book are designed to help you make a wise selection of age-appropriate gifts (toys, books, records, and tapes) for your grandchildren. I hope you will enjoy browsing through these appendixes and that you will find them helpful. They deal with the nuts and bolts of gift-giving. So I want to talk here about the philosophy of gift-giving.

Gifts are both an extension of the giver and an evaluation of the recipient. Some people give lavish gifts because they feel guilty about not giving time or attention. Or they may want to appear wealthier than they are. Some people give meager gifts because they have a great fear of appearing ostentatious. Or they may want to send a message: The person receiving the gift is getting just what he deserves—very little.

Some grandparents use gifts to try to buy love. But gifts don't buy love. They can only buy attention—and temporary attention at that.

Some grandparents give gifts with strings attached. They give a present, and then check to see if they think it's being used appropriately. For example, your grandson may be the sort of child who is careless with everything he owns. If you buy him an expensive ten-speed bike, you may be tempted to keep checking up on him (or his parents) to see if he is taking proper care of it. He probably won't be. If that's going to bother you, you shouldn't give the gift in the first place.

Money is often given with strings attached. If you make a loan, you certainly have every right to know how your money will be spent and how it will be repaid. But if you give a gift of money, you really shouldn't expect to influence what the recipient does with it. Say, for example, that your grand-daughter tells you she needs some clothes for college. You give her a birthday check, and she spends it for gold lamé jeans instead of a sensible woolen skirt. You're disappointed and frankly feel that she has wasted your money. But that's not the way she looks at it. It's *her* birthday money, and what she has bought has made her happy. (If you want her to have what will make *you* happy, you should find out her size and buy her the sensible wool skirt yourself.)

There's a difference between giving something with strings attached and putting limits on your gifts. Let's say your grandson is longing for new roller skates, and you tell him you'll buy him a pair. The last time you bought roller skates, you buckled and screwed them onto shoes, and kids wore skate keys around their necks. But things have changed! Skates now come attached to shoes, and the prices are high. You may find out too late that you can't afford what your grandson wants.

The moral of the story: Whenever you promise to buy a gift for your grandchild that he is picking out but you are paying for, let him know the price range you have in mind. (This means it's wise to find out the approximate cost of things before you volunteer to buy them.) Then, if you can't afford what the child has in mind, he has the option of choosing a less expensive model or a different gift, or of taking your contribution as part payment for what he wants.

You certainly do not have to wait for special occasions to give gifts. On birthdays and certain holidays, particularly Christmas and Chanukah, the child expects gifts and gets them from all his relatives. But sometimes the nicest gifts of all are those given when no special occasion prompts them. I call them un-birthday gifts, and they do not have to be large or expensive. The child will particularly like them because he is not expecting them.

Most people have to watch their gift budgets, especially if there are a large number of children to buy for. One grandfather told me that he buys his grandchildren small gifts for Christmas, "stocking stuffers" mostly. But on each child's birthday, he spends as much as his budget will allow. His rationale for this is that a birthday, the child's own special day, is more important than Christmas—and the child will get a multitude of gifts at Christmas anyway.

Sometimes it's not what you give, but how you give it. This is especially true with small token gifts, where style can play a larger part than substance. No matter what's inside, a nicely wrapped package usually seems more special than a bag from the store. Elaborate wrapping paper and ribbon can be somewhat expensive, but you can use your imagination and come up with something that's both festive and inexpensive. You can wrap gifts in Sunday comic strips, for example. Gummed notary seals and stars are available from stationery stores, and just a few of them can brighten up an ordinary gift package. Boxes enclosed in boxes until the gift is finally discovered are also fun, especially for young children. A small gift becomes even more special if the wrapping—a small ceramic or wooden box, a woven basket, a cloth pouch with a drawstring—is part of the gift. You can make or decorate these yourself if you are at all artistic. Boxes and decorations can be found at hobby stores.

Not all gifts are the kind you can wrap up and tie with a ribbon. You may want to take your grandchild out to dinner, just the two of you. Taking your grandchild on a fishing trip or sending her to a week-long summer camp can be an excellent gift. A high school graduation gift of a couple of weeks' vacation at a special place will probably be enthusiastically received by your teenage grandchild. (Naturally, you would consult the parents before giving such gifts.)

The older the child, the more particular he usually is, and the more attuned to fads and what's "in." If your grandchildren have reached this stage and can shop for themselves, sometimes it's best just to give them some money and let them pick out their own gifts. (If you think a gift check by itself is too impersonal, present it in a purse or wallet, a special box, or a box within a box within a box.)

If you give your grandson money as a gift, you may be tempted to take him shopping so he can spend it. I don't really recommend this. Letting the child go shopping by himself has several advantages. First, it's less tiring for you. If you've ever waited while a child tries to decide whether to buy the model or the game, and goes back and forth and back again, you know how exasperating it can be. And if you try to hurry him, he will invariably make the "wrong" choice and complain to you afterward that he would have chosen the model instead of the game if you hadn't rushed him.

Second, the amount of money you have given the child may not be enough to cover what he decides he wants. If you're along on the shopping trip, you may be conned into giving him more. Some grandchildren know just how to lay a guilt trip on their grandparents. It's not so bad if it's just one grandchild and a small amount of money, but if you have to give five or ten dollars more to each of several children, you may find yourself in a financial dilemma. (By the way, you may find it embarrassing to have to tell your grandchildren you can't afford something, but it doesn't hurt them to learn that you are not an ever-flowing fountain of money.)

Third, if you go along on the shopping trip you may influence your grandchild to buy something you want instead of something he wants. This will obviously defeat the purpose of giving him money so he can select his own gift.

And finally, the child may tell you he's allowed to have something when he's not. You may find yourself unwittingly helping him to break house rules, thereby putting yourself in the middle of a power struggle between the child and his parents.

It's a good idea to check with the parents about the suitability of any gift you are considering. They may not think the gift of a set of drums is the best way to encourage your grandchild's musical abilities. Grandparents who give candy cause difficulties for parents who don't want their children to have it. Some parents prefer that there be no cash gifts, especially in sizable amounts. They may think the child should put the money in the bank, while the child will probably want to spend it—and the result can be an unpleasant conflict.

You also have to consider whether your gift to your grandchild will count as a gift in her eyes as well. A savings bond for a nine-year-old girl to use for her college education isn't going to engender much enthusiasm on her part.

The Christmas my son Rusty was ten, his friend Eric was given a set of coins worth a hundred dollars by his grandfather. Eric was completely disgusted. "What kind of a Christmas present is that?" he grumbled. "Who wants a stupid set of coins for Christmas? And he won't even let me sell the dumb coins to get something I like. He says I can sell 'em when I get to college if I want to. Stupid!" This is a classic example of how *not* to give a gift. Eric's coins were an adult-type gift, totally unsuitable for him; they also had strings attached.

The younger the child, the more immediate gratification she wants from a present. If you insist on giving money or bonds to be earmarked for future use, it's often kinder not to let your grandchild know about it at all. You can bank the money in the child's name, in a savings account or a trust fund, and then give a small gift the child will really love.

Almost everybody loves to get presents. And usually giving them is a lot of fun, too. But much of the joy of giving is canceled out if the recipient acts in a negative way. Some children have an unfortunate habit of looking down their noses at anything they don't consider grand enough. And some children who are skilled at surfing or skiing or tennis seem absolutely incapable of the physical dexterity required to take a pencil or pen in hand and write a simple thank-you note.

If it really bothers you when your grandchild doesn't express gratitude, the best thing to do is to speak to her openly and up front: "If I go to the trouble of picking out a present and giving it to you, you can go to the trouble of writing me a thank-you note or calling me on the telephone to say thank you." And if she continues her loutish behavior, you can say something like, "You are hereby forewarned that I'm not sending gifts to people who don't take the trouble to say thank you. This doesn't mean that I love you less. It just means that I don't plan to send you any more presents until your behavior changes."

When I say speak to your grandchild, I mean just that. Speak to *her*, not her parents. Then, once you've given fair warning, you can stop sending gifts if you wish without seeming spiteful.

Now, what about gifts given to *you?* When your grandchildren are in grade school, they may give you pictures, handprints in plaster, and a variety of other items that have more sentimental than artistic value. If you have a limited amount of wall space and/or definite ideas about decorating, you may not want to display your grandchild's art over your living room couch, no matter how much you love the artist.

There are several solutions. One is to take a photograph of the work of art, and display that in a frame or album. Another is to use your refrigerator door as a revolving art gallery; most things can be put on it with magnets, shown for a limited period, and then replaced. This is an especially nice way to do things if you have several grandchildren who live close to you and visit frequently.

After displaying the items, keep at least some of them. Store them in a closet or a big box that slides under the bed. Preserving the art objects will be worth the trouble it takes to find a place to put them. Children are usually flattered to find that you have held on to these things for many years. And you may later decide that a few of the pictures deserve to be permanently preserved.

Be enthusiastic about receiving your grandchildren's gifts. They went to considerable time and trouble to make them for you. After all, nobody forced them to choose you as the recipient. They are giving the gifts to you solely because they want to. And if you expect thank-you notes from your grandchildren, be sure to set the example and write them yourself.

It's a terrible thing when gifts degenerate into obligations. Don't let that happen to you. In the final analysis, there is only one rule to follow: Do what your heart dictates. And this means give only when you are giving with love.

🙖 15 🙔

Grandparents, Grandchildren, and Family Roots

"Granny tells tales she told to Mother when she was a child . . . skating on the frozen park lake and riding on the top of an open-deck streetcar. All these more than make up for television."

Dawn Williams, age 10

The enormous success of the book *Roots* by Alex Haley and the subsequent TV series based on it underlined the fact that Americans are generally a rootless people, trying earnestly to find their origins. And don't make the mistake of thinking that only black Americans are looking for their roots; so are white, brown, and all other Americans.

Children like to know where they come from. They ask their parents to tell them what it was like when they were children. They like to think of themselves as part of a family line that goes back in time and has solidity and permanence.

This is where you, as a grandparent, can make a unique contribution to your own extended family. For who is better equipped than you to give your grandchild a sense of his roots? Who can impart a sense of "living history" better than you?

But if you asked most grandparents, "Would you consider yourself living history?" they would reply, "Oh, no. There's nothing special about me. I've led a very ordinary life."

Your life may seem ordinary to you, but it may not seem that way to your grandchildren at all. When you were a child, did you and your friends swim in the traditional "ole swimming hole"? Your granddaughter probably never will. She probably swims in swimming pools, with modern equipment. Most likely she's never in her life swung out over a swimming hole on an old tire and dropped into the water with a big splash.

You have no doubt ridden trains a number of times in the course of your life; maybe you have even slept in a Pullman berth. I remember telling my kids about the time I rode in a Pullman car from Baltimore across the

140

country to Portland, Oregon. They were fascinated, for they had never been on a train.

Your life may not have been full of the kind of personal adventures you could sell stories about to a magazine, but you have lived through eventful times. The Great Depression must have left its mark on your life. You may have fought in a war. Even if you didn't, you couldn't have helped being affected by one or more of them. Do you remember rationing? What did you do, growing up without television? Do you remember the first automobile you rode in? What was it like the first time you flew in an airplane? Even such little things as what you studied in school, how your mother cooked, and what you wore when you were young become fascinating to your grandchild simply because they are part of a time before she was born.

Many people do not share their childhood stories with their own children. Perhaps that's because they think their children wouldn't be interested. Sometimes the children aren't, because of the way the parents tell the stories. Often the same stories are repeated time and again; often the stories have a syrupy moralistic tone. Too many parents tell stories about doing chores and trudging through miles of snowdrifts to get to school, not about being mischievous and having fun. No wonder children are turned off.

Some parents are reluctant to talk about their childhoods because they were not very happy times. Some people cling tenaciously to the myth that children are supposed to be happy. So, if they *weren't* happy as children, they feel somehow guilty and don't want to talk about it. They may also hate to admit that their own children might be unhappy. If the children come to them with problems, they would rather shut them out.

The truth is that being a child—a small person in a world full of grown-ups whose rules often don't make sense—is frightening. Childhood is often a miserable time. That is why it might be of real help to your grandchildren to talk about your own life, both the happy *and* the difficult times. Knowing that other people have experienced hard times and that life is both hardship and delight is very helpful to children as they learn to face life's problems. You needn't moralize; just let your stories speak for themselves.

It may be easier for you to communicate with your grandchildren about life than it is for their parents to. You are a generation removed and not so deeply involved in the children's upbringing. You can do more, however, than just tell occasional stories about the times when you were young. You can build a real living history for your grandchildren. You can do this in person, on audio- or videotape, or by writing your story down.

Creating an oral history in person is wonderful and your grandchildren will love it, but there are advantages to recording or writing your story:

1. There are no interruptions or questions to make you lose your train of thought.

2. You can tell the story how and when you want to.

3. Some stories might be embarrassing if you told them face to face.

4. If you change your mind about including a story, you can remove it or redo it.

5. The stories can be enjoyed over and over by your grandchildren, and perhaps even by *their* children years from now!

6. The stories can be enjoyed by your grown children as well. Maybe you had difficulty communicating with them when they were kids. Hearing or reading about your life experiences can help them to understand you better. If they get a new view of you through your history, it can help enrich your relationship with them.

Talking into a tape recorder offers a simple way of creating a permanent oral history. In addition to telling stories, you might sing songs you knew when you were young, and have someone accompany you on a piano or guitar. Or you might speak some phrases of a foreign language you spoke when you were young. You will end up with a series of tapes that are a permanent living history.

Then again, you might prefer to write down your life history. "I'd like to," I hear you saying, "but I'm no writer." It's not as hard to write a book as you might think. Not, of course, the kind of book that would be published by a book publisher. But a *personal* book, your own special book for your grandchildren.

The idea of writing a book may seem overwhelming, but a book is only a series of chapters, which are in turn only a series of pages. If you write a page a day, you will have written a book-length manuscript in a year.

Starting at the beginning is sometimes the hardest thing to do, so start your story wherever it seems comfortable to you—where it's fun, where there's a memory that you'd like to share. You may find that the writing goes more easily if you think in terms of producing a series of easygoing, conversational letters.

In the future, most family histories will probably be recorded on videotapes—once the price of videotape machines comes down to the price of TV sets today. When you make a videotape, the machine records your picture and your voice at the same time. And the videotape can then be shown on a special video set, enabling you to watch it just as you would a television program.

There are many small companies that produce videotapes. If you can afford the cost, look in the Yellow Pages under TELEVISION FILM-PRODUCERS. If there are none listed there, people who sell television systems and equipment may be able to recommend someone. Or you might call the nearest college and see if anyone in the communications department can recommend a student producer. If you are really interested in home video productions, you can rent or buy your own video camera, but this will involve a rather hefty investment.

Actually, you don't have to decide on one form of story-telling exclusively. You can tell your story in person, on tape, or on paper. Now the question is, what do you talk about?

> Your own parents; your grandparents, sisters,
>   brothers, other relatives
> Where you were born
> Games you played as a child
> Places you've lived
> Your school days
> Your work experience
> Exciting events you have witnessed
> Sports you participated in
> Your own children when they were young
> Your grandchildren when they were young
> The most happy, frightening, sad, or funny
>   things you can remember

These are just some suggestions to get your imagination going. You will be amazed at how easy it is to think of things to talk about once you get started.

Your autobiography will be much more interesting if you include such personal museum pieces as:

> Photos (identify the people and their re-
>   lationship to you)
> Souvenirs (from a war, political campaign,
>   fairs, travel)
> Old letters
> Old magazine and/or newspaper articles,
>   or at least the headlines from these

"Personal museum pieces" of this kind can go along with your book or recorded story:

> Old clothing (for example, a christening dress that
>   has been in the family for several generations)
> Collectibles such as old toys, knickknacks,
>   license plates
> Objects you made or saved as part of a hobby

All these things will have much more value—sentimental and possibly monetary—if you can point out how you came to have them. Look in the attic and other storage places for things you might have forgotten you possess. Perhaps you have a cup and saucer that one of your great-grandmothers brought from Russia; a letter signed by Franklin D. Roosevelt in reply to one you wrote him supporting his first campaign for governor of New York; wings insignia from the time you were one of the first stewardesses for Pan American Airways (when stewardesses had to be registered nurses).

All of us procrastinate, and maybe you are thinking, "It sounds like it might be interesting. I'll do it someday." But don't wait too long. If you don't share your stories with someone in a permanent record, they may die with you.

Jewish tradition holds that you are alive as long as you live in someone's memory. By sharing your life, you are giving yourself a chance at immortality. And by making your living history available to your grandchildren, you are strengthening their roots!

~§ 16 §~

Grandparents, Divorce, and the Single-Parent Family

"Grandmas are always slow but they do not mind because they have all the time in the world."

Malcolm Andrew, age 10

Here are some jarring statistics that will show clearly why grandparenting is different in these changing times:

One out of every eight children in the United States now lives in a single-parent home.

An estimated four out of ten children born in the 1970s will live in a single-parent home during part of their childhood.

In 1951, only six hundred thousand children experienced the breakup of their families through separation or divorce. But in 1976, approximately two and a half million children experienced the psychological shock of the breakup of their families through separation or divorce.

Only 7 percent of the American population lives in what we persist in believing is the typical American family—one with a breadwinner father, a homemaker mother, and kids.

These are the facts as of today. But the divorce rate is continually going up. It looks as if there will be more and more single-parent families in the future.

If your daughter and her spouse go through a divorce, it will be one of the most traumatic events of their lives. Probably neither of them will have been through it before, and they won't have the faintest idea of what to expect. The divorce jungle is filled with venomous snakes and dangerous animals, as well as with banditos (otherwise known as lawyers). Your children have had no training in protecting themselves against any of these beasts.

To begin with, chances are that neither your child nor her spouse knows how to find a good lawyer—one who cares and who is intelligent, competent, and honest. But your daughter will have no trouble finding lawyers who do *not* fit that description.

145

According to the old-fashioned divorce concept, one party was supposed to be "innocent" and the other "guilty." Each lawyer in a divorce case tried to prove *his* party innocent and the other party guilty, so that his party would get the lion's share of the divorce settlement.

Now many states have adopted the so-called "no-fault divorce," in which neither party is presumed to be innocent or guilty. The marriage is merely dissolved because of "irreconcilable differences." One of the purposes of a no-fault divorce is to take some of the hostility and bitterness out of the procedure. But no-fault divorce laws have only partially succeeded in doing this. My own state, California, has had a no-fault divorce law for ten years. Nevertheless, I have seen an enormous amount of hostility in divorce cases I have worked with during that time in my clinical practice.

In a divorce situation, the cards are stacked against the couple, because even with no-fault divorce it is still an adversary system. If by some miracle the husband and wife are not angry and bitter at each other when they begin the legal process, by the time their respective lawyers finish egging them on, they certainly will be. The sad fact is that it is more profitable for lawyers to spend lots of time negotiating back and forth, firing off letters and phone calls, and conferring with their clients than it is for them to aid in a simple, clean divorce.

Then we come to judges. One divorce judge in Los Angeles is known as the "golf judge" because he has the reputation of wanting to get his cases wound up quickly so he can get out onto the golf course. One of my patients, a divorced father, told me about the verdict reached by another judge in his case. During the year-long divorce process, he and his wife, from whom he was separated, had gone by a mutually agreed-upon visitation schedule: The father would see his children every other weekend, and every Monday and Thursday night for dinner. The judge decided in court: "Monday and Thursday dinner visitations are too much; you can choose between them." Absolutely incredible! Where the children are losing a full-time father, but the father cares enough to want to see them twice a week for dinner, the judge rules that twice a week is "too much"!

Divorce judges are answerable to no one for the decisions they make. I've had a fair amount of experience with divorce judges, both through my clients' divorce cases and as an expert witness in custody cases. I find that most of them rule with all the finesse and competence of a gorilla playing the violin.

Why do I think it's important for grandparents to know these grisly facts about lawyers and judges? Because otherwise you will have no real understanding of the misery your grown children and grandchildren are going through, due to our archaic legal system. In addition, both of them are leaving the security of an established way of life and starting all over again on their own. One study showed that loss of a spouse through divorce or death is the most stressful thing an individual can experience. I don't need to go into all of the reasons for this; you will quickly become aware of them if there is a divorce in your family.

And don't assume that this will never happen to you. The chances are one in three that your married child will embark sooner or later on exactly that type of gut-wrenching experience.

All right, let's say you and your spouse have just found out your child is getting a divorce. Naturally you're upset, but you want to do the right thing. What is that?

First of all, you might issue a statement like this: "We're sorry things didn't work out for the two of you. But we're not going to take sides. We love you both and we know what a difficult time this is. So if you need somebody to talk to who will keep his mouth shut, or a baby-sitter, or if we can help in any other way, please call on us."

Not every divorcing couple gets that kind of emotional support from grandparents. It can be of great help in a time of crisis.

Remember that people can stop being married to each other, but they can never stop being parents to their children. And it is in your grandchildren's best interest for their father and mother, though divorced, to remain as amicable as possible. It does not do the children any good down through the years to be exposed to the spectacle of their parents' hatred for each other.

At this time, your child, his or her spouse, and your grandchildren will be going through the experience of mourning. If their father had died, the children and their mother would need to go through a period of what I call "grief work." Even though a divorce is not an *actual* death, it is the *psychological* death of a family, and there will be a need for mourning.

Working through grief takes time. As a rule of thumb, the sad, unhappy feelings persist for at least a year in both parents and children. You can help all of them simply by allowing them to ventilate their grief to you. You do not have to be a trained professional counselor to be helpful; just act as a sounding board for their feelings.

During a divorce, you probably won't be able to remain truly neutral in your heart. Your tendency will be to side with your child against his or her spouse. But outwardly you should try to maintain neutrality and treat both sides alike.

Even if you do feel very deeply that one person is in the wrong and deserves the blame, remember that you, like everyone else, can only look at the *outside* of the marriage. You cannot really know what is going on in the psychological interior of the relationship. So bite your tongue and keep quiet. You have no idea how much harm you can do yourself, the parents, and your grandchildren by taking sides. Grandparents sometimes feel the need to swing their weight around in such situations, and learn too late that they have made a huge mistake in doing so.

Here is an example from my case files. This was a divorce involving an executive father, his wife, and two children, aged three and seven. One set of grandparents lived in Wisconsin, while the grandparents on the mother's side lived forty minutes from the family in a Los Angeles suburb.

It was a messy situation. The father had been having an affair with a woman at work, and when the mother finally discovered the liaison (after about a year), she told her husband to pack up his belongings and leave. The husband had no deep interest in the other woman and did not want the marriage to break up. He came to see me to try to save his marriage. And he was finally able to persuade his wife to come see me, too.

While I was counseling the two of them, the maternal grandparents were beside themselves with rage. They told their daughter she was lucky to be getting rid of such a man, and that she was crazy even to think of reconciling with him. The grandfather phoned the husband and said, among other things, "If I was twenty years younger, I'd give you the thrashing of your life for what you've done to my daughter."

One of the things I've learned in my years of marriage counseling is that it's very difficult, if not impossible, to predict which way a couple will jump. And this case was no exception. I would have guessed that the marriage was "terminal" when the husband first came to see me. But after almost a year of counseling, during which the couple were living apart, they ended up getting back together again. We had to deal with some really hot emotions— rage, guilt, hurt—but we finally got all of them out in the open and worked through them. In the end, I felt that the couple were on really solid footing for the first time in their marriage.

But what about the grandparents? Well, they hadn't exactly made a friend of their son-in-law in the initial stages of the separation period. And their daughter wasn't too happy about the things they had said to her about him. So the parents put the deep freeze on the grandparents by preventing them from seeing the grandchildren. Oh, they relented at Christmas and Easter and on birthdays, but otherwise they were always "too busy" or doing something else when the grandparents wanted to see the children.

The grandparents were so upset about this that they wanted to consult me about it. I got the parents' permission and we set up an appointment.

The grandparents poured out their tale of woe, and I listened. Finally, I summarized the realities of the situation for them.

First, I agreed that not seeing their grandchildren was hard on them. Second, I said it was unfortunate for the grandchildren that they could not get together more often. But, as grandparents, they had no legal rights to see the children. I pointed out what a thorough job they had done in alienating their daughter and son-in-law. The only solution I could see was for them to try to get themselves back in their children's good graces. Until they did this, all of their pleas would fall on deaf ears.

It took these grandparents several years to establish a good relationship with the parents so that they could see their grandchildren on a regular basis again. They had certainly learned the hard way how *not* to handle a divorce situation.

Very few grandparents seem to realize that they have no legal rights to see their grandchildren. If the grandparents are reasonable, pleasant people to be around, the parents are going to want to see them and have the grandchildren see them. But if they're domineering, thoughtless, opinionated, or just uptight, chances are the parents are not going to want to have them around much, nor are they going to want the grandchildren to spend a lot of time with them. As a friend of mine in Los Angeles said to me recently when we were discussing this subject, "My parents are in Oregon, and that's just the way I want it. I don't want them messing around with my kids any more than is absolutely necessary."

I spoke a few pages ago of the "divorce jungle." There is another term that describes very well what a divorcing couple are going through: "divorce shock." Anthropologists speak of the "culture shock" that one may suffer when one is exposed to a completely foreign culture. Well, "divorce shock" is similar. It occurs when your child is exposed to the culture of a foreign land that I call "the country of the singles."

Not only will this territory be new and foreign and devastating to your child; it will probably be new and foreign and devastating to *you*. You will probably see your child living in ways she has never lived before, perhaps in ways you were raised to believe were wrong or immoral. Usually the behavior that will bother you is sexual. Your divorced daughter may have two young children and be living with a man she is not married to. Or perhaps she will allow men to stay overnight at her house from time to time when her children are there. Or your eight-year-old grandchild may tell you, "Last time I visited Daddy, he had a different girl friend staying there."

Once again, I can only caution you not to take sides or bad-mouth anyone. Remember, we are not talking about sixteen-year-olds. We are talking about men and women in their twenties and thirties or even forties. They are not children anymore, and they usually will not thank you for your advice on their life-styles. Do you seriously think that telling them that you disapprove is going to change their behavior? Of course not. And will it make your relationship with your grandchildren any better if you try to mold their father's and mother's behavior according to your wishes? Hardly.

If you are concerned, find someone you can talk to about your child's new and upsetting behavior—a trusted friend (possibly another grandparent whose children are in the same situation), or even a professional counselor. These people, *not* your children, are the ones to talk over your feelings with.

Now I'd like to go into something I touched on earlier in this book. During or after a divorce, you might be asked to become a part-time (or full-time temporary) parent to your grandchildren.

Ordinarily, a divorced mother gets custody of the children and the father gets visitation rights. Usually, both mother's and father's finances are drastically reduced after the divorce. This often means that in order to support herself and her children, the mother must go to work.

The experience of being a woman in the working world is not likely to do a great deal for the mother's economic or psychological well-being. But the divorced working mother's main problem is simply sheer *time!* She is somehow expected to do three things, each of which takes a great deal of time: earn her income, care for her children, and manage the household. And then, of course, she might like to have a social life of her own, and chances to meet a man who could replace her ex-husband and be a stepfather to her children.

To put it simply, with all of the incredible time pressures on them, many divorced women need help in caring for their children. (A divorced father with custody would need just as much help!)

And that, of course, is where grandparents come in. Mostly grandmothers, to be sure, but there's no reason why grandfathers can't help as well. The divorced mother may ask the grandparent to take over for her for at least part of the day or part of the week. Not as a baby-sitter, but as a genuine, emotionally involved, part-time parent.

Let's suppose your daughter has been divorced and she has two children, aged three and six. Her finances are tight, and she asks if you will help out with the kids. What are your options?

After thinking over the situation very carefully, you may decide you really don't want to help out. You could decide this for any number of reasons.

Perhaps you can't do it without quitting your job. Maybe you feel that raising your own children was enough—you want to spend your time now as you have in the past few years, relaxing, enjoying your leisure time, vacationing with your spouse. Or you may feel that taking care of two energetic children is too much for you physically. Or it may be that you like the three-year-old but you can't stand the six-year-old, who strikes you as a spoiled brat. Or you may simply have the gut-level feeling, for no reason you can put your finger on, that it's not wise for you to take on this responsibility.

Actually, it doesn't matter what your reason is. If you feel that agreeing to look after your grandchildren is the wrong thing to do, don't do it. If you decide not to do it yourself, maybe you can give your daughter financial assistance so she can hire a person to do the job. But if you can't, you can't. The important thing is to *avoid* taking on the children's care out of a sense of obligation, and then finding out you should have listened to your feelings.

If you do agree to take on the job, be sure to read some of the books on parenting for grandparents listed in Appendix D. You may be acting as a parent to the children for as much as five days a week, from perhaps seven in the morning until six at night, when their mother gets home.

Your task of parenting will obviously vary according to the ages of the children and the number of children involved. If there is only one grandchild and that child is a baby, you will probably have a relatively easy, uncomplicated job. If the child is a toddler, you may really have your hands full. If he is between three and six, you may want to turn him over for part of the day to a nursery school or day-care center. If he's six or older, he will be in the regular school system.

Let's say, for example, that you've got two grandchildren, a three-year-old and a six-year-old. You've agreed to look after them all day long five days a week. What do you do?

You pack the six-year-old off to first grade in the morning, and he gets home around two-thirty. He grabs a snack in the kitchen and is off to play with his friends. So he's taken care of rather easily until dinnertime.

But the three-year-old is another matter. You can spend all day with her, but you decide that's not really good for either of you. She needs time with her peer group, and having a three-year-old as a companion all day long five days a week is not exactly your idea of heaven. So you and your daughter talk about sending the child to a nursery school or a day-care center and how you can afford it. The day-care center will take your granddaughter early in the morning, at six-thirty or seven if you want, and keep her until you pick her up at five-thirty or six P.M. But you feel that's much too long a school day for a three-year-old. Besides, you've investigated the day-care centers in your area and you can't find a single good one.

That leaves the option of nursery school. These have morning or afternoon programs, but generally do not take children for a whole day. You and your daughter arrange to visit a number of nursery schools. One of them stands out head and shoulders above the others in terms of warmth of the teachers, easy and relaxed atmosphere, and breadth of the curriculum. So the two of you figure out how to finance it and decide to enroll your granddaughter there. You take the child to school at nine in the morning and pick her up at noon.

Now there's still the problem of what to do with the three-year-old in the afternoons. You decide to plan each afternoon around one central activity, such as a trip to the supermarket, an outing to a park or playground, or a visit to a museum or the library. This way the child will have something new and interesting to look forward to each afternoon. Of course, the activity does not need to take up the whole afternoon. Your granddaughter may want to spend part of her time playing with some friends. She may want to play games with you. She may want to watch some TV.

The crucial job of taking care of your grandchildren has many rewards. You will feel both useful and important, which many older people do not. You will have the opportunity to teach your grandchildren and to become influential in their lives. And of course you will have the advantage of being able to hand the children back to their mother at night, although in rare situations a grandparent might have the children nearly full-time.

Your grandchildren can benefit greatly from having you as a part-time parent. They will not have to spend all day at a day-care center, or become what are called "latchkey children" (carrying keys on strings around their necks to let themselves into the house when they get home from school), or suffer other unfortunate experiences that are the lot of many children of divorce. Instead of being in the care of a baby-sitter who may or may not take any real interest in them, they will have you, their grandparent, who loves them and volunteers for this job because you really want to take care of them and teach them. This can make all the difference in the world to a child.

One particular issue that comes up frequently is the psychological effect of divorce on children. Many people are convinced that a child of divorce is bound to develop emotional problems. If a youngster gets in trouble at school, you're likely to hear people say something like, "Oh, Danny comes from a broken home," as if that explained the problem. I have yet to hear a teacher or principal say, "Oh, yes, Harry comes from an intact home," as if that explained why Harry got into trouble. As a matter of fact, the evidence shows that intact families have a higher percentage of children with psychological problems than children coming from divorced families.

Instead of divorce, you might have to deal with a different problem: the death of your grandchildren's mother or father. A child reacts differently to the death of a parent than to losing a parent by divorce. A child's reaction to any kind of parental loss depends a great deal on her age. But, generally speaking, when a child loses a parent by death, she tends to idealize the missing parent and subconsciously resent anyone who replaces him. This would not apply to you, of course, because you are already firmly fixed in the child's mind as a grandparent, not as a father or mother.

The bitterness and wrangling of the typical divorce is missing from a family struck by death, of course. But there are other, different problems. The surviving spouse and the children need to go through their period of mourning and "grief work." You need to encourage them to let out their sad and unhappy feelings. Don't say things like, "Let's look on the cheerful side," or "Now come on, we've got to live in the present and stop thinking of the past." Both children and spouse *do* need to think about the past and remember with sadness and affection the person they have lost through death.

Divorced people usually remarry sooner than widows or widowers. Widows, especially, tend to become "stuck" in widowhood instead of getting back into dating and other social activities that can help them build a new life. A woman does not do herself or her children any good by remaining isolated. You can help the family by gently encouraging (but not nagging!) her to start dating again once the "grief work" is over.

Following a death or divorce, your daughter may remarry someone who has children of his own living with him. These children now become your step-grandchildren. You will quickly discover that dealing with them is quite different from dealing with your natural grandchildren, whom you have known from birth. "Instant" grandparenthood can be difficult; you will probably be expected to accept (and even love) the step-grandchildren without having any chance to get used to them.

Or your divorced son may remarry a woman with children, but *his* children may be in the custody of his ex-wife. In this situation, how often you see your natural grandchildren, and under what conditions, will depend to some extent on your relationship with your ex-daughter-in-law, the attitude of her new husband (if any), and where the family now lives. It can be very complicated. You may have to make special efforts to keep up your relationship with your natural grandchildren.

The step-family is an enormously complex psychological grouping. Jealousy exists in every nook and cranny of this complicated web of interpersonal relationships. As someone has said, "There are too many people in a step-family!" A step-family is inhabited by ghosts from the past—parental ghosts, resulting from divorce or death.

Because of this, grandparents should initiate relationships with their new step-grandchildren the way porcupines make love: very carefully!

Your tendency will be to favor your natural grandchildren, and you need to guard against this. Your step-grandchildren will probably be very wary of you or even hostile toward you at first. They are also quick to sense the psychological realities of their new family. If they feel that they are second-class citizens compared with your natural grandchildren, it is going to throw the proverbial monkey wrench into your relationship with them. So try not to devote a disproportionate amount of time or attention to your natural grandchildren. Your step-grandchildren will resent it. And above all, don't bad-mouth either parent to the step-grandchildren.

People I have worked with or talked to about stepparenting have all expressed the same thought: "I just didn't realize that a step-family was going to be so complicated!" And needless to say, most parents and grandparents are not prepared for the complications. If you are going to face this situation, I suggest that you read two excellent books: *Step-Parenting* by Jean and Veryl Rosenbaum; and *Living in Step* by Ruth Roosevelt and Jennette Lofas. These should help you to understand how, after the initial psychological fencing is over, you and your step-grandchildren can settle down to a solid and satisfying relationship.

Finally, what happens if the grandparents themselves—you and your spouse—get a divorce? Twenty years ago, such a question would have been almost unthinkable. At that time, people in their fifties and sixties simply did not split up after years of marriage. But now they do. In one unusual case I know of, a couple's divorce became final, by an unhappy coincidence, on their twenty-fifth wedding anniversary!

If your own divorce should become a bitter, acrimonious affair, it could adversely affect your role as a grandparent. Perhaps hostility between you and your ex-spouse is unavoidable. But you can see to it that the hostility does not spill over into your relationship with your grandchildren. Try your hardest not to speak ill of your ex-spouse. When you break the news of the divorce to your grandchildren, simply say something like, "Your grandfather and I weren't happy anymore being married and living together, so we decided to get a divorce and live apart." That's all you need to say. If the grandchildren ask searching questions based on rumors they have picked up, you can simply say, "That's something private, and I'm not going to answer any more questions."

But don't be under the illusion that your divorce will have no effect on your grandchildren. It will. They love you both and would rather see you stay married. It will upset them to realize that you may be angry at each other, or hate each other. They will mourn your divorce just as they would mourn the divorce of their parents. But I hope that, after the immediate bitterness of the divorce is over, you and your ex-spouse can each continue to play the role of a warm, loving grandparent to the grandchildren.

In closing this chapter, I want to emphasize how much children in single-parent families need their grandparents. They need you to give them love and teaching and extra parenting. They need you to help them get over their grief over the divorce or death. They need your emotional support to help them cope with an entirely new and scary family situation. And you need them to help make you feel loved, important, and useful. You will probably bring to the relationship some assets you did not have when you were raising your own children: more maturity of judgment, more leisure, and a more mellowed approach. The two of you—grandparent and grandchildren—make a wonderful fit. Enjoy!

❦ 17 ❧

Little Siblings, Big Siblings

"My grandmother is nice and comfortable and when she cuddles you, you can nestle down and feel safe and secure."
Angela Dobson, age 10

Most people think that "sibling rivalry" refers only to children. They think of the rivalry of young brothers and sisters—their jealousy of one another and their competition for their parents' love and approval.

But brothers and sisters often continue their competition right into adulthood. Their rivalry, just as when they were little, is usually for the love of the parents.

A woman patient once told me, "My invalid father has lived with me for years. It's been a drain on our financial resources and our emotions, especially as Dad has grown older and more difficult. I've got a brother and a sister no more than an hour's drive from here. Not only have they never offered to have Dad live with them—though they've both got more room than I do—they rarely come to see him. They almost never ask him to visit them, not even for a couple of hours a month. And yet on his birthday, you can't imagine the presents they send him! They spend all that money on stuff he'll never use. And he thinks it's wonderful. Everything they do is wonderful. But he takes me for granted. It's just not fair!"

Adult siblings frequently compete with each other through their children, using them as measures of their own achievement or status. For example, a man may be jealous because his brother's son gets straight A's while his son gets only C's.

And just as frequently, adults use their children as a means for keeping score on their parents' love.

"How come Mother gave a watch to my nephew Jimmy when he graduated from high school, and only a book to my son Fred?"

"My parents take my nieces camping, and they leave my kids at home. They've got plenty of room. My kids would love to go."

"My brother's sons will carry on the family name, my father tells me.

156

He completely ignores my daughters. They can't help but notice how differently he treats them, and they feel bad."

And sibling rivalry doesn't stop at the parental level. It is also characteristic of grandparents. The grandparents on the father's side often compete in various ways with those on the mother's side for the love of their shared grandchildren. For instance, the two sets of grandparents may try to outdo each other in the gifts they give for birthdays and at Christmas. They are more like two opposing teams, each trying to outdo the other, than like two families trying to work together for the good of their children and grandchildren.

And there is even intergenerational "sibling rivalry." Parents and grandparents often vie with one another, sometimes subtly, sometimes blatantly, for the love of the children.

So when we examine the psychological structure of the ordinary extended family—children, parents, and grandparents—we unfortunately see sibling rivalry, competition, and jealousy everywhere. In other words, little siblings and big siblings.

The parallel between the familiar sibling rivalry of young brothers and sisters and the intricate rivalry of children–parents–grandparents is amazingly close.

The rivalry of children is based on the fact that each one wants to have 100 percent of the love and affection of his parents. Down deep, your grandson wishes his siblings would vanish so he could have his parents all to himself. When he teases his brothers and sisters, disrupts their games, makes fun of them, hits or kicks them, he is saying in a disguised form, "Get out of here and let me have Mother and Dad all to myself!"

Parents can never eliminate their children's rivalry, no matter how effective their discipline methods may be. The only way to dispose of the problem would be to get rid of all of the children but one. The problem of sibling rivalry can only be *diminished,* never *eliminated.*

It's the same within the larger framework of children, parents, and grandparents. The people in the family cannot help feeling jealous of one another at least occasionally. Only if everyone went off to live as hermits could this rivalry be eliminated.

The problem is not so much that sibling rivalry exists, but that it exists mainly at the *unconscious* level. It is frequently the case that two sets of grandparents are competing with each other, but neither pair is aware of it. Parents and grandparents often do not realize they are competing with one another for the love of the children.

Though parents and grandparents are grown adults, they are really acting like eight-year-old children when they unconsciously play the sibling rivalry game.

And they cannot really do anything about their behavior until they become aware of it.

If you have an only child, and that only child is married to an only child, and they have only one child, you are going to be much less affected by the problem of sibling rivalry than the average grandparent. However, if you have two or more children, and they are married and have children, you are part of an intricate network of siblings—and rivalries. And the more children, spouses, grandchildren, and step-grandchildren there are, the more complicated and jealousy-laden that network becomes.

We need to be honest with ourselves about this situation. First, let's recognize that we do not like all people equally well. "Obvious," you say. But not quite so obvious is that this holds true even for members of your immediate family. If you are a parent or grandparent with three children or grandchildren, I guarantee you that you do not like all of them equally. In fact, if you had to, you could probably rank them in order of liking: one, two, three. This does not mean that you show preference to some and treat others unfairly. No, you probably show no outward signs of particular preference for any of the three. But don't try to tell yourself that you like a feisty, stubborn, nine-year-old grandson who is continually disobeying your rules and lipping off to you as much as you like his cheerful, easy to manage, seven-year-old sister who hardly ever rebels against you.

You cannot help feeling preferences for some of your grandchildren, any more than you can help the fact that you do not like all of your adult friends equally. But we have been brought up to believe that we must love our children and grandchildren equally. We were not raised to admit that we like some more than others. But that is nonsense. We can *treat* them all equally. But love them equally? Impossible.

It is this same type of social brainwashing that makes us believe it is wrong for us to be jealous of our children or our grandchildren, or other grandparents. Since we are taught that jealousy is a nasty feeling, we erect unconscious mental barriers to prevent us from becoming aware of such a feeling within us. But, as I have indicated, the mere fact of the *existence* of other family members makes it impossible for us *not* to feel jealousy.

Let me give you an example of "sibling rivalry" out of my own life. When my son Randy was three, I was very surprised to discover that I was feeling jealous of him. We had just enrolled him in nursery school and he was learning a number of things, such as math with the Cuisenaire rods, reading readiness, printing, and arts and crafts. I was very proud of him for learning these things at such an early age.

And yet, after a few weeks I realized I was also *jealous* of him, because I had not been fortunate enough to go to nursery school when I was three.

I was amazed to discover that the two sets of feelings—pride in Randy's accomplishments, and jealousy because he was getting things as a young child that I did not get could exist side by side.

That's an example at the father level. Here's one involving a grandfather I once counseled. I talked with him, his wife, and their college-age grand-daughter, who had lived with the grandparents since she was a youngster. When I interviewed the granddaughter, she spent most of the first hour in tears. She said, "We used to be so close, Grampy and I. But since I've been in college, he's just turned horrid to me. He accuses me of all sorts of sexual things I've never even done. To listen to him, you'd think I was some sort of sex monster or something. I'm *not* promiscuous, even though he accuses me of it. I don't sleep around with a bunch of different boys. I've got a boyfriend I've had for nine months, and the things we do are no different from what the other college kids do."

When I interviewed the grandfather, the whole first hour was devoted to his denunciation of college students' sexual immorality today, and his grand-daughter's immorality in particular. I worked with him for about two months before he was able to tell me what his own college life had been like. He was raised to believe in very strict moral principles, but he was a hot-blooded youth who was tempted more than once to violate them. Each time he managed to hold himself in check, but each time he felt very guilty about his sexual urges.

It was many months before I was able to introduce to him the idea that, unconsciously, he might feel jealous of the college students of today because they operate in an atmosphere of sexual freedom he never had.

As he began to accept the idea that it was normal to have such jealous feelings, his behavior toward his granddaughter changed. Because he could now admit his jealous feelings to himself, he no longer needed to let them out in destructive and unfair criticism of her.

If you, as a grandparent, have a problem with sibling rivalry, the first thing you need to do is admit to yourself that there are times when you may be jealous of *anybody* in your extended family: the other grandparents, your own children, or your grandchildren. And at various times, these same people will be jealous of you.

Social convention stands in the way of your admitting these feelings to yourself. But once you can, half the battle is won. For when you honestly recognize your feelings, you can begin to control them rather than letting them control you. And when jealousy is controlled, so is your need to be competitive.

Unfortunately, some grandparents assume that age automatically brings wisdom. It doesn't. Consider the case of the business executive who boasted, "I've had twenty years of experience in this business, and if anyone knows how to do something right around here, it's me." Another man overheard this and whispered to a friend, "No, he hasn't had twenty years' experience around here. He's had one year's experience twenty times! And if anyone knows how to do something wrong around here, it's him."

It's difficult for most of us to accept the fact that once our children are grown, our role as parent must change. But just as you are not responsible for your grandchildren's actions, you are not responsible for your grown children's actions. If you feel that you have to ask your adult children to behave in a certain way so they won't embarrass you in front of your friends, then you need to reevaluate your interpretation of your parental role.

The way your grown children and your grandchildren act, dress, work, and spend their leisure time is their own responsibility. You may not like it. You may not be proud of it. But what they do is up to them, not you.

Once you are able to relax your parental reins, life becomes easier for you. You can really begin to enjoy your children and grandchildren. Then your only responsibility is to worry about yourself.

Part of your responsibility, when you have more than one grandchild, is to be fair to each. This does not mean you have to do the same things in the same way for each and every grandchild. Interestingly enough, most grandchildren recognize this. It's their parents who don't. As I've said, a grown child will sometimes mentally keep score to make sure you're doing for his children what you do for your other children's children.

You may feel that no matter how scrupulously fair you would like to be, you face an impossible task. "My grandchildren are all different ages, and they have so many different interests," I hear you saying. I repeat: To be fair does *not* mean treating each child in exactly the same way. But there are some areas (gift-giving is one) in which you need to be especially careful so you don't unconsciously foster jealousy.

Suppose you have several grandchildren or step-grandchildren in the same family. Even if you don't do the same thing for each child, try to even things out. Don't give a special gift to the same grandchild every time. If you can't give special treats to all the grandchildren at the same time, make sure that each one gets a special treat at *some* time.

If you do give one grandchild something special, give the others at least token gifts. It's not fair to leave the others out completely. And word of who gets what travels very quickly through the family sibling grapevine!

If one of your grandchildren complains about your token gift and says,

"Scott's set of cars is a lot better than my present!" say something like, "Tony, sometimes Scott gets the more expensive toy, sometimes you do. It all evens out in the long run."

What do I mean by "token gifts"? They are inexpensive gifts, but ones that convey to the child that you are thinking of him. Depending on the ages and tastes of your grandchildren, you could give as token gifts things like a set of jacks, a kite, a puzzle, a model to build, a set of colored felt-tip pens, art supplies, a small blackboard and colored chalk, a game that can be played by one person, a game that can be played by two or more, small cars or trucks, a set of plastic barnyard animals, a xylophone, an inexpensive doll, or a book.

At this point, dollar signs may well be floating before your eyes. Even the cost of token gifts mounts up. "My income is limited, and I have more important things to spend it on," you may be thinking. Or you may say, "It's not the money, but if I always bring gifts when I come to see the grandchildren, it will just encourage them to be materialistic."

If your grandchildren fight over who gets to sit next to you when you read aloud, or in the car, or at the movies, or whatever, you may need to make rules about equal time. But if they don't compete this way, you can let the grandchild who wants to be close have her way most of the time. Some children always seem to want to climb up on your lap or give the longest hug or sit next to you at dinner. Don't be too fussy about trying to be scrupulously fair about these things, because they have a way of sorting themselves out as time goes by.

Few things fan the flames of sibling rivalry like gossip. You may feel it's only natural for family members to want to know how other family members are doing. And you may think that if it's "all in the family," you are not gossiping. Obviously, if a brother, sister, niece, or nephew has been mentioned, you are not expected to clap your hands over your ears and run out of the room. But you can be boring and make trouble if you spend your time with your daughter Barbara relating in detail your last visit with your son Ben. And this is true whether your report is favorable or not.

"I saw Ben and his family. They're feeling fine and it was good to see them all." This fairly neutral comment is a lot easier for Barbara to take than "Ben had the most marvelous news! He got a raise and both kids got straight A's last semester. And the family promised me they'd take me to Europe with them this summer for a month's vacation." On the other hand, don't tell Barbara "Ben's doing awful; he's not like you at all." Even if Barbara feels praised by the comparison, your comments are bound to make her feel uncomfortable. She won't be able to help suspecting that if the time ever comes when *she* is doing poorly, you won't hesitate to tell Ben all about her troubles.

I would say that you can't be too careful when you are talking with one child or grandchild about another. You will be amazed at how your son, for example, can take the simplest thing you say about another family member and twist it into something that makes him angry or jealous, or hurts his feelings. Why do people do this? Because they are siblings! Big people or little people, the members of your family are still siblings.

The first step toward resolving sibling rivalry is to stop kidding ourselves and to admit that children, parents, and grandparents are all competing with one another. We are all full of jealous feelings; we are all easily angered or hurt. This is human nature; it is also one of the major causes of the failure of the old-fashioned extended family. As I have said, no family can completely eradicate the problem. But by using the suggestions in this chapter, you can help to minimize sibling rivalry in your family. Then, with the rivalry and jealousy under control, both little siblings and big siblings can play less the role of rivals and more their true and fulfilling roles as children, parents, and grandparents.

❦ 18 ❧

How to Desensitize Yourself to Problem Situations

"Grannies are very necessary for letting you do things you are not allowed to do generally, like watching 'The Late Night Horror Show.' "

Kate Clancy, age 14

In this chapter I'd like to discuss a rather touchy subject. What if you find yourself stuck with a grandchild, a parent, or another grandparent whom you simply cannot stand? How do you handle it? What do you do? If this person were just an acquaintance, you could simply drop him. But you can't do that when the person is part of the family. What in the world *can* you do?

What you need is a magic button to push that would desensitize your feelings toward the person. If, for example, on a scale of one to ten, you had negative feelings of eight, it would help a great deal to be able to desensitize them down to two or three. The person would seem less annoying, and you would feel much better.

There is a procedure that can accomplish this. I call it "negative thinking." The germ of the idea came from a UCLA psychologist named Dr. Knight Dunlap, who was learning to type. As he practiced his typing, he found he was persistently making the same error. Instead of typing "the," he found he was typing "hte." Anybody else would have simply tried hard to eliminate the error. But Dr. Dunlap tried a little experiment with himself. He deliberately typed "hte" about two hundred times. Then he found he could type "the" with no problem.

How did this work? Dr. Dunlap had tried to type "the," but, against his conscious control, "hte" came out. So he consciously and deliberately typed the error repeatedly. By doing this, he put the involuntary and unconscious error under his voluntary and conscious control. He no longer unconsciously typed "hte."

Using this principle, Dr. Dunlap had great success working with people

163

who were making persistent errors in learning to type, play the piano, or do Morse code. I have extended this principle to the field of human feelings and emotions. I teach it as a technique to get rid of undesirable feelings and replace them with more desirable ones. Here is an example of how this applies to grandparenting.

For six years, a man I'll call Bob was a happy grandfather. He enjoyed his relationships with his son and daughter-in-law and his young grandson, Andrew. He and his wife, Helen, who lived in California ten minutes away from their grandchild, thought of themselves as the only grandparents in the picture. And they were, for the other grandparents lived far away in Massachusetts.

But then the other grandparents, Peter and Emma, moved out to California, within a twenty-minute drive of the grandchild's family. It took only one family get-together for Bob to have enough of Peter to last a lifetime. He found him an obnoxious bore who talked on and on about how successful he was in his business as a salesman. One thing particularly galled Bob. Peter would point to little Andrew and say, "That kid's the spitting image of me. I just know he's going to be a success. After all, he's a chip off the old block." It was all Bob could do to make it through the evening. It didn't even help much when Shelley, his daughter-in-law, took him aside toward the close of the evening and said, "Bob, I know my father is difficult to take at times, but try to bear with him. After all, he is Andrew's grandfather, too."

Bob didn't know what to do. He didn't want to avoid family gatherings, but, on the other hand, he didn't think he could take very much of Peter.

I said to him, "Obviously Peter isn't going to change, so if anybody does the changing it's going to have to be you." I asked him to rate his sensitivity to Peter's obnoxiousness on a scale of one to ten. He picked nine. Then I asked him, "If I could press a magic button to get your sensitivity down to two or three, wouldn't that improve things greatly?" He agreed, somewhat reluctantly, that it would. I said, "Of course I don't have a magic button, but I do have a technique you can use to decrease your sensitivity to Peter." I explained how it worked and he agreed to try it.

Bob was *not* to try to think positively about Peter and improve his feelings that way. (The trouble with such an approach is that the negative feelings keep breaking through the positive ones.) Instead, he was to deliberately *increase* his negative feelings and recite to himself all of the things Peter did that bugged him. Then he was to let his imagination run riot. He was to picture himself lying on the floor in a nervous breakdown, all due to Peter's insufferable behavior. He was then to imagine himself begging Peter for mercy and imploring him to change his obnoxious ways before they caused him to have another nervous breakdown.

After mentally rehearsing all these scenes in the privacy of his own home, Bob was to recall them silently the next time he was with Peter.

Can you see how it worked? Instead of just feeling annoyed and exasperated by Peter's behavior, Bob took his spontaneous angry feelings and put them under his deliberate, voluntary control. By consciously exaggerating the feelings and picturing himself as a helpless victim of them, he took command of the situation.

Bob told me that the first time he tried recalling these scenes in Peter's presence, he felt like laughing. "I thought, 'If only the insufferable old jerk knew what's going through my head!' " In the scenes he was imagining, Bob was at Peter's mercy. But *in reality,* Bob no longer thought of himself as a helpless victim of Peter's boring personality. He was in charge, and that made Peter somehow easier to take.

Bob did not suddenly begin to find Peter a completely acceptable fellow. But after five or six months, Bob reported that his degree of annoyance with Peter had decreased markedly. Bob had, in effect, desensitized himself to Peter's annoying personality. It was now much easier for him to tolerate Peter's presence in the family group.

Here's another case. Martin had been a fifth-grade schoolteacher for many years and was now retired. He had really looked forward to being a grandfather, and had been disappointed that his only son's marriage had proved to be childless. He was genuinely sorry to see the marriage break up after four years, because he was very fond of both his son and daughter-in-law. But when Hank was married again a year later to a divorcée with two children, Martin was a happy man. He was going to be a grandparent at last.

As a schoolteacher, Martin had handled all sorts of children for many years, and he boasted, like Will Rogers, "I never met a kid I didn't like." Unfortunately, those words were soon to stick in Martin's throat.

Hank's new stepchildren were two boys, Mike (aged twelve) and Stephen (aged ten). Martin began taking the two boys on camping and fishing trips with him, which both of them liked. But Martin was shocked to discover that although he liked Mike, who was a typical feisty twelve-year-old full of mischief, his feelings about Steve were very different. Martin had had a great deal of experience with children of all sorts, but there was one kind of youngster with whom he had never had any intimate experience: a goody-goody. And Steve was a first-class, A-1, certified goody-goody.

When they came home from one camping trip, Martin heard Steve boast to his mother, "I said 'Thank you' twenty-seven times, more than anyone else did." And what did his mother say? "That's wonderful, darling. You keep that up and you'll be the most thoughtful boy anyone can find!" Martin resisted the urge to throw up.

Martin was in a dilemma. He had a fine time with Mike and enjoyed having him along on the trips. But at the same time, he was stuck with one of the most irritating and exasperating prigs he had ever encountered. And the prig was only ten years old! Once Steve said to him, "Grandpa, you know what I try to do?"

"No, I don't."

"I try to do at least one good deed for someone every day, because that way I can become a finer spiritual person."

"Well, what do you know," said Martin feebly.

"Yes, and I was thinking what kind of a good deed I could do for you, Grandpa, and you know what I thought of?"

"By all means, tell me," said Martin.

"Well, I've noticed that you belch sometimes and I don't think you know that you're doing it. Because it's a bad habit and shows a lack of good manners. So if it's all right with you, Grandpa, I could remind you every time you do it and help you get over the habit. Would you like me to do that?"

Martin felt a strong temptation to pick up Steve by the scruff of the neck and dunk him an appropriate number of times in the creek. But he resisted the temptation and merely said, "Much as it touches my heart, Steve, I must turn down your generous offer."

Steve also had a habit of regaling Martin with tales of the bad habits and misbehavior of children at school, and especially those of his brother Mike. Mike's bad behavior was inevitably contrasted with Steve's own good behavior.

But probably the thing that grated on Martin's nerves the most was Steve's determination to love his grandpa in spite of all his shortcomings—and to tell him about it interminably. Martin had never before had the experience of taking a child to task about something and having the child tell him he loved him even though he had faults and imperfections. And Martin did not especially cotton to people who tried to reform him. He had resisted the efforts of his wife, Liz, to do this for many years, and she had finally given up. So it was rather a shock to have an unctuous ten-year-old attempt it.

Steve had singled out overeating as his main area of reform. Martin had been twenty pounds overweight for many years. But Steve informed him on one camping trip that eating too many starchy foods was hazardous to his health, and it would be best if Grandpa would give up that habit and stop eating sweets. Martin was incensed.

"Look here, young man. I'm a responsible adult, and I've been eating the way I please for many years. I *am* a little bit overweight, but so are a lot of other people in this country. And my eating habits are none of your blankety-blank business, so from now on, I'll thank you to shut up about them."

"But, Grandpa, your habits *are* my business, because I love you and I want to help you to be the finest person you can become."

Martin lapsed into a glum silence. He now began to realize what he was dealing with—a ten-year-old Pharisee. Martin had been a churchgoer and a Bible student for years. And he was very familiar with the Pharisees— the smug, uptight, holier-than-thou group condemned by Jesus for their moral harshness and their inability to love. He saw that Steve had precisely the same rigid, unloving, holier-than-thou attitudes, in spite of his constant claim to love everybody.

No wonder I find it hard to like him, thought Martin. How could anyone like a kid like Steve?

When they got home that weekend, Martin did some hard thinking. In one sense, he knew, Steve wasn't totally responsible for being the way he was. His mother, Janice, had done a good job of changing a child who had probably started out as a normal, fun-loving, mischievous boy into Steve, the world's greatest kid angel. And he knew there was no use taking his case to Janice. She saw Steve as a sensitive, thoughtful, considerate little boy, altruistic and self-sacrificing, always doing good deeds for others. No, Janice would never see Steve the way others saw him. Mike was lucky that somehow he hadn't turned out the same way.

This was the situation when Martin first consulted me. "Dr. Dodson," he said, "I'll bet you've never had a case like this before. The problem is that I've got a step-grandson who's such a goody-goody, he makes me want to throw up."

After Martin had finished telling his story, I explained negative thinking to him. Then we designed a strategy for decreasing his sensitivity to Steve. I told Martin to deliberately exaggerate his feelings about Steve. Since he felt helpless before Steve's angelic do-goodism, he was to exaggerate his helplessness. He was to tell himself that there was no way he could resist Steve, that he was fated to give in and live the way Steve wanted him to. He was to feel particularly helpless when Steve used the love gambit on him, because how could he resist someone who loved him so much?

At the same time, I instructed Martin in a turn-around strategy for dealing with Steve. For example, Martin was to tell Steve that, after long consideration, he had decided Steve was right and he should give up overeating. . . .

Steve was overjoyed when he heard this news.

"Yes, indeed, Steve. I'm going to give up overeating for good. And to celebrate my giving up overeating, I'm going to eat a luscious chocolate doughnut now."

Steve was aghast.

"But, Grandpa, you shouldn't eat a doughnut at all if you're going to give up overeating."

"Now, don't you fret about it. The best way to give up overeating is to have a farewell doughnut to do it."

Steve was baffled. In his narrow world of do-goodism, he had not encountered such a bewildering maneuver. How could something that was supposedly bad suddenly turn around and become good?

For the rest of the weekend trip, Martin continued eating as he always had. When Steve objected, Martin would say something like, "Now, don't you worry, Steve. I'm going to stop overeating just like I promised. But, you see, if you stop overeating all at once, it's a shock to your nervous system. So I have to stop gradually so my nervous system can get accustomed to it."

Steve would look at him as if he were speaking Greek.

From then on, each time Steve tried to reform Grandpa "for his own good," Grandpa told him he was absolutely right and thanked him profusely for his advice. Then he went right on doing what he was doing, giving Steve truly outlandish reasons for why it was necessary for him to do so.

Steve finally told Martin he should go on a strict diet. Martin told Steve that he was absolutely right and that he was going to begin that very day. So, for breakfast, he cooked up a mess of bacon and pancakes slathered in butter for the three of them. Steve protested that the breakfast was high in calories and very fattening. But Martin again explained patiently that if you rushed your system when you went on a diet, it was bad for your body, so you had to go at it slowly.

The combination of negative thinking and this turn-around technique did wonders for Martin in his relationship with Steve. He no longer felt helpless. When Steve attempted to control him or reform him, Martin was able to turn the tables and take charge of the situation. When Martin used negative thinking, he was able to realize that he had control over his own feelings and that Steve was only a ten-year-old boy who was mildly irritating, not someone who was going to make a disaster out of his life. And, fortunately, Steve finally realized that his grandfather had no intention of giving up his bad habits, and gradually decreased his efforts at salvation.

It is really amazing how easily negative emotions can crop up in the parent–child–grandparent relationship. Here is another case in which I used negative thinking.

Harley was a grandparent, and basically a good one, who cared deeply for his ten-year-old granddaughter and twelve-year-old grandson. His wife had died two years before and he was the only grandparent living near the children. He read stories to them, took them out to dinner, to the movies, and on weekend trips. They all got along well together, and were very fond of one another.

That was before the coming of electronic football games. Jerry, the twelve-year-old, had the game on his Christmas list, so Grandpa Harley dutifully bought it for him, little dreaming what the consequences would be.

Two days after Christmas, Harley took the children on a weekend trip to the nearest large city. As soon as they got in the car, Jerry started playing his new game. He played it throughout the four hours it took to drive to the city. Harley found that the constant *beep-beep-BEEP-be-beep* of the electronic game grated horribly on his nerves, but he said nothing about it. He figured that Jerry was utterly fascinated with the game because it was so new, and that the fascination would eventually wear off.

Harley quickly learned that this was not to be the case. When Jerry got up the next morning, there was the beeping of the game again. Jerry played the game through breakfast, lunch, and dinner. And he played it late at night, until Harley finally ordered him to stop and go to sleep.

It was three months after the coming of The Game into their lives that Harley consulted me. He was very apologetic about coming to see me. "I hardly feel I have a problem that's worth consulting you about, but, nevertheless, it's something that's bothering the living daylights out of me." And he told me his feelings about Jerry's electronic football game and its beeping sounds.

I suggested that Harley simply tell Jerry how much the sounds bothered him and ask him not to play the game around him. But Harley had already tried that. "I told him the beeping of the game bothered me, and you know what the little monster said to me? He said, 'Well, Grandpa, I think you have some sort of a problem. The sound doesn't bother my mom and dad, and it doesn't bother my sister, and it doesn't bother any of my friends' parents. You're the only one it bothers. Maybe your ears are extra sensitive.' Did you ever hear anything like that?" asked Harley. "I would never have dared talk to my grandfather like that."

I sympathized with Harley, but pointed out that it was good that Jerry was able to put his feelings into words. From the *tone* of the words, however, I got the feeling it would be difficult to budge Jerry from his position. So I suggested that Harley talk with Jerry's mother, Sue.

Harley's conversation with his daughter-in-law was no more satisfactory than his earlier conversation with Jerry. He explained his situation, saying that the loud beeping got on his nerves.

"Loud?" Sue said. "I think you would have to stretch things considerably to call it loud. It's actually a very soft beeping. I ought to know, because I hear it almost every day."

"You're right, Sue. I misspoke. I shouldn't have called it loud. But it is *persistent* and it gets on my nerves, and I think he should give it up out of respect for my nerves."

"What!" said Sue. "That's the most ridiculous thing I've ever heard. Nobody else is bothered by it. You're the only one. And I hope you're not going to suggest that the rest of us govern our lives by what gets on *your* nerves. I've never mentioned it to you, but there are a few things you do that get on my nerves. Are you prepared to give up those things for the sake of my nerves?"

Harley brought the conversation to an abrupt end and took his departure.

He was feeling quite defeated when he saw me next. "I feel boxed in by the situation," he said. "In one sense, it's really not a big problem, but it sure does bother me. And it's obvious I'm not going to get any backing from Sue. I think my only alternative is to tell Jerry that either he stops playing that lousy game around me, or I'm not going to take him anywhere with me.

"I think I'm in a no-win situation. I don't think Jerry's going to leave his game at home. He loves it too much. He might just say he doesn't want to go places with me anymore, and I don't want that. He's a good kid, and I love him and want to see him. And, if he did agree not to take the game along, I think he'd be angry with me, and that would take the fun out of our experience. So I really don't know what to do."

"There is a way out," I said to Harley. I told him about the negative thinking technique, and explained how he could desensitize himself to the beeping by deliberately exaggerating his feelings and expressing them out loud to himself twice a day, something like this:

"Harley, you've got to do something about those beeping sounds. They don't bother other people, but your nerves are more sensitive than most people's. If Jerry keeps playing with that game and you have to listen to those beeping sounds, you will surely go stark raving mad. You will end up in a straitjacket. There's no way you can get around it—more beepings spell INSANITY for you! You'll *never* be able to get accustomed to that beeping! That beeping is going to result in palsy, epilepsy, schizophrenia, and just plain psychosis!"

In addition, whenever Jerry played the game, Harley was to imagine that the sound of the beeping was going up ten decibels every minute or so. Then, after he had imagined the sound at a very high level, he was to imagine it gradually going down in decibels.

After two months of this procedure, Harley told me things were much better. "When I first came to see you, I didn't think there was any way out. You've gotten me to see that part of what was wrong was that I was thinking of myself as a passive victim of Jerry and that damn game. But now I see I'm not helpless. I can control things with my mind. I can make the sounds of the game seem louder or softer by using my imagination. I can imagine negative situations, like ending up in a mental hospital because of that stupid beeping, and feel how silly they are.

"I still don't like that damn beeping, but it's a minor annoyance now, like a mosquito, not a major thing that's going to ruin a weekend trip for me."

As we have seen, when there is a person or situation in your extended family that bothers you, you can try to change that situation or person. But where the person or situation cannot be changed, negative thinking can come to your rescue.

᭜ 19 ᭚

A Special Chapter for Parents

"You can tell them secrets of all the bad things you have done and they won't tell our mothers. Then they tell you about all the wicked things they did when they were little."

Helen Smith

You, as a parent, are one-third of the new extended family. You are, in a sense, the most important third, because you are in the middle, between your children and their grandparents. In the new extended family the name of the game is communication. And the message of this chapter is:

Talk with your children.

Talk with your parents.

Sounds simple, doesn't it? It is simple. Yet very few people know how to do it.

Let's start with your children. In Chapter 4, "How to Talk with Children," I dealt with grandparents and grandchildren—but everything I said there applies equally to you and your children.

The most important thing to learn, as Chapter 3 points out, is to talk *with* your children rather than *at* them. This means talking on their level, about things that are interesting to them.

The object here is to break the ice so that your children will feel free to give their comments on life as *they* experience it. Too many parents unwittingly talk to their children in ways that throw roadblocks into the path of communication.

Let's look at some of the major roadblocks.

1. Being judgmental.

If your child says, "You know, my new teacher Mrs. Wilson has a face like an alligator," and you say, "Timmy, that's no way to talk about your teacher," you are being judgmental. Your child wants your approval, and when you are judgmental, you discourage him from making any more comments that might draw judgmental responses. By talking to your child this way, you can easily cut off all future conversation about things that are deeply important to him. (For instance, fear of disapproval is the reason there is so little talk between parents and children on the subject of sex. Children quickly sense that it's a forbidden subject, and stay off it.) So if you want to encourage your child to talk with you freely about everything and anything, try to avoid making shocked or negative responses when he's talking.

2. Denying your child's feelings.
"Surely that little problem can't still be bothering you?" (If it weren't bothering her, she wouldn't still be talking about it. And to her, it's *not* a little problem!)

3. Reassuring your child.
"Don't worry, Sally, things will work out fine; you'll see." (How can you be sure? Unless you're sure, this is a form of Pollyanna-like dishonesty, and your child knows it.)

4. Handing your child a free, gift-wrapped solution.
"Listen, here's what I would do about Herb the next time he tries to bully you." (You are not your child, and your glib solution probably does not fit his situation. But maybe his problem with Herb is something you can help him work out by encouraging him to talk to you about it.)

5. Lecturing.
"Everybody has problems with their teachers. I remember when *I* was in the fifth grade. . . ." (But he isn't in *your* fifth grade, and he never can be. Your fifth grade and his fifth grade are worlds apart.)

6. Attacking with questions.
"Okay, now, let's be honest. What did you do to Janice to provoke her into tearing up your paper?" (You're acting as if you are omniscient and know exactly who's to blame.)

7. Moralizing, telling your child what he ought to do.
"I think you should go over to Steve and shake hands and make up and forget the whole thing ever happened." (You probably know as much about social relationships among seventh-graders as you know about rock formations on the other side of the moon, and you're sharing your knowledge with your son.)

8. Threatening.
"Look, I'm telling you for the last time. You tease your sister once more and you'll wish you were in outer space." (Threats do very little to change future conduct, although many parents seem to believe devoutly in their efficacy.)

9. Playing amateur psychoanalyst.

"Beth, I think your whole problem is that you're just plain jealous of Jennie. That's why you're doing all these things to bug us." (Because of your seven years of psychoanalytic training, you can figure out the motives behind Beth's behavior? Stick around, and when Beth is old enough to go to an analyst, we can save thousands of dollars and use you instead!)

Now let's move to the positive side and talk about what you need to do in order to encourage your child to talk to you, and make her want to listen when you are talking.

1. Take a physical stance that sends your child the message that you are actively listening to her. Don't try to dust or watch TV or repair your fishing tackle. She will know she is not really the focus of your attention, and her conversation will fade out. When you and she are talking, maintain eye-to-eye contact that lets her know you are really concentrating on what she has to say.

2. Use the feedback technique discussed in Chapter 4 to show her you are really listening. Nothing is so powerful as this technique in demonstrating to your child that you are right there when she is talking.

3. Interject comments into the conversation that will keep your child talking, such as, "Tell me more about those feelings that it wasn't going to work out," or "What happened next?" or "He really did that, huh?"

4. Try to talk to one child at a time. You will probably have plenty of opportunities to talk to more than one at once (at the dinner table, for example), but children do not open up as readily when another child is present. So strive for one-to-one conversations; through them, your sharing with your child will be deepest.

5. Be brief when you respond. Most adults are much too long-winded with children. As one child said, "Daddy, why do you give such long answers when I ask you such short questions?" Try to let your child do most of the talking.

6. Grant your child genuine respect as a small human being. Children have much less information about the world than you do, but they still have unique points of view to share with you if you will let them. You have only to listen to parents talking to children in stores, at playgrounds, and at home to realize how few parents give their children this kind of respect.

7. Have the courage to disclose yourself as a real person with human feelings and weaknesses. Most young children picture their parents as powerful,

superior beings who don't face the fears, worries, and indecision that they, as children, face. One reason for this kind of misconception is that parents usually don't reveal their fears and weaknesses. If you have the courage to disclose these things to your child, it will do wonders for both of you. Your child will perceive you as more human and will feel closer to you. And you will have very good feelings about your own openness. Also, research shows that when one person makes a disclosure to another, the second person usually makes a reciprocal disclosure. This is bound to happen with your child and you. And when we disclose our feelings and weaknesses to our children, it enhances their self-confidence, and helps them to realize they can succeed at things in spite of their fears and weaknesses.

When you truly communicate with your young child, you will be given a peek into a new and strange and fascinating culture you never knew existed. In fact, you will experience many different cultures as your child grows, for a child changes cultures rapidly as she grows up. The culture of the three-year-old is emphatically not that of the six-year-old, and the culture of the eleven-year-old is another one altogether. If you really begin to listen to your child talk, you will be fascinated by what you hear. And this will be one of the things that will make child-raising a delight for you.

Now, what can you and your child talk about?

First, about anything and everything the child wants to talk about. Let's say you have a seven-year-old daughter, and the two of you are having an after-school conversation. You should try to act like a talk-show host, to get your "guest" to reveal her vision of the world. This means asking helpful questions, but, mostly, letting the child talk about whatever is on her mind at the moment—school and teachers and friends, movies and TV programs she has seen, adult conversations that have puzzled her, experiences that have frightened her, her feelings about the members of her family. If she wants to ask you questions, answer them, but remember not to be long-winded! Even questions on such all-important topics as sex may not require long answers.

You can begin conversations with your child by telling her about your "adventures in life," from the time you were a little kid on. Try telling her about things parents ordinarily don't think of as being of interest to their children: nice teachers and mean teachers you had as a child, fights you had with other kids, places you went to see, scout hikes and camping trips, your special hobbies and how you started them, your first efforts to learn to drive a car, how scared you were on your first date and when you applied for your first job, what that first job was like, what going to college was like. These things and others like them, which most parents and grandparents take for granted and do not think of as particularly fascinating, will be of keen

interest to your children. And in the telling of these things, you will be present-
ing a picture of yourself as a three-dimensional human being who has faults,
makes mistakes, gets upset, and worries just like other human beings.

BUT REMEMBER: Don't moralize when you tell your stories. Tell them
purely for the sharing.

When is a good time to begin telling these parental adventure tales? I
would say when your child is three. Of course, the stories will have to be
kept simple when the child is that young. But they can grow and fill out as
your child grows older.

Remember, when you are raising your children, that you and your spouse
are your children's most important teachers and their most important role
models. As your children grow and mature, good relationships with you will
help them in all their dealings with their peers and with other adults. And
if your children have good relationships with you, they are almost sure to
have good relationships with their own children later on. This is the basis
for a close, warm extended family.

That brings us to the other part of your own extended family—your
parents. They can contribute immeasurably to the richness of your family's
emotional life. You yourself will be enriched by getting input from two worlds
that are quite different from your own—the world of children and the world
of older people. And, of course, the more you talk and listen to your children
and your parents, the more intimacy you build among all three generations.
That's what this book is all about.

Unfortunately, many adults think that older people have nothing to teach
them, nothing of value to contribute. I was like this when I was twenty-two
years old. I was a minister; I had just completed my first year of theological
school, and I was assigned to a summer pastorate in a small town in southern
Oregon called Phoenix. I'll never forget that summer. At that time, I was
very prejudiced against older people. My secret attitude was something like
this: "Young people (like myself) are the ones with courageous, inquiring
minds, the ones who are willing to face the social issues of our times. I guess
I can learn from people in their forties, but, after that, forget it! People fifty
and over are old fuddy-duddies who have nothing to teach me, so there's no
sense messing around with them."

I learned a great deal that summer. And I revised my beliefs considerably.
For a large proportion of my little congregation were those people over fifty
(and sixty!) whom I had written off as having nothing to teach me. One of
my duties was to call on my parishioners (younger and older) and talk with
them. I was amazed to discover that they were not boring at all; in fact,
they were quite fascinating. They told me stories of their early lives and of
what Oregon had been like in the early days and of how they had come to

live in Phoenix. I discovered that I really enjoyed talking to these people—and I learned a great deal from them.

If you have the same kind of prejudice about talking with your parents that I had about talking with my older parishioners, I hope you will manage to get over it as I did.

I can't offer a money-back guarantee that, after you have talked extensively with your parents for a couple of months, you won't conclude that they are a couple of boring, rigid, uptight, opinionated people. You may decide that further efforts to talk with them are strictly blowing in the wind. So be it! Who can contradict your firsthand experience?

But I'll bet that 95 percent of you will discover that your parents are far more interesting people than you thought. And that their special experiences in life have a unique meaning to you because you are seed of their seed. I would also guess that you will discover something else about them: that because of their age and experience in life, they have a kind of quietness of mind and centeredness that people of your age do not yet have. And a mellowness you do not usually find among people in their thirties and forties.

The same methods and techniques that you use to encourage your children to talk with you will also encourage your parents to talk. Don't be judgmental, don't lecture; don't attack with questions; don't moralize; use the feedback technique; and learn to develop a genuine interest in what the other person is saying. When you talk, be sure to grant respect to your parent as a human being, and also try to have the courage to disclose yourself as a real person with problems as well as joys.

Naturally, talking with your parents is not the same experience as talking with your children. In fact, you may have problems doing it at first, if you're not used to it.

When talking with their parents, many people unconsciously revert to feeling the way they used to when they were little, and this gets in the way of effective communication. Just remember that you are no longer your parents' little child, but an adult in your own right.

If your parents are the kind who still remind you to take your umbrella when it's raining, you will have to learn to assert yourself as an adult. Not in an obnoxious way, of course. Say something like, "Mother, it really makes me feel odd when you remind me to take my umbrella or brush my teeth, as if I were still a child. I'm thirty-seven years old. I learned many important things from you when I was a child. But now I'm responsible for myself, and I'm raising my own children." Some parents take longer to get the message than others, so just hang in there. If your mother says, "But you're still my darling little girl to me," express your appreciation of her, but remind her again of your adult status.

When you talk to your parents about your problems and your successes, you may need to set a limit on the extent to which you reveal the details of your life. Parents are often very quick to give advice if they think you need it. So try not to talk about yourself in a way that will encourage them to come to your rescue, unless you are really seeking their advice and help. You will have to learn just how far you want to go with self-disclosure. You can still have a close and rewarding relationship with your parents, even if you don't share every little (or big) thing. Some personal life-space and privacy is healthy for everybody.

It is certainly just as well not to talk very much with your parents about problems you may be having in raising your children. I have already advised grandparents not to give unasked-for advice about their grandchildren. Be sure not to give them an excuse to do so unless you really do want their help.

Many grown children have one big problem with their parents: They feel that the parents are overly critical of them. And it is true that some parents just never stop finding fault.

Janet, who is forty-three years old, has two children, a daughter, eighteen, and a son, fourteen. "My mother comes to see us twice a year and stays for three weeks," says Janet. "And the whole time she's here, it's nothing but nag, nag, nag. She seems to take great delight in telling me everything I do wrong, from the way I look to the way I cook. But most of all, she seems to find fault with the way I bring up my children. If you want to know the truth, I think I'm a much better mother than she is."

Eleanor, aged twenty-nine, is the mother of a six-month-old daughter. She says, "My mother-in-law seems to start every sentence with 'I don't mean to interfere, dear, but . . .' And then she starts interfering."

Do these statements sound familiar?

Such problems can be solved. They occur with mothers, mothers-in-law, fathers, and fathers-in-law. Since grown children seem to complain the most about mothers, the following discussion will deal with them. But the methods of coping I am going to discuss can be used with anyone who finds fault, related or not.

If your mother's criticism bothers you, it is because you are still, in effect, wishing for her approval. You may not be coming right out and saying, "Mother, am I doing this right?" but you are probably sending out messages that you want her to tell you you're doing okay. If she weren't your mother, and if you *knew* that what you were doing was okay, you wouldn't care whether she approved or not. So if you do feel pretty sure you're doing a good job, try to let any criticism she gives you fall on deaf ears.

First of all, try to stop thinking of this person as your mother. Think of her as an older friend. Learn to detach yourself. This may take time and effort, but you can do it.

Secondly, remember that everyone is entitled to her own share of mistakes. Your mother must have made plenty of them in her life. You're entitled to make some, too. They probably won't be the same mistakes she made. You'll make your own. But you can be sure that your children will tell you all about them when *they* become adults, if not sooner.

What I'm saying is that one way to deal with a critical parent is to grow up yourself.

Adults who feel confident about what they are doing do not have to seek approval. They may seek advice. But that is a far different thing. Advice is something you can consider and take or not take. Approval is something you need in order to give yourself credibility. You should not have to depend on anyone except yourself for approval. When you continue to depend on your parents for approval, you regress to childhood. As long as you approve of yourself and your actions, your mother's opinions should be immaterial.

At this point, you are probably thinking, "That's easy enough to say, but I need some help if I'm going to make it work." I think one thing that will help you immensely is my Creative Listening Plan.

1. When your mother criticizes you, listen attentively to what she says. Then state, in your own words, what she has said.

Sometimes when you repeat the criticism this way, your mother will say, "That isn't what I *meant*. You're twisting my words." Then ask her to say it again, so you can get it right.

Repeat the process until you can pinpoint the problem, as your mother sees it.

Try to listen carefully to what your mother is saying. Most people feel they are not listened to. This problem occurs not only between parents and children, but also between husbands and wives, employers and employees, doctors and patients—almost any time two people are talking and one feels he has something important to say. If you are lucky, all your mother really wants to do is air a complaint she feels is legitimate. If that's the case, and she gets a fair hearing, perhaps she'll keep quiet—at least for the time being.

2. Once you have defined the problem to your mutual satisfaction, ask your mother for a solution. This takes some mothers by surprise, because they think their only duty is to point out faults and let you worry about correcting them.

3. Never dismiss a solution as being ridiculous or wrong, even if you have no intention of seriously considering it. Instead, ask for an alternative solution. Repeat this process until your mother runs out of solutions.

4. Thank her for her concern.

5. Promise to give careful attention to what she has said, but don't feel you have to make a commitment. Just because you've listened, it doesn't mean you're going to put her suggestions into effect.

The Creative Listening Plan may not work the first time—or the second, or even the third. But gradually it should begin to show results for you.

The Creative Listening Plan works in two different ways. First, anyone is likely to feel better if she knows her complaints have really been heard. Second, no one lives in a vacuum. For every action there is a reaction. If you change your reaction to criticism, the people around you usually react to your change.

The Creative Listening Plan can also be useful if your children are being critical of you, especially if they are going through that adolescent stage of making it clear that their parents can do absolutely nothing right. If you use the Creative Listening Plan and really listen to your teenager's complaints, without being defensive, you will go a long way toward defusing the situation. Your teenager may merely need to blow off steam; on the other hand, you may discover something about yourself that you would like to change. Or you may gain some insight into how you can successfully negotiate with your teenager on a particular behavior problem.

Suppose, though, that you have the kind of parents whose habits are set in granite. They won't change, it seems, no matter what. And they continue to criticize you no matter what you do. How do you live with that?

As I see it, you have three options.

1. You can continue to feel resentment. This is the least satisfactory approach, because you are going to be suffering inside.

2. You can accept your parents' behavior and shrug it off. "It's their problem, not mine." This is a better approach. In essence, you are remaining neutral.

3. You can maximize your parents' good qualities as grandparents. This is the best approach of all. Most of our parents are much different with our children than they were with us. They have more patience. They are not nearly as critical. They are willing to share their time and abilities. Mothers who wouldn't let their own children in the kitchen may happily endure smudgy fingerprints as they teach their grandchildren how to make fudge. Fathers

who wouldn't let anyone near their fishing gear will show grandchildren how to tie flies.

When we adults act in harmony with our parents, grandparents, parents, and children have a much better chance of achieving the closeness that is the goal of the new extended family.

⊸§ 20 §⊸

Birthing Your Extended Family

I've covered an enormous amount of ground in this book, just as you will in being a grandparent to a child from birth through adolescence.

I began by issuing a call for a new structure in the American family, a structure I refer to as the *new* extended family. We have good historical evidence that the old extended family, with grandparents, parents, and children all living in the same house, has many psychological drawbacks. We have equally good evidence that in the modern nuclear family, the generations often live in psychologically watertight compartments, separate from one another. It seems clear that we must go beyond the structure of the isolated nuclear family if we are to get the most out of the emotional and intellectual enrichment that the three generations—children, parents, and grandparents—can offer one another.

In this book I have taken you step by step, from infancy through adolescence, and shown you how all three generations can work and play together, and learn from one another. I have talked about the many ways in which you, as a grandparent, can contribute to your extended family and receive great pleasure from doing so. But as joyfully and enthusiastically as you may enter into this idea, you can't create the new extended family all by yourself. It takes all three generations to bring it up to its full potential. So there is one more thing you can do.

This is a simple idea, but a scary one. Call a meeting of your family, and I mean *all* the family: children, parents, and grandparents (as many who live close enough to come). Either you or the parents can set up the meeting, as long as it is at a convenient time for everyone.

At the meeting, share your feelings about wanting the three generations to be close and open with one another. Say something like, "We've got three generations here, and each person is special, and each generation is special and different from the others. Each of us has things we can contribute to the family that will help us to have more fun together and to be closer and warmer." If some of the material in this book has had special meaning to you, share that, too. If you're nervous or scared about being the person to initiate this project, everyone will like you better for admitting that. And talking about it will help you to relax.

After you have spoken, pass out pieces of paper and ask everyone to write out the answers to three questions. Each person writes about the other two generations, not just about one child or parent or grandparent. Children too young to write can dictate their ideas and feelings to a parent.

Here are the questions:

1. What are the things that my parents (or grandparents or children or grandchildren) do that I like and hope they'll keep on doing?

2. What do I wish they would do less of, or stop doing?

3. What do I wish they'd do more of?

To show you what the lists might be like, here is what a child might answer.

1. I like it when my parents take me out to dinner and to the movies. I like the way we have fun at the dinner table and joke around.

I like it when everybody gets together and we play games and tell stories to each other.

I like it when my grandparents invite me to stay with them overnight.

2. I wish my parents would quit nagging me about my homework.

I wish my grandparents wouldn't lecture me about how long my hair is, or the clothes I wear.

I wish my parents wouldn't make me come home by ten o'clock on Saturday nights, when all my friends get to stay out till eleven.

I wish my parents would quit worrying about me when I ride my bike in traffic.

3. I wish my parents would understand that I can do more things for myself and quit overprotecting me.

I wish my grandparents would take me with them on more of their fishing trips.

I wish my parents would let me have my own telephone if I paid for part of it myself.

Probably the children should read their lists first (including lists dictated to parents by children who are too young to write). If the adults go first, the children may tend to feel intimidated. They may be fearful anyway, so you may need to encourage them to say what they feel. It's important that when the lists are read, everyone listen without comment, argument, or disagreement, no matter what is said.

After the lists have been read, there will be plenty to talk about. Explain that everyone is to try to be constructive. The idea is to try to clear up problems that may be getting in the way of good relationships, and to look for ways of enjoying one another more. Nobody is trying to force somebody to change or to be a particular way.

This meeting can end with something good to eat—that will help draw the children in and be pleasant for everybody. Don't let this meeting go on more than about an hour unless important things are being said. You don't want people to leave feeling bored or exhausted. You do want them to leave with good feelings and plenty to keep thinking about. Try to set up a regular meeting time for the future: once every two weeks, or once a month for as many as can attend. Future meetings can also end with something good to eat.

You might want to have a different person chair each meeting. (Include children eight or older in your roster of chairpeople.) This is good training for everybody, as well as good democratic procedure for the group.

In future meetings, you will talk about how to get rid of the stumbling blocks between the generations, and how to do more things that bring you closer together. You will probably have fun thinking up new things you'd like to do together as a family. You may also uncover new problems from time to time. If some of the problems seem really difficult to solve, you may need to use the mutual problem-solving technique I discussed in Chapter 3. Even young children can often contribute very good ideas in a problem-solving session.

If you can keep the atmosphere constructive, the rewards of these meetings, in terms of joy and satisfaction and warmth and closeness, can be very great.

You may be wondering, "Will this really work?"

There are several answers to that question. The main one is that you won't know unless you try it. In the immortal words of the famous Hungarian philosopher Zsa Zsa Gabor, "If you haven't tried it, don't knock it!" If you do try having a meeting and it is successful, you will be surprised and delighted. You'll find you belong to a *real family* (compared to those isolated clumps of parents and children living in houses all around you). If you try and the meeting is a failure because your family members aren't ready to open up, then you will have lost nothing by trying. You may discover that holding an unsuccessful preliminary meeting is a step in a process that yields rewards later.

When you do find out what it's like to be a part of a *real family,* you'll wonder why you didn't get your family together to talk like this years ago.

I'm sitting here typing this in my office and it's getting dark outside, and I'm wondering how many families are actually going to be daring enough to try what I've just suggested. Every time I write a book I regret very much that the audience before me is unknown. I am confined to the impersonal world of the printed word, when I'd like to be able to communicate with you over a cup of coffee, or as we walk leisurely along a forest trail. That way we could talk back and forth, you and I, about the new extended family, about your concerns for your grandchildren and your family, and about my suggestions.

When I am limited to the printed word, I have to write about grandchildren-in-general and parents-in-general and grandparents-in-general. But of course you are not grandparents-in-general. You are your own unique selves with your own unique grandchildren and family. I realize that this book may not cover some important aspects of grandparenting you are concerned with in your individual family. Or you may disagree with some of the things I've said and want to challenge me.

If you want to write to me for any reason, I would be happy to hear from you. You can write me in care of my original publisher, Harper & Row, 10 East 53rd Street, New York, New York 10022.

My sincere wish to all of you is for happy grandparenting!

❧ Part Four ❧

Appendixes

✺§ *Appendix A* ৡ✹
A Grandparent's Guide to Toys and Play Equipment

Sad to say, in the ten years since I compiled my first guide to toys in *How to Parent,* the quality of toys in the United States, with very few exceptions, has gone steadily down. Good wooden toys are the hardest to find. They are being replaced by hard plastic toys, and hard plastic toys are being replaced by softer plastic ones. American toys are beginning to look as though they were designed not by skilled toy designers, but by accountants. Fewer and fewer toys appeal to a child's intelligence and stretch her imagination and creativity. More and more toys violate the dictum that most of the play should be in the child and not in the toy. Battery-powered atrocities continue to dominate the field.

In 1978, I served as one of three judges at the International Creative Toy Contest held in Miami Beach, Florida. We judges surveyed 110 entries, nearly all of which were imaginative, creative, and well designed. Unfortunately, few of the entries bore any relationship to the current crop of toys being produced by toy companies in the United States.

There is one note of optimism. I think the age of the electronic computerized toy is coming. We see a little bit of this now, with thinking games for preschoolers and electronic football and baseball and basketball games for older children. I foresee the day when the computer will revolutionize the toy industry as it has revolutionized other industries—a day when we will teach logic, history, science, and almost everything else by computerized games. Watch for these kinds of computerized toys and games, for they have much to offer your grandchildren.

The toy scene today is not completely bleak, of course. There are a few companies still producing well-designed, durable toys that have lots of play value. And I want to mention them by name before I begin to list the toys that fit the ages and stages of your grandchild's development.

Fisher-Price specializes in toys for babies and for children under the age of six. The whole Fisher-Price line is well-designed and durable; the toys all have great play value for the child.

Tonka Toys specializes in toy cars, trucks, and earth-moving equipment. These toys are well-designed and will withstand very hard usage by a preschooler. (I remember several Tonka trucks that lasted through two of my kids.)

Fisher-Price toys and Tonka toys are sold in retail toy stores and the toy sections

189

of department stores. I recommend these companies' full lines of toys.

Other toy companies that sell through retail outlets make individual good toys; I will mention these toys in the following pages.

Interestingly, some of the best toy companies in America sell only by mail order. What I would say is *the* best one, Childcraft, sells mostly by mail order, though some Childcraft toys are available in a few retail stores.

Those of you who live in rural areas or in small towns, where the selection of toys in accessible stores is limited, should welcome the opportunity to buy good toys by mail order. But even those of you who live in big cities can obtain toys from these mail-order companies that you might not be able to find in your local toy or department stores.

All of the following companies are excellent, and you won't go wrong in buying toys from any of them. Their catalogs are usually free, and I suggest you send for a catalog from each of them.

1. Childcraft, 20 Kilmer Road, Edison, New Jersey 08817. For overall excellence and coverage of children from babies to adolescents, I think Childcraft is the best of the American toy companies. Childcraft also has the dome climber and the indoor gym house, which I think are the two best buys for preschool children available anywhere. You can call Childcraft toll-free at (800) 631-5652.

2. Child Life Play Specialties, 55 Whitney Street, Holliston, Massachusetts 01746. Phone: (617) 429-4639. This fine company specializes mainly in outdoor play equipment: jungle gyms, tree houses, firemen's gyms, a ladder jungle, and a "commando climber." If you prefer, you can get the play equipment in the form of a kit, put it together yourself, and save 20 percent. This company is particularly important to know about, because the average parent or grandparent has a hard time buying good outdoor play equipment. It's just not available many places.

3. The Children's Design Center, Geyser Road, Saratoga Springs, New York 12866. Superb design is the hallmark of all Children's Design Center toys, which are for children from infancy to early adolescence. The prices may seem rather high, but you are buying quality. This company has a toll-free number, (800) 833-4755, so that you can order by phone or get more information about a particular toy quite easily.

4. Community Playthings, Rifton, New York 12471. Phone: (914) 658-3142. Community Playthings is well-known for the fine quality of all their toys. The firm sells a great deal to nursery schools and kindergartens as well as parents. The fact that their toys can stand up to the beating that a class of three- or four- or five-year-olds gives them says a lot for the sturdiness of their construction!

5. Constructive Playthings, 1040 East 85th Street, Kansas City, Missouri 64131. Phone: (816) 444-4711. Another company that sells mainly to nursery schools and kindergartens, but will sell to parents and grandparents, too. The firm has a multitude of good toys, including the hard-to-find dome climber and indoor gym house.

6. Debo Toys, 24401 Redwood Highway, Cloverdale, California 95425. Phone: (707) 857-3693. This company makes a set of handcrafted natural wood animals for ages three to six. An excellent toy for preschoolers.
7. Different Drummer Workshop, Solon, Maine 04979. Phone: (207) 643-2572. This is a group of craftspeople who make wooden toys from native pine. The toys are sturdy; they feel good; and they even smell good! Different Drummer's brochure states: "We take pride in the quality of our work and will gladly repair or replace any toy which breaks in the course of normal play." There are toy cars, trucks, railroad trains, and airplanes, and even a rocking horse. This company is a particularly valuable source, because good wooden toys are hard to find.
8. Educational Teaching Aids, 3905 Bohannon Drive, Menlo Park, California 94025. Phone: (415) 322-9934. This company's catalog is used mainly by nursery schools and kindergartens, but parents and grandparents will find many items of interest in it. This firm's Superblocs, Lock 'N' Stack Blocks, Snap Wall, Educubes, dollhouse and dollhouse furniture, puppets, and Versa-Tiles (educational games in reading readiness, language arts, and math) are all excellent for preschoolers.
9. Galt Toys. This company is one of the finest in England, and they now have a branch in the United States at 63 Whitfield Street, Guilford, Connecticut 06437. Phone: (203) 453-3366. Their catalog has excellent toys for children from infancy to age ten. They also have several pages of "stocking stuffers," which are often hard to find.
10. Jonti-Craft Educational Play Equipment, 416 Summit Avenue South, Sauk Rapids, Minnesota 56379. Phone: (612) 251-7503. This company specializes in wood toys, and has a number of excellent and sturdy toys for preschool-age children.
11. Learning Games, Inc., Box 820-C, North White Plains, New York 10603. Phone: (914) 428-7336. This company puts out the fabulous Cuisenaire Home Mathematics Kit, as well as Quick Master Chess, an excellent way to teach a child as young as five how to play chess. In fact, in my opinion, Quick Master Chess is psychologically *the* best way to teach a youngster of any age to play chess.
12. Milo Products Corporation, Grantham, Pennsylvania 17027. Phone: (717) 766-6451. This company manufactures Dado, the modular space block. These precisely cut, oil-finished, birch plywood blocks are slotted so they fit together and allow children to build almost anything their imaginations can conceive of. Dado blocks have been used successfully in a number of nursery schools, and it would be a rare preschooler who would not take to them enthusiastically.
13. Novo Toys, 11 Park Place, New York, New York 10007. Phone: (212) 255-1061. Novo's catalog is a virtual encyclopedia of fun toys that are also educational.
14. Playper Corporation, Box 312, Teaneck, New Jersey 07666. Phone: (201) 836-7300. Here is a company that manufactures only one piece of play equipment for children: items called Fun Covers. You start out with empty half-gallon milk cartons, tape Fun Covers around them, and wind up with a miniature

city that preschoolers will love. There are Fun Covers Big City, Fun Covers Downtown, Fun Covers Bricks, and Fun Covers Trucks. A most ingenious idea, and one with enormous play value for your grandchild. (Fun Covers are also delightfully inexpensive.)

15. The Toy Works, Middle Falls, New York 12848. Phone: (518) 692-9666. This firm specializes in a unique type of toy: antique-style dolls with features hand-printed on natural fabrics. Their current catalog shows twenty dolls, in color. I assure you that the actual cloth dolls are many times more charming than their pictures in the catalog. My favorites are the Edward Gorey cat and the Edward Gorey pig, the tabby cat, the toucan, and the bunny. You can purchase any of these dolls ready-made, or more inexpensively in sew-it-yourself kit form. By the way, teenage girls are not too old to welcome these dolls as gifts.

16. Wooden Toys by R. Voake, Toymaker. Thetford Center, Vermont 05075. Phone: (802) 785-2837. Another fine maker of wooden toys, including cars, trucks, boats, airplanes, trolley cars, and earth-moving equipment such as bulldozers and road graders. These toys are usually big enough for a young child to ride on. Quality construction throughout, built for rugged play.

Now that I have given you all these excellent sources for good toys and play equipment, I want to say a few words about "expensive" and "inexpensive" toys and equipment.

Often parents or grandparents will see an excellent piece of play equipment such as the dome climber, which is currently priced at about $75, and say, "Oh, that's too expensive. I couldn't afford that." Then they will go out at Christmastime and buy about $40 worth of poorly designed, poorly constructed, easily breakable, chintzy toys, which will be demolished by their children in two days.

I call the dome climber an excellent but "inexpensive" toy, whereas the $40 worth of "junk" toys I would call "expensive," because they have little play value to begin with and, in fact, they usually do last about two days.

Consider this bit of arithmetic. I bought a dome climber when my older son, Randy, was two. He used it till he was nine. My younger son, Rusty, used it from the time he was three till he was nine. So it was used for a total of thirteen years. If I had paid today's price of $75 for it, it would have ended up costing me about $5.75 per year of its use. Now *that* is what I would call an inexpensive toy!

So please, my friends, when you come across what you consider a high price tag for a toy, either in a store or a mail-order catalog, remember that good toys may last through several children, but poor toys may not even last from Christmas to New Year's Day.

And now let's proceed to an analysis of what toys are appropriate and helpful for your grandchild at each age and stage of development.

Remember, I obviously do not know your grandchild personally, and so I will speak of what is appropriate for a one-year-old or a four-year-old or an eleven-year-old *in general.* But your grandchild is not a child-in-general; she is a child-in-particular. Your grandson is his own unique self; your granddaughter is her own unique self. And of course you will need to allow for that in matching your grandchildren to my lists of toys for different age groups, especially as the children grow older and develop individual tastes.

On that note of caution, here we go!

I. Infancy (from birth until the child learns to walk, usually around the end of the first year)

Many grandparents and parents think of babies as passive, helpless creatures. They sleep a lot; they are fed; they have their diapers changed; they are given baths. But they are not learning anything important because, at this stage of their lives, they are only babies.

This is a very mistaken view. Babies are not passive at all. They are actively exploring their environment every moment of the day that they are not asleep. And the first year of life is an important year for learning. Your infant grandson actively studies his environment, constantly using his eyes, ears, mouth, nose, hands, and body to see, hear, taste, smell, and touch everything he can make contact with.

Before he acquires the ability to attach names to objects through spoken language, he is busy creating models of these objects in his mind. He explores the softness, hardness, and shape of a given object. He compares it with his mental models of other objects. He takes measurements of an object in his own crude way, puts it in his mouth, and smells it. Passive? Ridiculous! The baby is ceaselessly exploring and manipulating his environment.

Here are some good toys that can aid babies greatly in their sensory exploration of the environment:

1. Crib mobiles, bought or homemade (Fisher-Price has some excellent ones)
2. Modular crib rod (Childcraft)
3. Cradle gym (Fisher-Price; Children's Design Center)
4. Baby trainer (Childcraft)
5. Rattles (Fisher-Price; Children's Design Center)
6. Rubber squeeze toys (Fisher-Price; Children's Design Center)
7. Teething toys (Child Guidance; Fisher-Price)
8. Small, soft texture ball (Calico Clutch Ball, Children's Design Center; Childcraft's Clutch Ball)
9. Texture pad: a homemade toy consisting of swatches of cloth of different textures sewn on a two-foot-square piece of rubber matting
10. Musical carousel or musical mobile (Fisher-Price)
11. Musical pull toys that hang from the crib (Fisher-Price)
12. Soft, cuddly toy animals or dolls (Fisher-Price; Childcraft)
13. Sponges for bath play
14. Tub and pool toys (Fisher-Price)
15. Busy box or activity center with a number of things for the baby to do (Fisher-Price; Gabriel). For roughly ages three months to eighteen months,

one of the best and most practical toys ever designed for the baby and toddler. You will find this toy especially helpful if you're taking an active baby on a long trip.

II. Toddlerhood (from the time the child learns to walk till approximately the second birthday)

At this stage, your granddaughter is no longer hampered in her exploration of her environment by having to wait for it to come to her. Now that she can walk, she can go to the environment!

The basic developmental task of the toddler stage is *to learn self-confidence*. Toddlers also need to develop their large and small muscles. Several kinds of toys and play equipment will help them do both these things.

A. Outdoor Play Equipment

Obviously, some of the toys I list below can be used indoors, too. And some of the toys I list in Section B can be used outdoors. These two categories are only rough groupings; what toys you will let your grandchild bring indoors will depend to some extent on how big your house or apartment is.

1. Dome climber (Childcraft; Constructive Playthings). This is the best single item of outdoor play equipment you can buy for a toddler. It is based on Buckminster Fuller's geodesic dome concept, and it can safely support the weight of as many children as can climb on it. It is simply great for a toddler's large-muscle development. Put a piece of canvas or cloth over it and it can serve as a tent, playhouse, tepee, or anything else your grandchild can dream up. It will last throughout the preschool years.
2. Slide
3. Tyke Bike (Playskool)
4. Hollow wooden blocks
5. Small but sturdy boards, sanded down
6. Sandbox and sand toys: cups, spoons, pie pans, sifters, etc.
7. Plastic toy people and animals for sand and water play
8. Small toy cars and trucks for sand play (Tootsietoy)
9. An old coffee percolator (marvelous for toddlers!)
10. Water toys: plastic boats, dishes, scoops, measuring cups, etc.
11. Small but sturdy shovel for digging and sand play
12. Large wooden or metal cars, trucks, and earth-movers (Different Drummer wooden toys; R. Voake Wooden Toys; Tonka Toys)
13. Playhouse, bought or homemade
14. Cardboard boxes big enough for toddlers to get inside
15. Climbing Frame (Galt Toys)
16. Climbing House (Galt Toys)
17. Pet dog. I grant you that a dog is not exactly a "toy" or piece of play equipment, but running and playing with a friendly dog is great for a toddler's large-muscle development. A pet cat, on the other hand, is not a very good

idea for young children; they usually don't know how to play with cats and just wind up getting scratched.

B. Indoor Play Equipment
1. Indoor gym house (Childcraft; Constructive Playthings; Novo Toys). I consider this the outstanding piece of indoor play equipment for a toddler. It has a ladder, a slide, a tunnel for crawling through, and a "house" inside. Toddlers love it, and it's great for their large-muscle development.
2. Pull toys of various sorts. Toddlers love these, and Fisher-Price excels at making them.
3. Beanbags
4. Hollow cardboard or plastic blocks for building (Galt Toys; Constructive Playthings; Fun Covers Bricks by Playper)
5. Cardboard boxes of various sizes (from your friendly neighborhood market)
6. Stacking and nesting blocks (Playskool; Fisher-Price)
7. Hammering and pounding toys (Playskool; Childcraft)
8. Large beads to string
9. Balloons
10. Very simple puzzles (Fisher-Price; Childcraft)
11. Nerf ball
12. Small rubber ball
13. Toy cars and trucks that come with toy people (Fisher-Price)
14. Soft, cuddly toy animals and dolls. Many dolls are just plain awful. The play is not in the child, but in the doll, which cries, wets, or takes her hat off. But Childcraft has three nice ones: Terry Baby, Terry Teddy, and Bunny Ball, a toy rabbit. Galt Toys has a guinea pig, a hedgehog, a rabbit, a kangaroo with baby, a panda, a lamb, and a bear. Fisher-Price has Cholly, Lolly, and Freddy Bear. The Children's Design Center has a handcrafted clown doll, and Paddington Bear.
15. Dress-up clothes (Goodwill, Salvation Army—or your own closet!). Many nursery schools provide dress-up clothes for girls, but not for boys. Don't make that mistake. Both boys and girls like to dress up and play out adult roles.
16. Soap flakes or liquid detergent for water play, plus water play toys listed in Section A
17. Music boxes (Fisher-Price)
18. Toy xylophone (Fisher-Price)
19. Wooden blocks (Playskool; Child Guidance). Some children will be ready for wooden block play at this age; others will not. If your grandchild isn't interested in wooden blocks now, just hang on to the blocks until a little later.

III. First Adolescence (from approximately the second to the third birthday)
   The toys and play equipment you provided for your grandchild in toddlerhood will still be used with eagerness and gusto in first adolescence. But the child is now ready

for new toys as well. For example, you didn't give your grandson crayons and chalk and paint earlier, because he might have eaten them; however, he has now reached a new developmental level and can handle these art media. He is also ready for more sophisticated building toys, and for such "toys" as his own inexpensive record player.

A. Outdoor Play Equipment
Again, some of these toys can be used indoors if you have the room.
 1. Workhorse tricycle (Community Playthings) This is called a "workhorse" because it is built to last and last and last. Don't faint at the price, but consider that it may last you through several grandchildren.
 2. Irish Mail (Constructive Playthings, Childcraft). An unusual type of riding toy that exercises arms and shoulders with the pump action and is steered by the feet.
 3. Dart-About Racer (Constructive Playthings)
 4. Fourway Transport (Community Playthings). One sturdy wooden truck kids can ride on in four different ways.
 5. First wagon (Childcraft)
 6. Ride 'Em Car (Childcraft). Sturdily built of one-inch heavy-gauge tubing, this is a very durable car.
 7. Activity Bike (Childcraft). Like the Ride 'Em Car, very durably constructed.
 8. Trestle slide (Galt Toys). This climbing apparatus can be used in a number of different ways. Children can climb up the rungs on the trestle, and crawl or walk across the wide bridge.
 9. Snap Wall (Childcraft). Big, colorful panels for building play structures with swinging doors and crawl-through hatches.
 10. Notched Play Planks (Childcraft). These fit together without posts, bolts, or pegs, and can be used to build various types of playhouses, taken apart, and used again.
 11. Play-All (Childcraft). Three curved sections of unbreakable polyethelene can combine in different ways to form a rolling circle, a sit-astride see-saw, a reclining seat, or an individual rocker. A remarkably versatile toy.
 12. Easel for painting and drawing outside. Make an easel that will go on a fence in your yard; see suggestions below about paper and paint.
 13. A large rubber ball for outdoor play.

B. Indoor Play Equipment
 1. Blackboard. You can paint all four walls of your grandchild's room with blackboard paint, and really give him room to scribble! Or buy an easel-type blackboard or one to hang on the wall; one *at least* four by four feet is best. This is the most basic item of play equipment you can get for your grandchild at this stage.
 2. Painting easel
 3. Paper. Newsprint is fine—a first adolescent does not require high-quality paper. At this age your grandchild will be perfectly happy to paint right

over the printing on ordinary newspaper. Also plain newsprint is excellent.

4. Crayons and chalk
5. Watercolor felt-tip pens
6. Water-soluble paint and large, sturdy paintbrushes
7. Finger paints
8. Play-Dough
9. Clay, bought or homemade
8. Plasticene
10. Lego beginner set
11. Bristle Blocks (Playskool). Colorful plastic shapes with flexible bristles that interlock when pressed together to form all sorts of constructions.
12. Hardwood or softwood blocks (Playskool; Childcraft; Community Playthings). If your grandchild began to play with wooden blocks in toddlerhood, you may want to increase your collection of them at this stage.
13. Blockbusters blocks (Childcraft; Educational Teaching Aids). Large, lightweight blocks made from specially constructed corrugated cardboard. These blocks are sturdy enough to stand on, yet easy for a young child to manipulate.
14. Toys dealing with sounds and music
    a. Rhythm instruments: pans and cigar boxes to beat, tin cans with dry beans or pebbles in them to shake; drums, cymbals, triangles, bought or homemade
    b. Toy xylophone or accordion
    c. Inexpensive record player. Get one that cannot possibly scratch the records, such as the Music Box record player by Fisher-Price.
    d. Inexpensive records the child can play by herself
    e. Good family record player, which you do *not* allow the child to play until she is five or older
    f. Good children's records you play for the youngster

C. Other Equipment You May Wish to Get
    1. Bulletin board to pin up your grandchildren's paintings and drawings on
    2. Child-sized table or desk for painting and drawing on
    3. Sturdy child-sized chairs. I recommend Efebino children's chairs, made in Italy and sold by the Children's Design Center. Good children's furniture is hard to find, and these chairs are better than good. They are made of molded plastic reinforced with fiberglass; they come in attractive colors, stack easily, and are very durable.

IV. The Preschool Stage (from approximately the third to the sixth birthday)

During these years your grandchild develops at a fantastic rate, both emotionally and intellectually. Preschoolers are able to play cooperatively with other children. And they are particularly responsive to intellectual stimulation. Ideally, your preschool-age grandchild's home will have in it the kind of indoor and outdoor play equipment found in a good nursery school.

If there is a good nursery school near you, it would certainly be a good idea to visit it. Pay particular attention to the play equipment and think about how you can duplicate it in your grandchild's home. Much of this equipment you can make yourself, with a little ingenuity.

A. Outdoor Play Equipment
1. Tree house, built near the ground, with ladder and slide.
2. Tricycle. The Workhorse tricycle by Community Playthings (mentioned earlier in this appendix) is, in my opinion, the best. The Childcraft Trike and the Childcraft Ground Hugger are also excellent.
3. Irish Mail (Childcraft; Constructive Playthings)
4. Dart-About Racer (Constructive Playthings)
5. Wagons (Childcraft; Community Playthings)
6. Rope ladders or cargo netting
7. Large hollow blocks
8. Boards (sanded down)
9. Tunnel of Fun (Childcraft; Constructive Playthings). A tunnel made of durable, nonflammable fabric on a spring steel frame. Children hide in it, crawl through it, use it as a tunnel or a tent.
10. A large rubber ball

B. Construction Toys
1. Tools: hammer, saw, etc., plus nails and screws. Don't get toy tools, but real ones that a child can use under supervision.
2. Put-together construction toys
   a. Lego
   b. Tinkertoy (Gabriel)
   c. Giant Tinkertoy (Gabriel). Kids love Tinkertoy, but they love Giant Tinkertoy even more. This is one of the most delightful toys you can get for a preschooler.
   d. Swedish Variplay Set (Community Playthings). Unstructured building pieces to stimulate a child's imagination.
   e. Young Erector Set (Gabriel). Be sure to get the Young Erector Set, which is for children three to six, rather than the regular Erector Set, which is for children six and older.
      NOTE: There are three excellent construction toys for preschoolers made in Europe—Brio, Bilofix, and Baufix—which I have left out of this list only because there are so few toy stores in the United States where you can get them. However, if you happen to run across these toys, get them!
3. Additional hardwood or softwood blocks (Playskool; Childcraft; Community Playthings). A large number of wooden blocks can be used for elaborate block building by an individual child, or for cooperative block play by several children. Now is the time to add to your grandchild's supply of blocks, for a really super block collection will act as an enormous stimulus to the child's creativity. Remember: Frank Lloyd Wright was inspired to become an archi-

tect by the collection of blocks his mother gave him to play with when he was a preschooler.

4. Fun Covers Big City and Fun Covers Downtown (Playper). With Fun Covers you can turn milk cartons into "buildings" your grandchild can use in connection with block play.

5. Playtown (Galt Toys). This is a heavy vinyl base on which children can arrange and rearrange the buildings of their play cities.

6. Miniature interlocking wooden railway with miniature cars (Galt Toys; Educational Teaching Aids; Constructive Playthings). Children love this toy, and it's solid and durable.

7. Toy people and animals for use in connection with block play or sand play (Childcraft)

8. Wooden cars and trucks for use in the block cities children will create (Different Drummer; R. Voake, Toymaker; Childcraft; Community Playthings; Constructive Playthings)

9. Metal and plastic cars, trucks, and earth-movers for block play or sand play (Fisher-Price; Tonka)

10. Very small metal cars and trucks (Tootsietoy; Corgi; Matchbox)

C. Toys for Role-Playing and Creative Fantasy Development
1. Puppet stage (Childcraft; Galt)
2. Hand puppets (Childcraft; Educational Teaching Aids)
3. Flexible family figures for dollhouse or block city play (Childcraft)
4. Dress-up clothes (Salvation Army; Goodwill)
5. Doctor kit, hospital kit
6. Play store. A play store is expensive to buy (Childcraft), but you can make a simple one yourself.
7. Flannel cutouts and flannel board (educational supply store)
8. Fisher-Price Play Families. Children can act out roles through the use of little toy people in an assortment of environments. These well-designed, sturdy toys are also excellent for keeping preschoolers entertained on trips.
   a. Play Family Minibus
   b. Play Family Fun Jet
   c. Play Family School Bus
   d. Play Family Fire Engine
   e. Play Family Nursery School
   f. Play Family Farm
   g. Play Family School
   h. Play Family Action Garage
   i. Play Family Children's Hospital
   j. Play Family House
   k. Play Family Circus Train
9. Adventure People by Fisher-Price. Similar to the Play Families line, also first-rate, and equally popular with preschoolers.
   a. The Adventure People and Their North Woods Trailblazer

    b. The Adventure People and Their Wild Animal Safari
    c. The Adventure People and Their Wilderness Patrol
    d. The Adventure People and the TV Action Team
    e. The Adventure People and Their Emergency Rescue Team
    f. The Adventure People and Their Air-Sea Rescue Copter
    g. The Adventure People Rescue Team
    h. The Adventure People and Their Sea Explorer
    i. The Adventure People Construction Team
    j. The Adventure People Scuba Divers

D. Toys for a Homemaking Corner and for Doll Play
1. Child-sized play stove, sink, and refrigerator, bought (Jonti-Craft) or home-made
2. Child-sized pots and pans, silverware (Childcraft)
3. Dollhouse. Childcraft has an excellent open-top dollhouse of modern design. This allows even a very young child to manipulate the furniture and dolls easily.
4. Dollhouse furniture. Childcraft has a complete and well-made set of dollhouse furniture: suites for living room, dining room, kitchen, bedroom, bathroom.
5. Dollhouse dolls. Childcraft has a set of five small flexible dolls to go with its dollhouse: father, mother, infant, brother, and sister.
6. Other dolls
    a. Playskool's Dapper Dan and Dressy Bessy are nice. Dressing and undressing these dolls gives preschoolers valuable practice in working snaps, zippers, buttons, and ties—skills they need to dress themselves.
    b. The Children's Design Center has an anatomically accurate boy doll that can aid a parent or grandparent in toilet training. After the doll drinks from his bottle, you push a button on his back and he's ready for his potty.
    c. Childcraft has anatomically correct little brother and little sister dolls.
    d. Childcraft has a number of other excellent dolls to choose from:
        i. Raggedy Ann and Raggedy Andy
        ii. Florie and Alfie
        iii. Christopher and Debbie, black dolls
        iv. José and Chiquita, Latin American dolls
        v. Asian girl and boy dolls

E. Arts and Crafts Equipment
1. Play-dough
2. Plasticene
3. Clay, bought or homemade
4. Crayons, chalk, pencils, felt-tip pens
5. Paint and large paintbrushes
6. Light-colored paper for painting and drawing on; bright-colored construction paper

7. Colored tissue paper and scrap materials for making collages. Don't throw anything away; put it in the collage box for your grandchild to use later.
8. Glue and paste
9. Gummed paper stickers and seals
10. Various materials for block printing: lemons, oranges, carved potato, key, wire, leaf, etc.
11. Etch-a-Sketch (Ohio Art Company). A "classic" creativity toy for children, and particularly useful to take on trips.

F. Cognitive Stimulation Toys and Equipment
　1. Reading and Language Development
　　a. Magnetic letters and numerals (Fisher-Price; Child Guidance; Childcraft). A good place to use these is on the door of the refrigerator.
　　b. Plastic letters and numerals (Mattel)
　　c. Sandpaper letters and numerals. Cut your own out of cardboard or wood and glue the sandpaper on them.
　　d. Rubber stamps of letters and numerals, plus stamp pad and paper
　　e. Cardboard signs with familiar words printed on them: "door," "chair," "table," "TV," etc. (a wonderfully cheap homemade "toy"!)
　　f. Puzzles of all sorts (Fisher-Price; Childcraft)
　　g. Matching games that teach the child shapes, colors, and relationships (Childcraft has many of these)
　　h. Games to aid in reading readiness and language development (again, Childcraft has a number of excellent ones)
　　i. Put-together, take-apart clock (Child Guidance) to aid the child in learning to tell time
　2. Mathematics and Numbers
　　a. The Cuisenaire Home Mathematics Kit (Learning Games, Inc.). A terrific educational toy that will introduce your preschool-age grandchild to math in a delightful way. Children learn arithmetic concepts by manipulating colored rods of different lengths, representing the numbers one to ten. A step-by-step instruction book is part of the kit. The address of Learning Games, Inc., is Box 820-C, North White Plains, New York 10603. Phone: (914) 428-7336.
　　b. Math readiness games (Childcraft). The Childcraft catalog has nine solid pages of interesting math games for young children.
　3. Science
　　a. Magnets
　　b. Science materials from Childcraft; Constructive Playthings. Both catalogs devote several pages to science materials—excellent ones—for young children.

G. Music and Dance Toys
　1. Childcraft has an excellent selection of rhythm and musical instruments for young children, including rhythm sticks, maracas, claves, finger cymbals,

sand blocks, triangles, tambourines, cymbals, a koko (African) drum, a wooden xylophone, tom-toms, bongo drums, and steel drums.

V. Middle Childhood (from approximately the sixth to the eleventh birthday)

At this stage, the child's developmental task is to achieve *mastery* and thereby avoid a feeling of *inadequacy*. If your grandson feels secure that he can do what is demanded of him at school, with his peer group, and at home, then he will develop a sense of mastery. If he is not able to master the tasks demanded of him, he will develop a sense of inadequacy.

What are the toys that will help a child develop a sense of mastery, and which ones will exert a particular fascination at this stage?

Remember that your middle childhood grandchildren have by no means outgrown all the wonderful toys that delighted them in the preschool stage. They will still love to dig in the sand, build cities of blocks, play with puppets, play with toy cars and trucks and boats, dolls and dollhouses. But in middle childhood they are ready for toys, games, and play materials they were not mature enough to enjoy as preschoolers.

A. Games

At this stage, your grandchildren love to play games—with you, with their parents, with their friends, with the whole family. Intellectually, a middle childhood youngster has come a long way since the beginning of the preschool stage, and he is capable of playing moderately sophisticated games.

1. Checkers
2. Quick Master Chess (Learning Games, Inc.). An excellent way to teach a youngster to play chess. (The address of Learning Games, Inc., is given on page 201 of this appendix.)
3. One or two decks of playing cards
4. *Fifty Card Games for Children* by Vernon Quinn. Many of the card games in this book are played by only two people. You and your grandchildren can learn to play them together, and the youngster can also play them with a parent or a friend.
5. Pick-up sticks
6. Dominoes
7. Parcheesi
8. Monopoly
9. Roulette
10. Blockhead
11. Cross-Fire (Ideal). This is an exciting two-person game with particular appeal for boys.
12. Air Hockey (Ideal). Another two-person game that especially appeals to this age group.
13. Mattel electronic games. These are perfect not only for middle childhood youngsters, but for preadolescents and early adolescents (up to the age of about fourteen) as well. Look for more of these games to come out in the near future.

      a. Baseball

      b. Football I

      c. Football II

      d. Hockey

      e. Soccer

      f. Basketball

      g. Auto Race

      h. Space Alert

14. Othello (Gabriel). A unique two-person game of strategy played on a sixty-four-square board with sixty-four discs that are black on one side and white on the other. Eight-year-olds can enjoy it, and so can adults.

B. Sports Equipment

1. Nerf ball. This soft foam ball can safely be thrown around the house.
2. Whiffle ball. Another special kind of ball your grandchild can use in learning to throw and catch.
3. Softball and/or baseball. Parents and grandparents often don't realize how long it takes for a middle childhood youngster to develop true proficiency in throwing and catching a baseball. You can help your grandchild by practicing with him.
4. Baseball bat. Children also need lots of practice in order to hit the ball skillfully.
5. Football and/or soccer ball. If you can teach your grandchild football and/or soccer skills, or practice with the child, by all means do so.
6. Basketball, or ball of the same general type. Again, if you can help your grandchild to learn or improve skills, that's great. Hint: A middle childhood youngster may feel more comfortable shooting and dribbling a ball that is a little smaller than a regulation-size basketball—a volleyball, for example. Encourage your grandchild to save the "real" basketball till he or she feels truly ready to play with it.
7. Baseball glove for practice in catching
8. Bicycle. Some children will be ready to learn to ride a bike at six; others will not be ready till seven.
9. Roller skates
10. Jump rope
11. Marbles
12. Spinning tops
13. Pogo stick (Gabriel). It's best to wait till your grandchild is eight or nine to give her a pogo stick.

C. Crafts Equipment

1. Plastic or wooden model kits. Model-making may not be particularly creative, but at this stage many children, especially boys, go ape over putting together models of airplanes, cars, ships, prehistoric scenes, dinosaurs, horror characters, and you-name-it. Some of the models simply snap together; others must

be put together with plastic glue. Don't believe all the claims in the directions that the model will simply snap together—buy some glue to be safe. And try to find models with *simple* instructions.

2. Equipment for modeling clay. Gabriel has a nice electrically motorized potter's wheel called Potterycraft.
3. Supplies for doing papier-mâché (paper and glue)
4. Weaving equipment and yarn or other materials to weave
5. Woodworking equipment and supplies
6. Leatherwork equipment and supplies

D. Intellectual Stimulation Toys
   1. Scrabble for Juniors (Selchow & Righter)
   2. Scrabble (Selchow & Righter) (starting about age 7 or 8)
   3. Scribbage (Lowe). These three games can help children improve their spelling and learn new words.
   4. Probe (Parker Brothers)—a game of words
   5. WFF 'N Proof: The Beginner's Game of Modern Logic by Layman E. Allen. WFF 'N Proof is a series of math and logic games. It's probably best to start playing WFF 'N Proof when your grandchild is about ten. You will need to read the directions and familiarize yourself with the simplest game before attempting to teach it to your grandchild. Children cannot learn to play this by themselves, but once they have learned it, it will hold its fascination for them up into adolescence. An excellent learning toy, but not many stores carry it—you may have to look awhile before you find it.
   6. First Multiplier (Child Guidance). A fascinating introduction to the multiplication table.
   7. Biology Lab (Skilcraft)
   8. Chemistry Chemcraft (Gabriel), or Chemistry Lab (Skilcraft)
   9. Geology Lab (Skilcraft)
  10. Microscope (Constructive Playthings), Microcraft (Gabriel)
  11. Telescope (Gabriel)
  12. Big I, little i (Constructive Playthings). A lens containing a concave reducing lens and a convex magnifying lens is fascinating to children.
  13. Stethoscope (Constructive Playthings)
  14. Giant Super Magnet (Constructive Playthings)
  15. Primary Science Kit (Constructive Playthings). This kit—for children through age eight—contains over forty pieces of equipment and a manual of experiments. This kit is not something you can simply hand over to a child to play with; adult supervision is required.
  16. Elementary Science Kit (Constructive Playthings). For ages nine to thirteen. Seventy pieces of equipment, with chart manual showing how to perform one hundred fifty different experiments. Once again, not a toy to be handed over to a child to play with; young scientists need adult supervision.

E. Miscellaneous Toys

    1. Cassette tape recorder. Not exactly a "toy," but one of the most useful and versatile gifts you could ever give a child. For example, your grand-daughter might use it in her schoolwork, to tape a speech or a music lesson she is practicing so she can listen to her performance, and to communicate with you, through an exchange of tapes, if you are a long-distance grandparent (or even if you aren't!).

    2. Now is the time to add to the supply of tools you bought for your grandchild in the preschool stage. Real tools: hammer, crosscut saw, coping saw, screw-driver, pliers, brace and bit, hand plane, wood file and rasp, hand drills. I also suggest that you provide a pegboard for your grandchild to hang these on, rather than a toolbox to stuff them in.

    3. Electric train set. It's not wise to give this to your grandchild until he is nine or ten, because before that age the child probably won't take proper care of it.

    4. The full-fledged Erector Set (Gabriel)

    5. Flower Fun and Creepy Crawlers (both Mattel). Neither of these toys is particularly educational or inspirational, but they exert an incredible fascina-tion for children of middle childhood.

    6. Hot Wheels (Mattel). These souped-up little cars are just right for middle childhood children, particularly boys, who love to collect and play with them.

    7. Matchbox and Corgi cars. Middle childhood youngsters collect these small cars and play with them in a more sophisticated manner than when they were preschoolers.

    8. Superman Spinball Pinball (Mattel). If there's one thing kids love at this stage, it's a pinball machine, and this is a good one.

    9. Vertibird S.W.A.T. Patrol (Mattel). This toy includes a Vertibird helicopter with dual controls, a car, a roadblock, and a highway intersection. The Vertibird set can be used with a block city built by the youngster, and with plastic people or animals the Vertibird can pick up with its sky-hook.

VI. Preadolescence and Adolescence (from approximately the eleventh birthday to age twenty-one)

I will not recommend any particular toys for these stages for several reasons. Preado-lescents and adolescents are quite individual and unique in their choice of toys and games. Therefore, you need to know your grandchild's particular likes and dislikes in order to buy a toy or game he will like. Then, too, when youngsters reach the stage of preadolescence or adolescence, they are highly sensitive to anything that even remotely reminds them of being younger. So it's safest for you to consult with your grandchild before buying a Christmas or birthday present, to make sure you are on his wavelength.

I know from my experience with other books I have written that when I include an appendix on toys for children of different ages and stages, people are almost always sure to write me asking where they can buy a particular toy they find recommended. The trouble is that the answer to their question is usually found in the appendix they have just read! I welcome your questions on anything else, but please don't write and ask me where to buy a certain toy. Check the name of the manufacturer in the appendix and then ask for the toy by name and manufacturer at a retail toy outlet, or order it from the appropriate mail-order company. Remember that the addresses of sixteen excellent mail-order companies are listed near the beginning of this appendix.

৫§ *Appendix B* ৡ৵
A Grandparent's Guide to Children's Books

This guide to good fiction and nonfiction for children is meant to help you in selecting books from the library or at a bookstore.

Even though you have this bibliography, you should get to know the children's librarian of your local library. She is thoroughly trained in the field of children's literature. If you need a good nonfiction book on dinosaurs for a four-year-old or a good novel about horses for a ten-year-old, the librarian will be able to suggest titles to you. The librarian will also help your grandchild to pick out books that will especially appeal to her.

If you live near your grandchild, start the habit of taking her on weekly visits to the public library. You can do this as early as the preschool stage. By taking your grandchild to the library regularly (whether it's every week or every time she comes to visit you from out of town), you will be getting her into the habit of going. And going to the library will acquaint your grandchild with the world of books in a more comprehensive way than exposure to one book at a time will. At the library, your grandchild can have the wonderful experience of picking her own books from a seemingly vast collection. (You will probably want to check out more than one book on each visit, depending on the difficulty of the material and the time available for reading. For example, books for preschoolers are very short—you will be able to read a whole book to your youngster at bedtime.)

After your library visit, take your grandchild somewhere for a special treat. This might mean the ice cream store, a brief trip to someplace she particularly likes, or perhaps a trip to the park. Remember the positive reward system. Following the library visit with something very pleasurable will strengthen the appeal of the library in your grandchild's mind.

Every book in this appendix can be obtained from your library, even if they do not have it on their shelves. Ask the librarian to order titles you want on interlibrary loan. Any book that is in print, and many that are out of print, can be gotten on interlibrary loan.

Too many parents and grandparents take their youngsters to the library but don't think about buying them books of their own. What a mistake! You *always* buy toys for your grandchildren. If you don't buy books as well, the children may conclude that toys are more important than books. Surely you don't want them to believe that!

So, take your grandchildren to the bookstore to buy some books to keep and cherish. And don't forget that books make fine gifts.

If you don't live near a bookstore that has a good selection of children's books, you can buy them by mail. One of our best sources for children's books by mail is the Children's Book and Music Center, 2500 Santa Monica Boulevard, Santa Monica, California 90404; phone (213) 829-0215. They have a wide and comprehensive selection of children's books—over fifteen thousand, in fact. They also have an excellent selection of books on parenting. This is the same children's speciality store that I recommend in Appendix C for their fine selection of children's records, which you can also buy by mail. I urge you to send for their free catalog.

You can also buy children's paperback books from Scholastic Book Service, 904 Sylvan Avenue, Englewood Cliffs, New Jersey 07632, or 5675 Sunol Boulevard, Pleasanton, California 94566. Ask for their free catalog, which lists more than five hundred good paperbacks for children.

I. Toddlerhood (from the time the child learns to walk till approximately the second birthday)

A. Books for Labeling the Environment

At this age, children are usually too young for a book that has a continuous narrative. Rather, they will enjoy books containing pictures of people, animals, or objects, and words labeling them. Books are useful in playing the Label the Environment Game I mentioned in Chapter 5.

1. Sears or Montgomery Ward catalog, toy catalog, or trading stamp catalog. Although most people would not think of these as books, your toddler will, and he will love to use them to play the Label the Environment Game with you.

2. *Richard Scarry's Best Word Book Ever* (Western Publishing). Richard Scarry's books are wonderful for children, and this is one of his best. When you have finished playing Label the Environment with this book of fourteen hundred gaily illustrated objects and words to match, your grandchild will have learned a vocabulary of 1,400 words. An enormous aid in his language development!

3. *The Cat in the Hat Beginner Book Dictionary,* Dr. Seuss (Random House). Another fine picture dictionary to use in playing Label the Environment. Funny pictures and phrases in the inimitable style of Dr. Seuss make clear the meaning of a thousand words.

4. Other books that can be used to play Label the Environment and to enlarge your grandchild's vocabulary:

    a. *Words, Words, Words, Words,* illustrated by Judith Corwin (Platt & Munk)

    b. *Strawberry Word Book,* Richard Hefter (Grosset & Dunlap; also paperback)

    c. *My Very First Book of Words,* Eric Carle (Crowell)

    d. *Words,* Selma Chambers (Western Publishing)

    e. *Early Words,* Richard Scarry (Random House; also paperback)

    f. *Little Word Book,* Richard Scarry (Random House paperback)

    g. *My First Picture Dictionary,* Richard Scarry (Random House)

B. Nursery Rhymes

When you buy books for children of this age, make sure they are sturdy, because the first thing toddlers will do with books is to put them in their mouths!

    1. *Brian Wildsmith's Mother Goose,* Brian Wildsmith (Franklin Watts; also paperback). Traditional Mother Goose rhymes beautifully illustrated by the famous British artist.

    2. *I Wish I Had a Computer That Makes Waffles,* Fitzhugh Dodson (Oak Tree Publications). Modern educational nursery rhymes that teach such things as counting, addition, subtraction, colors, and days of the week. Contains a section describing how to teach your grandchild to write her own do-it-yourself nursery rhymes and free-verse poems. With marvelous illustrations by Al Lowenheim. For ages one and a half to six.

    3. *Hi Diddle Diddle* (Scholastic paperback). Mother Goose rhymes.

C. Other Books for the Toddler

    1. *The Giant Nursery Book of Things That Go,* George Zaffo (Doubleday)

    2. *Baby's First Golden Books* (Western Publishing)

    3. *Anybody at Home?,* H. A. Rey (Houghton Mifflin; also paperback)

    4. *Farm Animals Board Book* (Grosset & Dunlap)

    5. *Who Lives Here?,* Pat and Eve Witte (Western Publishing)

    6. *The Touch Me Book,* Pat and Eve Witte (Western Publishing)

    7. *Baby's Lap Book,* Kay Chorao (Dutton)

    8. *Baby's Toys and Games,* illustrated by N. Jo Smith (Platt & Munk)

    9. *Find Out by Touching,* Paul Showers (Crowell)

D. Bedtime Books for the Toddler

    1. *Goodnight Moon,* Margaret Wise Brown (Harper & Row; also paperback)

    2. *A Child's Goodnight Book,* Margaret Wise Brown (Addison-Wesley)

    3. *Bedtime for Frances,* Russell Hoban (Harper & Row; also paperback)

    4. *Bedtime,* Beni Montresor (Harper & Row)

    5. *Dr. Seuss's Sleep Book,* Dr. Seuss (Random House)

    6. *Goodnight Andrew, Goodnight Craig,* Marjorie Weinman Sharmat (Harper & Row)

II. First Adolescence (from approximately the second to the third birthday)

Some of the books that were your grandchild's favorites in the stage of toddlerhood will continue to be loved at this stage. Many books listed for the preschool stage would probably be too advanced for first adolescents. But they might be delighted by others and beg you to read them again and again. So this or any other book list is only a rough-and-ready guide to selecting books for children of a particular age. Your grandchild is the final authority on what book is appropriate for him. Be guided by the child's response.

A child in the stage of first adolescence is fascinated by words and word play. And he will continue to love nursery rhymes, with their rhythm, their cadence, and their repetition of words and phrases. At this age your grandson loves to repeat things until he feels he has mastered them. He likes the repetition in familiar nursery tales such as "The Three Little Pigs" or "Chicken Little." He likes to recognize what is coming next in the story and to chant it with you as you read it to him. He also delights in sounds of all sorts, particularly unusual or funny sounds. When you read books of sounds to him, emphasize the sound.

The first adolescent enjoys stories of the here and now of his everyday world: riding in a car or bus, playing in the park, shopping in the market, or going to the zoo. Animal stories are especially popular at this age.

Reading to a first adolescent should be a cooperative affair. He likes to look at the book and touch it. He enjoys finding things in the illustrations.

A first adolescent often has favorite books he will want you to read to him day after day. Sometimes it is difficult to get him to agree to let you read to him from a new book. And it is characteristic of this stage that you are in deep trouble if you dare to change a phrase or leave out a sentence in a familiar book!

A. ABC and Counting Books
1. *Brian Wildsmith's ABC,* Brian Wildsmith (Franklin Watts)
2. *Brian Wildsmith's 1, 2, 3's,* Brian Wildsmith (Franklin Watts)
3. *ABC of Cars and Trucks,* Anne Alexander (Doubleday)
4. *ABC of Buses,* Dorothy Shuttlesworth (Doubleday)
5. *Bruno Munari's ABC,* Bruno Munari (Collins + World)
6. *Richard Scarry's ABC Word Book,* Richard Scarry (Random House)
7. *Richard Scarry's Best Counting Book Ever,* Richard Scarry (Random House)
8. *Richard Scarry's Find Your ABC's,* Richard Scarry (Random House)
9. *Dr. Seuss's ABC,* Dr. Seuss (Beginner Books)
10. *Counting Carnival,* Feenie Ziner and Paul Caldone (Coward, McCann)
11. *Brown Cow Farm,* Dahlov Ipcar (Doubleday)
12. *The Nutshell Library,* Maurice Sendak (Harper & Row)
13. *Anno's Alphabet,* Mitsumasa Anno (Crowell)
14. *Curious George Learns the Alphabet,* H. A. Rey (Houghton Mifflin; also paperback)
15. *What Do You Think I Saw? A Nonsense Number Book,* Nina Sazer (Pantheon)
16. *Count and See,* Tana Hoban (Macmillan)

B. Books About Sounds
1. *The Noisy Book,* Margaret Wise Brown (Harper & Row)
2. *The Indoor Noisy Book,* Margaret Wise Brown (Harper & Row)
3. *The City Noisy Book,* Margaret Wise Brown (Harper & Row)

4. *The Country Noisy Book,* Margaret Wise Brown (Harper & Row)
5. *The Seashore Noisy Book,* Margaret Wise Brown (Harper & Row)
6. *The Summer Noisy Book,* Margaret Wise Brown (Harper & Row)
7. *The Winter Noisy Book,* Margaret Wise Brown (Harper & Row; also paperback)
8. *The Quiet Noisy Book,* Margaret Wise Brown (Harper & Row)
9. *What Does the Rooster Say, Yoshio?,* Edith Battles (Albert Whitman)
10. *Look Around and Listen,* Jay Friedman (Grosset & Dunlap paperback)
11. *I Hear: Sounds in a Child's World,* Lucille Ogle and Tina Thoburn (American Heritage)
12. *Bow Wow! Meow! A First Book of Sounds,* Melanie Bellah (Western Publishing)
13. *It Does Not Say Meow,* Beatrice DeRegniers (Seabury)
14. *What I Hear,* June Behrens (Addison-Wesley)

C. Nursery Tales
1. *Tall Book of Nursery Tales,* illustrated by Feodor Rojankovsky (Harper & Row)
2. *Catch Me and Kiss Me and Say It Again,* Clyde Watson (Collins + World)
3. *It's Raining, Said John Twaining,* N. M. Bodecker (Atheneum; also paperback)

D. Animal Stories
1. *The Tale of Peter Rabbit,* Beatrix Potter (Frederick Warne)
2. *Millions of Cats,* Wanda Gag (Coward, McCann; also paperback)
3. *Little Bear,* Else Minarik (Harper & Row; also paperback)
4. *No Ducks in Our Bathtub,* Martha Alexander (Dial Press; also paperback)
5. *Harry the Dirty Dog,* Gene Zion (Harper & Row; also paperback)
6. *The Story About Ping,* Marjorie Flack (Viking Press; also Penguin paperback)
7. *Swimmy,* Leo Lionni (Pantheon; also paperback)
8. Brian Wildsmith's books (Franklin Watts)
   a. *Fishes*
   b. *The Lazy Bear*
   c. *The Little Wood Duck*
   d. *The Owl and the Woodpecker*
   e. *Python's Party*
   f. *Squirrels*
9. *Bruno Munari's Zoo* (Collins + World)
10. *Bear Book,* Jan Pfloog (Western Publishing)
11. *Puppies Are Like That,* Jan Pfloog (Western Publishing)
12. *Bunny Book,* Richard Scarry (Western Publishing)
13. *Animal, Animal, Where Do You Live?,* Jane Moncure (Child's World)
14. *Animals and Their Babies,* David Roberts (Grosset & Dunlap)
15. *Johnny Crow's Garden,* Leslie Brooke (Franklin Watts; also paperback)

16. *Bread and Jam for Frances*, Russell Hoban (Harper & Row; also Scholastic paperback)
17. *A Birthday for Frances*, Russell Hoban (Harper & Row; also paperback)
18. *The Runaway Bunny*, Margaret Wise Brown (Harper & Row; also paperback)
19. *Where Have You Been?*, Margaret Wise Brown (Hastings House)
20. *The Cat in the Hat*, Dr. Seuss (Beginner Books)
21. *The Cat in the Hat Comes Back*, Dr. Seuss (Beginner Books)

E. Books About the Child and the Everyday World
 1. *Play With Me*, Marie Ets (Viking Press; Penguin paperback)
 2. *Just Me*, Marie Ets (Viking Press; also Penguin paperback)
 3. *Umbrella*, Taro Yashima (Viking Press; also Penguin paperback)
 4. *Big Red Bus*, Ethel Kessler (Doubleday)
 5. *A Friend Is Someone Who Likes You*, Joan Walsh Anglund (Harcourt Brace)
 6. *The Carrot Seed*, Ruth Kraus (Harper & Row; Scholastic paperback)
 7. *Daddy Book*, R. Stewart and D. Madden (McGraw-Hill)
 8. *The Day Daddy Stayed Home*, Ethel and Leonard Kessler (Doubleday; also paperback)
 9. *Everybody Has a House and Everybody Eats*, Mary McBurney Green (Addison-Wesley)
 10. *Summer Night*, Charlotte Zolotow (Harper & Row)
 11. *Animal Daddies and My Daddy*, Barbara Hazen (Western Publishing)
 12. *Days with Daddy*, Pauline Watson (Prentice-Hall)
 13. *We're Going to Have a Baby*, Doris and John Helmering (Abingdon Press)
 14. *Friends*, Satomi Ichikawa (Parents' Magazine Press)
 15. *That's What a Friend Is!*, P. K. Hallinan (Addison-Wesley)
 16. *Grover and the Everything in the Whole, Wide World Museum*, Norman Stiles and Daniel Wilcox (Random House paperback)
 17. *Have You Seen My Mother?*, Anne Maley (Carolrhoda Books)

F. Miscellaneous
 1. *The Very Hungry Caterpillar*, Eric Carle (Collins + World)
 2. *Don't Forget to Come Back*, Robie H. Harris (Knopf)
 3. *I Am Adopted*, Susan Lapsley (Bradbury Press)
 4. *The Temper Tantrum Book*, Edna Preston and Rainey Bennett (Viking Press)

III. The Preschool Stage (from approximately the third to sixth birthday)
 You need to read both nonfiction and fiction to your preschool-age grandchild. Nonfiction provides the child with basic concepts that help him understand the world; fiction enlarges the child's imagination and creative thinking.

A. "Double-Duty" Beginning to Read Books
 I call these books "double-duty" for a very simple reason. You can read them to your grandchild in the preschool years before he has learned to read, and, later, they

can help the child master the strange new task of learning to read. The child will regard these books as old familiar friends, ratner tnan as frightening newcomers full of unfamiliar words, and will be interested in trying to read them alone.

I have listed each of these eighteen beginning-to-read series by publisher, to make it easy for you to become familiar with them.

If you read even a few of these books to your preschool-age grandchild, he (and you!) will absorb an amazing amount of information about the world in which we live.

1. Harper & Row: I Can Read Books
   a. *Policemen and Firemen: What Do They Do?*, Carla Greene
   b. *Doctors and Nurses: What Do They Do?*, Carla Greene
   c. *Cowboys: What Do They Do?*, Carla Greene
   d. *Animal Doctors: What Do They Do?*, Carla Greene
   e. *Truck Drivers: What Do They Do?*, Carla Greene
   f. *Father Bear Comes Home*, Else Minarik (also paperback)
   g. *Little Bear*, Else Minarik (also paperback)
   h. *Little Bear's Friend*, Else Minarik
   i. *Little Bear's Visit*, Else Minarik
   j. *No Fighting, No Biting!*, Else Minarik (also paperback)
   k. *Oliver*, Syd Hoff
   l. *Julius*, Syd Hoff
   m. *Danny and the Dinosaur*, Syd Hoff
   n. *Sammy the Seal*, Syd Hoff
   o. *Stanley*, Syd Hoff (also paperback)
   p. *Grizzwold*, Syd Hoff
   q. *Last One Home Is a Green Pig*, Edith Hurd
   r. *Dinosaur, My Darling*, Edith Hurd
   s. *Hurry Hurry*, Edith Hurd
   t. *Johnny Lion's Book*, Edith Hurd
   u. *Harry and the Lady Next Door*, Gene Zion
   v. *Who's a Pest?*, Crosby Bonsall
   w. *A Picture for Harold's Room*, Crockett Jackson (also paperback)
   x. *Harold and the Purple Crayon*, Crockett Jackson
   y. *Morris the Moose Goes to School*, B. Wiseman (also Scholastic paperback)
   z. *The Happy Birthday Present*, John Heilbroner
   aa. *Little Runner of the Longhouse*, Betty Baker
   bb. *Oscar Otter*, Nathaniel Benchley
   cc. *Tom and the Two Handles*, Russell Hoban
   dd. *Spooky Tricks*, Rose Wyler and Gerald Ames
   ee. *Magic Secrets*, Rose Wyler and Gerald Ames (Harper & Row; Scholastic paperback)
   ff. *Amelia Bedelia and the Surprise Shower*, Peggy Parrish
   gg. *Small Pig*, Arnold Lobel

hh. *How the Rooster Saved the Day*, Arnold Lobel

ii. *Arthur's Pen Pal*, Liilian Hoban

jj. *Arthur's Prize Reader*, Lillian Hoban

2. Harper & Row: I Can Read science books

   a. *Greg's Microscope*, Millicent Selsam

   b. *Tony's Birds*, Millicent Selsam

   c. *Plenty of Fish*, Millicent Selsam

   d. *Terry and the Caterpillars*, Millicent Selsam

   e. *Seeds and More Seeds*, Millicent Selsam

   f. *Let's Get Turtles*, Millicent Selsam

   g. *When an Animal Grows*, Millicent Selsam

   h. *More Potatoes!*, Millicent Selsam

   i. *Is This a Baby Dinosaur and Other Science Puzzles*, Millicent Selsam

   j. *Prove It!*, Rose Wyler and Gerald Ames

   k. *Ants Are Fun*, Mildred Myrick

   l. *The Penguins Are Coming*, R. L. Penney

   m. *Steven and the Green Turtle*, William Cromie

   n. *Donald and the Fish That Walked*, Edward Ricciuti

   o. *Fish Out of School*, Evelyn Shaw

   p. *Nest of Wood Ducks*, Evelyn Shaw

   q. *Octopus*, Evelyn Shaw

   r. *Look for a Bird*, Edith Hurd

3. Harper & Row: I Can Read history books

   a. *Hill of Fire*, Thomas P. Lewis

   b. *Clipper Ship*, Thomas P. Lewis

   c. *George, the Drummer Boy*, Nathaniel Benchley

   d. *Sam the Minuteman*, Nathaniel Benchley

   e. *Wagon Wheels*, Barbara Brenner

4. Harper & Row: I Can Read sports books

   a. *On Your Mark, Get Set, Go!*, Leonard Kessler

   b. *Kick, Pass, and Run*, Leonard Kessler

   c. *Here Comes the Strikeout*, Leonard Kessler

   d. *Last One in Is a Rotten Egg*, Leonard Kessler

   e. *Play Ball, Amelia Bedelia*, Peggy Parrish

5. Harper & Row: I Can Read mystery books

   a. *The Binky Brothers and the Fearless Four*, James Lawrence

   b. *The Binky Brothers, Detectives*, James Lawrence

   c. *The Case of the Hungry Stranger*, Crosby Bonsall

   d. *The Strange Disappearance of Arthur Cluck*, Nathaniel Benchley

   e. *A Ghost Named Fred*, Nathaniel Benchley

   f. *The Homework Caper*, Joan Lexau

6. Harper & Row: Early I Can Read books

   a. *Dinosaur Time*, Peggy Parrish

   b. *Who Will Be My Friend?*, Syd Hoff

    c. *The Horse in Harry's Room*, Syd Hoff

    d. *Barkley*, Syd Hoff

    e. *Cat and Dog*, Else Minarik

    f. *Come and Have Fun*, Edith Hurd

    g. *The Day I Had to Play with My Sister*, Crosby Bonsall

    h. *And I Mean It, Stanley*, Crosby Bonsall

    i. *Hattie Rabbit*, Dick Gackenbach

7. Crowell: Let's Read and Find Out science books

It is difficult to praise this series too highly. The scientific information is accurate and up-to-date, for the editor of the series is Dr. Franklyn Branley, coordinator of educational services for the American Museum of Natural History–Hayden Planetarium, and he himself has written a number of books for the series. Educationally, the books are superb and meet the child on her own level, for the series special advisor is Dr. Roma Gans, Professor Emeritus of Childhood Education at Teachers College, Columbia University. The format of the books is splendid, and the illustrations are eye-catching.

    a. *A Baby Starts to Grow*, Paul Showers (also paperback)

    b. *Your Skin and Mine*, Paul Showers (also paperback)

    c. *The Listening Walk*, Paul Showers

    d. *Me and My Family Tree*, Paul Showers

    e. *Look at Your Eyes*, Paul Showers (also paperback)

    f. *How You Talk*, Paul Showers (also paperback)

    g. *Find Out by Touching*, Paul Showers

    h. *Hear Your Heart*, Paul Showers (also paperback)

    i. *Follow Your Nose*, Paul Showers (also paperback)

    j. *Where Does the Garbage Go?*, Paul Showers

    k. *Before You Were a Baby*, Paul Showers and Kay Showers

    l. *What Makes a Shadow?*, Clyde Bulla

    m. *Caves*, Roma Gans

    n. *It's Nesting Time*, Roma Gans (also paperback)

    o. *Birds Eat and Eat and Eat*, Roma Gans (also paperback)

    p. *What the Moon Is Like*, Franklyn Branley (also paperback)

    q. *What Makes Day and Night?*, Franklyn Branley (also paperback)

    r. *The Sun: Our Nearest Star*, Franklyn Branley

    s. *Snow Is Falling*, Franklyn Branley

    t. *North, South, East and West*, Franklyn Branley

    u. *Rockets and Satellites*, Franklyn Branley

    v. *Rain and Hail*, Franklyn Branley

    w. *The Moon Seems to Change*, Franklyn Branley

    x. *Air Is All Around You*, Franklyn Branley

    y. *The Beginning of the Earth*, Franklyn Branley

    z. *Seeds by Wind and Water*, Helene Jordan

  aa. *How a Seed Grows*, Helene Jordan (also paperback)

  bb. *Animals in Winter*, Henrietta Bancroft and Richard Van Gelder

cc. *Watch Honeybees with Me*, Judy Hawes
dd. *Ladybug, Ladybug*, Judy Hawes (also paperback)
ee. *Bees and Beelines*, Judy Hawes (also paperback)
ff. *Camels: Ships of the Desert*, John F. Waters
gg. *Hungry Sharks*, John F. Waters
hh. *My Hands*, Aliki
ii. *My Five Senses*, Aliki (also paperback)
jj. *A Map Is a Picture*, Barbara Rinkoff
kk. *Energy from the Sun*, Melvin Berger
ll. *Where the Brook Begins*, Margaret Bartlett
mm. *Hot as an Icecube*, Philip Balestrino

8. Follett: Beginning Science series
a. *Earth Through the Ages*, Philip Carona
b. *Water*, Philip Carona
c. *Electricity*, Edward Victor
d. *Friction*, Edward Victor
e. *Fishes*, Loren Woods
f. *Light*, Isaac Asimov
g. *The Moon*, Isaac Asimov
h. *The Solar System*, Isaac Asimov
i. *Rocks and Minerals*, Lou Page
j. *Weather*, Julian May
k. *Your Wonderful Body*, Robert Follett
l. *Your Wonderful Brain*, Mary J. Keeney

9. Coward, McCann: Science Is What and Why series
a. *Sound*, Lisa Miller
b. *Levers*, Lisa Miller
c. *Atoms*, Melvin Berger
d. *Computers*, Melvin Berger
e. *Stars*, Melvin Berger
f. *Time After Time*, Melvin Berger
g. *Fitting In: Animals in Their Habitats*, Gilda and Melvin Berger
h. *Friction*, Howard Liss
i. *Heat*, Howard Liss
j. *Motion*, Seymour Simon
k. *Look! How Your Eyes See*, Marcel Sislowitz
l. *Rocks All Around*, Margaret Bartlett
m. *Sunlight*, Sally Cartwright
n. *Sand*, Sally Cartwright
o. *Water Is Wet*, Sally Cartwright
p. *What's in a Map?*, Sally Cartwright
q. *Sunpower*, Norman Smith
r. *Who Will Clean the Air?*, Thomas R. Perera
s. *Your Brain Power*, Gretchen and Thomas Perera

    t. *Who Will Drown the Sound?*, Carleen Hutchins

    u. *Who Will Wash the River?*, Wallace Orlowsky

10. Childrens Press: The True Book series

    a. *The True Book of the Mars Landing*, Leila Gemme

    b. *The True Book of Metric Measurement*, June Behrens

    c. *The True Book of the Moonwalk Adventure*, Margaret Friskey

    d. *The True Book of Dinosaurs*, Mary Lou Clark

11. Childrens Press: Stepping into Science series

    a. *Sounds All About*, Illa Podendorf

    b. *Easy or Hard? That's a Good Question*, Tobi Tobias

    c. *Liquid or Solid? That's a Good Question*, Tobi Tobias

    d. *Quiet or Noisy? That's a Good Question*, Tobi Tobias

    e. *Ecology and Pollution: Air*, Martin Gutnick

    f. *Ecology and Pollution: Land*, Martin Gutnick

    g. *Ecology and Pollution: Water*, Martin Gutnick

12. Random House: Beginner Books

    a. *Fox in Socks*, Dr. Seuss. This is an especially good book for a child just learning to read. With it, she can practice phonics in the most painless way possible. Read it to your grandchild in the preschool years, and let the child read it to you as she is learning how.

    b. *The Cat in the Hat*, Dr. Seuss

    c. *The Cat in the Hat Comes Back*, Dr. Seuss

    d. *My Book About Me*, Dr. Seuss

    e. *One Fish, Two Fish, Red Fish, Blue Fish*, Dr. Seuss

    f. *Dr. Seuss's ABC*, Dr. Seuss

    g. *Foot Book*, Dr. Seuss

    h. *Green Eggs and Ham*, Dr. Seuss

    i. *Dr. Seuss's Sleep Book*, Dr. Seuss

    j. *Hop on Pop*, Dr. Seuss

    k. *Cat's Quizzer*, Dr. Seuss

    l. *I Can Read with My Eyes Shut!*, Dr. Seuss

    m. *Oh! The Thinks You Can Think*, Dr. Seuss

    n. *Please Try to Remember the First of Octember*, Dr. Seuss

    o. *Book of Laughs*, Bennett Cerf

    p. *Book of Riddles*, Bennett Cerf

    q. *Animal Riddles*, Bennett Cerf

    r. *Go Dog Go!*, P. D. Eastman

    s. *Are You My Mother?*, P. D. Eastman

    t. *Sam and the Firefly*, P. D. Eastman

    u. *Snow*, Roy McKie and P. D. Eastman

    v. *A Fish Out of Water*, Helen Palmer

    w. *I Was Kissed by a Seal at the Zoo*, Helen Palmer

    x. *Why I Built the Boogle House*, Helen Palmer

    y. *The Bear Scouts*, Stanley and Janice Berenstain

    z. *The Bears' Picnic,* Stanley and Janice Berenstain

  aa. *The Bears' Vacation,* Stanley and Janice Berenstain

  bb. *Inside Outside Upside Down,* Stanley and Janice Berenstain

  cc. *The Bear Detectives,* Stanley and Janice Berenstain

  dd. *The Bears' Christmas,* Stanley and Janice Berenstain

  ee. *The Berenstain Bears Go to School,* Stanley and Janice Berenstain

  ff. *The Big Jump,* Benjamin Elkin

  gg. *Ann Can Fly,* Fred Phleger

  hh. *Put Me in the Zoo,* Robert Lopshire

  ii. *The Beginner Book of Things to Make,* Robert Lopshire

  jj. *Hugh Lofting's Travels of Doctor Dolittle,* Al Perkins

  kk. *Hugh Lofting's Doctor Dolittle and the Pirates,* Al Perkins

  ll. *Babar Loses His Crown,* Jean de Brunhoff

13. Wonder Books Easy Readers series

  a. *Will You Come to My Party?,* Sara Asheron

  b. *When I Grow Up,* Jean Bethell

  c. *The Monkey in the Rocket,* Jean Bethell

  d. *The Boy, the Cat, and the Magic Fiddle,* Tamara Kitt

  e. *Adventures of Silly Billy,* Tamara Kitt

  f. *A Surprise in the Tree*

  g. *Question and Answer Book*

  h. *Jokes and Riddles*

  i. *The Birthday Party,* P. Newman

  j. *Let Papa Sleep,* Crosby Bonsall and E. Reed

14. Putnam's: See and Read biography series

  a. *George Washington,* Vivian Thompson

  b. *Daniel Boone,* Patricia Martin

  c. *Abraham Lincoln,* Patricia Martin

  d. *John Fitzgerald Kennedy,* Patricia Martin

  e. *Pocahontas,* Patricia Martin

  f. *Thomas Alva Edison,* Patricia Martin

  g. *Annie Sullivan,* Mary Malone

  h. *Ben Franklin,* Estelle Friedman

  i. *Booker T. Washington,* William Wise

  j. *Buffalo Bill,* Eden Y. Stevens

  k. *Davy Crockett,* Anne Ford

  l. *Frederick Douglass,* Charles P. Graves

  m. *The Wright Brothers,* Charles P. Graves

  n. *Jacques Cousteau,* Genie Iverson

  o. *John Muir,* Glen Dines

  p. *Johnny Appleseed,* Gertrude Norman

  q. *Martin Luther King,* Beth Wilson

  r. *Richard E. Byrd,* Helen Olds

  s. *Walt Disney,* Greta Walker

    t. *The Great Houdini*, Anne Edwards

    u. *Theodore Roosevelt*, Sibyl Hancock

15. Follett: Beginning to Read series

    a. *The Birthday Car*, Margaret Hillert (also paperback)

    b. *The Funny Baby*, Margaret Hillert (also paperback)

    c. *Little Runaway*, Margaret Hillert (also paperback)

    d. *The Magic Beans*, Margaret Hillert (also paperback)

    e. *Come Play with Me*, Margaret Hillert (also paperback)

    f. *Happy Birthday, Dear Dragon*, Margaret Hillert (also paperback)

    g. *Little Puff*, Margaret Hillert

    h. *The Boy Who Wouldn't Say His Name*, Elizabeth Vreeken (also paperback)

    i. *One Day Everything Went Wrong*, Elizabeth Vreeken (also paperback)

    j. *The Curious Cow*, Esther Meeks (only Scholastic paperback)

    k. *The First Thanksgiving*, Lou Rogers

    l. *George Washington*, Clara Judson (also paperback)

    m. *Have You Seen My Brother?*, Elizabeth Guilfoile

    n. *Nobody Listens to Andrew*, Elizabeth Guilfoile (also paperback)

    o. *Kittens and More Kittens*, Marci Ridlon (also paperback)

    p. *A Frog Sandwich: Riddles and Jokes*, Marci Ridlon

    q. *The No-Bark Dog*, Stanford Williamson

    r. *Banji's Magic Wheel*, Letta Schatz

    s. *Beginning to Read Riddles and Jokes*, Alice Gilbreath (also paperback)

    t. *Crocodiles Have Big Teeth All Day*, Mary Smith

    u. *An Elephant in My Bed*, Suzanne Klein (also paperback)

    v. *The Ice Cream Cone*, Mildred Willard

    w. *The Strange Hotel: Five Ghost Stories*, Marcy Carafoli (also paperback)

    x. *You Are What You Are*, Valjean McLenighan (also paperback)

16. McGraw-Hill: Science books by Tillie Pine and Joseph Levine

    a. *Energy All Around*

    b. *Friction All Around*

    c. *Gravity All Around*

    d. *Heat All Around*

    e. *Water All Around*

    f. *Rocks and How We Use Them*

    g. *Scientists and Their Discoveries*

    h. *Simple Machines and How We Use Them*

17. Other McGraw-Hill science books

    a. *All Around You*, Jeanne Bendick

    b. *What Could You See?*, Jeanne Bendick

    c. *What Made You?*, Jeanne Bendick

    d. *Science Fun with a Flashlight*, Jeanne Bendick

    e. *Magnify and Find Out Why*, J. Schwartz

    f. *Science Fun for You in a Minute or Two*, Herman and Nina Schneider

    g. *Investigating Science in the Swimming Pool and Ocean,* Norman Anderson

    h. *Investigating Science Using Your Whole Body,* Norman Anderson

18. Franklin Watts: The Let's Find Out books

    a. *What Electricity Does,* Martha and Charles Shapp

    b. *The Moon,* Martha and Charles Shapp

    c. *The Sun,* Martha and Charles Shapp

    d. *Water,* Martha and Charles Shapp

    e. *Space Travel,* Martha and Charles Shapp

    f. *Animal Homes,* Martha and Charles Shapp

    g. *What's Light and What's Heavy,* Martha and Charles Shapp

    h. *What's Big and What's Small,* Martha and Charles Shapp

    i. *Babies,* Martha and Charles Shapp

    j. *Cavemen,* Martha and Charles Shapp

    k. *Indians,* Martha and Charles Shapp

    l. *Weather,* David Knight

    m. *Mars,* David Knight

    n. *Telephones,* David Knight

    o. *Earth,* David Knight

    p. *Subtraction,* David Whitney

    q. *The City,* Valerie Pitt

    r. *The Family,* Valerie Pitt

    s. *Communications,* Valerie Pitt

    t. *Hospitals,* Valerie Pitt

    u. *Manners,* Valerie Pitt

    v. *Bees,* Cathleen Fitzgerald

    w. *Frogs,* Corinne Naden

    x. *Let's Find Out About Christmas,* Franklin Watts

    y. *Let's Find Out About Easter,* Franklin Watts

B. Books Dealing with Intellectual or Emotional Development

These books can be read to your preschool-age grandchild to stimulate her intellectual development. They are categorized according to the particular aspect of development they deal with. Since some books cannot be categorized precisely, you may find a particular title listed in more than one place.

1. Sensory Awareness and Perceptual Acuity

    a. *The Listening Walk,* Paul Showers (Crowell)

    b. *Follow Your Nose,* Paul Showers (Crowell)

    c. *Things We Hear,* Anthony Thomas (Franklin Watts)

    d. *Do You See What I See?,* Helen Borten (Abelard-Schuman)

    e. *Do You Move as I Do?,* Helen Borten (Abelard-Schuman)

    f. *The Headstart Book of Looking and Listening,* Shari Lewis and Jacqueline Reinach (McGraw-Hill)

    g. *My Five Senses,* Aliki (Crowell; also paperback)

2. Concept Formation: Comparisons

    a. *High Sounds, Low Sounds,* Franklyn Branley (Crowell; also paperback)

    b. *The Very Little Girl,* Phyllis Krasilovsky (Doubleday paperback)

    c. *The Very Little Boy,* Phyllis Krasilovsky (Doubleday paperback)

    d. *So Big,* Eloise Wilkin (Western Publishing)

    e. *Fast Is Not a Ladybug,* Miriam Schlein (Addison-Wesley)

    f. *Heavy Is a Hippopotamus,* Miriam Schlein (Addison-Wesley)

    g. *Which Is Biggest?,* Mary Brewer (Child's World)

    h. *Over, Under and All Around,* Sylvia Tester (Child's World)

    i. *Up Above and Down Below,* Irma Webber (Addison-Wesley)

    j. *Playing with Opposites,* Iris Grender (Pantheon paperback)

    k. *Push, Pull, Empty, Full: A Book of Opposites,* Tana Hoban (Macmillan; also paperback)

3. Concept Formation: Classification by Color

    a. *Let's Find Out About Color,* Ann Campbell (Franklin Watts)

    b. *The Color Kittens,* Margaret Wise Brown (Western Publishing)

    c. *Little Blue and Little Yellow,* Leo Lionni (Astor-Honor)

    d. *A Color of His Own,* Leo Lionni (Pantheon)

    e. *The Great Blueness and Other Predicaments,* Arnold Lobel (Harper & Row)

    f. *Ant and Bee and the Rainbow,* Angela Banner (Franklin Watts)

    g. *My Very Best Book of Colors,* Eric Carle (Crowell)

    h. *See What I Am,* Roger Duvoisin (Lothrop, Lee & Shepard)

    i. *Green Says Go,* Ed Emberley (Little, Brown)

    j. *What Color Is Your World?,* Bob Fill (Astor-Honor)

    k. *Orange Is a Color,* Sharon Lerner (Lerner Publications)

    l. *Richard Scarry's Color Book,* Richard Scarry (Random House)

    m. *The Color Factory,* John Denton (Penguin paperback)

    n. *Color Me Brown,* revised edition, Lucille Giles (Johnson Publishing)

    o. *Is It Red? Is It Yellow? Is It Blue?,* Tana Hoban (Greenwillow Books)

4. Concept Formation: Classification by Shape

    a. *Shapes,* Miriam Schlein (Addison-Wesley)

    b. *A Kiss Is Round,* Blossom Budney (Lothrop, Lee & Shepard)

    c. *The Wing on a Flea,* Ed Emberley (Little, Brown)

    d. *On My Beach There Are Many Pebbles,* Leo Lionni (Astor-Honor)

    e. *Circles, Triangles and Squares,* Tana Hoban (Macmillan)

    f. *Shapes and Things,* Tana Hoban (Macmillan)

    g. *My Very First Book of Shapes,* Eric Carle (Crowell)

    h. *Playing with Shapes and Sizes,* Iris Grender (Knopf paperback)

    i. *The Shape of Me and Other Stuff,* Dr. Seuss (Random House)

    j. *Square Is a Shape: A Book About Shapes,* Sharon Lerner (Lerner Publications)

    k. *Hello, This Is a Shape Book,* John Trotta (Random House)

5. Concept Formation: Time
   a. *Do You Know What Time It Is?*, Roz Abisch (Prentice-Hall paperback)
   b. *Ant and Bee Time*, Angela Banner (Franklin Watts)
   c. *Just a Minute: A Book About Time*, Leonore Klein (Harvey House)
   d. *What Time Is It?*, John Peter (Grosset & Dunlap)
   e. *Time*, Harlan Wade (Raintree Publishers)
   f. *Time and Clocks*, Herta Breiter (Raintree Publishers)
   g. *Time and Mr. Bass*, Eleanor Cameron (Little, Brown)
   h. *What Time Is It Around the World?* Hans Baumann (Scroll Press)
   i. *Time: A Book to Begin On*, Leslie Waller (Holt, Rinehart & Winston)
6. Concept Formation: Numbers and Counting
   a. *One Is No Fun, But Twenty Is Plenty!*, Ilse-Margaret Vogel (Atheneum paperback)
   b. *I Can Count*, Dick Bruna (Methuen)
   c. *I Can Count More*, Dick Bruna (Methuen)
   d. *One, Two, Three with Ant and Bee*, Angela Banner (Franklin Watts)
   e. *One Is One*, Tasha Tudor (Rand McNally)
   f. *Berenstain Bears' Counting Book*, Stanley and Janice Berenstain (Random House)
   g. *Moja Means One: The Swahili Counting Book*, Muriel Feelings (Dial Press paperback)
   h. *Three by Three*, James Krauss (Macmillan; also paperback)
   i. *One, Two, Three: An Animal Counting Book*, Margaret Wise Brown (Atlantic Monthly Press)
   j. *10 Bears in My Bed: A Goodnight Countdown*, Stan Mack (Pantheon)
   k. *Ten Little Elephants: A First Counting Book*, Robert Leydenfrost (Doubleday)
   l. *Anno's Counting Book*, Mitsumasa Anno (Crowell)
   m. *Ants Go Marching*, Berniece Freschet (Scribner's)
7. Concept Formation: Seasons of the Year
   a. *Let's Find Out About Fall*, Martha and Charles Shapp (Franklin Watts)
   b. *Let's Find Out About Winter*, Martha and Charles Shapp (Franklin Watts)
   c. *Let's Find Out About Spring*, Martha and Charles Shapp (Franklin Watts)
   d. *The Bears' Almanac*, Stanley and Janice Berenstain (Random House)
   e. *All Year Long*, Richard Scarry (Western Publishing; also paperback)
   f. *Sunshine Makes the Seasons*, Franklyn Branley (Crowell)
   g. *A Year Is Round*, Joan Walsh Anglund (Harcourt Brace)
   h. *Winter Bear*, Ruth Craft (Atheneum)
   i. *Fall Is Here!*, Jane Moncure (Child's World)
   j. *Summer Is Here!*, Jane Moncure (Child's World)
   k. *Winter Is Here!*, Jane Moncure (Child's World)
   l. *Spring Is Here!*, Jane Moncure (Child's World)
   m. *All for Fall*, Ethel and Leonard Kessler (Parents' Magazine Press)

n. *Summers Fly, Winters Walk,* Charles Schulz (Holt, Rinehart & Winston)

o. *Wintertime for Animals,* Margaret Cosgrove (Dodd, Mead)

p. *Summer Is,* Charlotte Zolotow (Abelard-Schuman)

8. Concept Formation: Basic Science Concepts That Tie a Large Number of Events Together in One Concept

    a. *Energy All Around,* Tillie Pine and Joseph Levine (McGraw-Hill)

    b. *Friction All Around,* Tillie Pine and Joseph Levine (McGraw-Hill)

    c. *Gravity All Around,* Tillie Pine and Joseph Levine (McGraw-Hill)

    d. *Heat All Around,* Tillie Pine and Joseph Levine (McGraw-Hill)

    e. *Friction,* Howard Liss (Coward, McCann)

    f. *Heat,* Howard Liss (Coward, McCann)

    g. *Motion,* Seymour Simon (Coward, McCann)

    h. *Atoms,* Melvin Berger (Coward, McCann)

    i. *Friction,* Edward Victor (Follett)

    j. *Electricity,* Edward Victor (Follett)

    k. *Electricity,* Harlan Wade (Raintree Publishers)

    l. *Heat,* Harlan Wade (Raintree Publishers)

    m. *Levers,* Harlan Wade (Raintree Publishers)

    n. *Sound,* Harlan Wade (Raintree Publishers)

    o. *Gravity Is a Mystery,* Franklyn Branley (Crowell)

    p. *The Fresh Look Series,* J. Curtis (British Book Centre)

        i. *A Fresh Look at the Solar System*

        ii. *A Fresh Look at Gravity*

        iii. *A Fresh Look at Evolution*

        iv. *A Fresh Look at Atoms and Molecules* (also paperback)

        v. *A Fresh Look at Water*

9. Other General Books on Science

    a. *Let's Look at Reptiles,* Harriet Huntington (Doubleday)

    b. *Let's Look at Insects,* Harriet Huntington (Doubleday)

    c. *Sounds All About,* Illa Podendorf (Addison-Wesley)

    d. *In the Days of the Dinosaurs,* Roy Chapman Andrews (Random House)

    e. *Insects Do the Strangest Things,* Leonora and Arthur Hornblow (Random House)

    f. *Animal Habits,* George Mason (William Morrow)

    g. *Earthquakes,* Charles Cazeau (Follett)

    h. *Where Are You Going with That Energy?,* Roy Doty (Doubleday)

    i. *Nature's Squirt Guns, Bubble Pipes and Fireworks: Geysers, Hot Springs and Volcanoes,* Alice Gilbreath (David McKay)

    j. *Nature at Its Strangest,* James Comell, Jr. (Sterling)

    k. *Dr. Beaumont and the Man with the Hole in His Stomach,* Beryl and Samuel Epstein (Coward, McCann)

    l. Lerner Publications: First Fact books

        i. *First Facts About Animal Attackers,* Brenda Thompson and Cynthia Overbeck

ii. *First Facts About Monkeys and Apes*, Brenda Thompson and Cynthia Overbeck

iii. *First Facts About the Spaceship Earth*, Brenda Thompson and Cynthia Overbeck

iv. *First Facts About Volcanoes*, Brenda Thompson and Cynthia Overbeck

v. *First Facts About Under the Sea*, Brenda Thompson and Cynthia Overbeck

vi. *First Facts About Rockets and Astronauts*, Brenda Thompson and Rosemary Giesen

10. Problem-Solving

a. *What Makes Day and Night?*, Franklyn Branley (Crowell; also paperback)

b. *What Makes a Shadow?*, Clyde Bulla (Crowell)

c. *Are You My Mother?*, P. D. Eastman (Beginner Books)

d. *Why Can't I?*, Jeanne Bendick (McGraw-Hill)

e. *The Shadow Book*, Beatrice DeRegniers (Harcourt Brace)

f. *What Can You Do with a Shoe?*, Beatrice DeRegniers (Harper & Row)

g. *Why: A Book of Reasons*, Irving and Ruth Adler (John Day)

h. *Why and How: A Second Book of Reasons*, Irving and Ruth Adler (John Day)

i. *Sometimes I Worry*, Alan Gross (Addison-Wesley)

j. *Mom's New Job*, Paul Sawyer (Raintree Publishers)

k. *Help!*, Susan Riley (Child's World)

l. *What If I Couldn't: A Book About Special Needs*, Janet Kamien (Scribner's)

m. *Up Day, Down Day*, Jacquie Hann (Four Winds Press)

n. *Why Didn't I Think of That?*, Web Garrison (Prentice-Hall)

o. *What Would You Do?*, Leland Jacobs (Garrard)

11. Scientific Methods for Preschoolers

a. *The Headstart Book of Thinking and Imagining*, Shari Lewis and Jacqueline Reinach (McGraw-Hill)

b. *Greg's Microscope*, Millicent Selsam (Harper & Row)

c. *Benny's Animals and How He Put Them in Order*, Millicent Selsam (Harper & Row)

d. *Prove It!*, Rose Wyler and Gerald Ames (Harper & Row)

e. *How Can I Find Out?*, Mary Bongiorno and Mable Gee (Childrens Press)

f. *What Could You See?*, Jeanne Bendick (McGraw-Hill)

g. *The Real Magnet Book*, Mae Freeman (Scholastic paperback)

h. *ABC Science Experiments*, Harry Milgrom (Macmillan paperback)

i. *Adventures with a Cardboard Tube*, Harry Milgrom (Dutton)

j. *Simple Science Fun: Experiments with Light, Sound, Air and Water*, Bob Ridiman (Parents' Magazine Press)

k. *Got a Minute? Quick Science Experiments You Can Do*, Nina Schneider (Scholastic paperback)

l. *Berenstain Bears' Science Fair*, Stanley and Janice Berenstain (Random House)

m. *The Smallest Life Around Us*, Lucia Anderson (Crown)

n. *Magnify and Find Out Why*, J. Schwartz (McGraw-Hill)

o. *Look! How Your Eyes See*, Marcel Sislowitz (Coward, McCann)

p. *Finding Out with Your Senses*, Seymour Simon (McGraw-Hill)

12. Mathematics

a. *Let's Find Out About Subtraction*, David Whitney (Franklin Watts)

b. *Count and See*, Tana Hoban (Macmillan)

c. *The True Book of Metric Measurement*, June Behrens (Addison-Wesley)

d. *Measure with Metric*, Franklyn Branley (Crowell; also paperback)

e. *How Little and How Much? A Book About Scales*, Franklyn Branley (Crowell)

f. *Metric Can Be Fun*, Munro Leaf (Lippincott; also paperback)

g. *How Did Numbers Begin?*, Mindel and Harry Sitomer (Crowell)

h. *Zero Is Not Nothing*, Harry and Mindel Sitomer (Crowell)

i. *The Greatest Guessing Game: A Book About Dividing*, Robert Froman (Crowell)

j. *About the Metric System*, Alma Filleo (Child's World)

k. *Solomon Grundy, Born on One Day: A Finite Arithmetic Book*, Malcolm Weiss (Crowell)

l. *Humphrey, the Number Horse*, Rodney Peppe (Viking Press)

m. *Numbers, Signs and Pictures: A First Number Book*, Shari Robinson (Platt & Munk)

n. Series of six books by Vincent O'Connor (Raintree Child)
   i. *Mathematics at the Farm*
   ii. *Mathematics in Buildings*
   iii. *Mathematics in the Circus Ring*
   iv. *Mathematics in the Kitchen*
   v. *Mathematics in the Toy Store*
   vi. *Mathematics on the Playground*

13. The Alphabet and Learning to Read

a. *Follett's Picture Dictionary*, Alta McIntire (Follett)

b. *The Headstart Book of Knowing and Naming*, Shari Lewis and Jacqueline Reinach (McGraw-Hill)

c. *Alligators All Around*, Maurice Sendak (Harper & Row)

d. *Loud-Noisy, Dirty-Grimy, Bad and Naughty Twins: A Book of Synonyms*, Sylvia Tester (Child's World)

e. *What Did You Say?*, Sylvia Tester (Child's World)

f. *Never Monkey with a Monkey*, Sylvia Tester (Child's World)

g. Jane Moncure's Series of Five (Child's World)
   i. *Play with "A" and "T"*
   ii. *Play with "E" and "D"*

iii. *Play with "I" and "G"*

iv. *Play with "O" and "G"*

v. *Play with "U" and "G"*

h. Jane Moncure's Series of Ten (Child's World)

i. *My "B" Sound Box*

ii. *My "D" Sound Box*

iii. *My "F" Sound Box*

iv. *My "H" Sound Box*

v. *My "L" Sound Box*

vi. *My "P" Sound Box*

vii. *My "R" Sound Box*

viii. *My "S" Sound Box*

ix. *My "T" Sound Box*

x. *My "W" Sound Box*

i. *ABC of Monsters,* Deborah Niland (McGraw-Hill)

j. *Alphabrutes,* Dennis Nolan (Prentice-Hall)

k. *All About Arthur: An Absolutely Absurd Ape,* Eric Carle (Franklin Watts)

l. *Pooh's Alphabet Book,* A. A. Milne (Dutton; also Dell paperback)

m. *Zag: A Search Through the Alphabet,* Robert Tallon (Holt, Rinehart & Winston)

n. *The Magic World of Words* (Macmillan)

o. *I'll Teach My Dog 100 Words,* Dick Gackenbach (Harper & Row)

p. *Silent E Man: Sesame Street Book of Letters* (Random House)

14. Richard Scarry

Richard Scarry is so unique and wonderful, he deserves a category all to himself. He has a series of absolutely enchanting books that teach children about the world and the people who live in it. I advise buying a number of these books for your preschool-age grandchild. The child will use them for years and receive enormous intellectual stimulation from them.

a. *Richard Scarry's Great Big Air Book* (Random House)

b. *Richard Scarry's Busiest People Ever* (Random House paperback)

c. *Richard Scarry's Great Big Schoolhouse* (Random House)

d. *Busy, Busy World* (Western Publishing)

e. *Hop Aboard, Here We Go!* (Western Publishing)

f. *All About Animals* (Western Publishing)

g. *All Day Long* (Western Publishing)

h. *At Work* (Western Publishing)

i. *My House* (Western Publishing)

j. *On the Farm* (Western Publishing)

k. *On Vacation* (Western Publishing)

l. *Storybook Dictionary* (Western Publishing)

m. *Richard Scarry's Please and Thank You Book* (Random House)

n. *Richard Scarry's Postman Pig and His Busy Neighbors* (Random House)

o. *Animal Nursery Tales* (Western Publishing)

p. *Richard Scarry's Best Mother Goose Ever* (Western Publishing)

q. *Richard Scarry's Best Storybook Ever* (Western Publishing)

r. *Richard Scarry's Best Word Book Ever* (Western Publishing)

s. *Richard Scarry's Favorite Mother Goose Rhymes* (Western Publishing)

t. *Richard Scarry's Egg-in-the-Hole Book* (Western Publishing)

u. *Richard Scarry's Cars and Trucks and Things That Go* (Western Publishing)

v. *Richard Scarry's Just for Fun* (Golden Press)

w. *Richard Scarry's Find Your ABC's* (Random House)

x. *Richard Scarry's ABC Word Book* (Random House)

y. *Richard Scarry's Best Counting Book Ever* (Random House)

z. *Richard Scarry's Silly Stories* (Random House)

aa. *Richard Scarry's Great Big Mystery Book* (Random House)

bb. *Things to Know* (Western Publishing)

cc. *Things to Learn* (Western Publishing)

dd. *Going Places* (Western Publishing)

ee. *Nicky Goes to the Doctor* (Western Publishing)

ff. *Rabbit and His Friends* (Western Publishing)

gg. *Fun with Words* (Golden Press)

15. The Self-Concept

a. *My Book About Me,* Dr. Seuss (Beginner Books)

b. *My Hands,* Aliki (Crowell)

c. *My Five Senses,* Aliki (Crowell; also paperback)

d. *What's Inside Me?,* Herbert Zim (William Morrow)

e. *Any Me I Want to Be,* Karla Kaskin (Harper & Row)

f. *Who Am I?,* a Sesame Street book (Western Publishing)

g. *How I Feel,* June Behrens (Addison-Wesley)

h. *Katie's Magic Glasses,* Jane Goodsell (Houghton Mifflin)

i. *Look at Me Now,* Jane Watson (Western Publishing)

j. *About Me,* Jane Moncure (Child's World)

k. *All by Myself,* Jane Moncure (Child's World)

l. *The Boy with the Special Face,* Barbara Girion (Abingdon Press)

m. *To Be Me,* Barbara Hazen (Child's World)

n. *But Names Will Never Hurt Me,* Bernard Waber (Houghton Mifflin)

o. *Hooray for Me!,* Remy Charlip and Lillian Moore (Parents' Magazine Press)

16. Relationships Within the Family and with Peers

a. *My Family,* Felicity Sen (Bradbury Press)

b. *When I Have a Son,* Charlotte Zolotow (Harper & Row)

c. *When I Have a Little Girl,* Charlotte Zolotow (Harper & Row)

d. *If It Weren't for You,* Charlotte Zolotow (Harper & Row)

e. *It's Mine: A Greedy Book,* Crosby Bonsall (Harper & Row)

f. *Daddies: What They Do All Day,* Helen Puner (Lothrop, Lee & Shepard)

g. *Mommies,* L. C. Carton (Random House)

h. *Daddies,* L. C. Carton (Random House)

i. *Mommies Are for Loving,* Ruth Penn (Putnam's)

j. *Mommies at Work,* Eve Merriam (Knopf; also Scholastic paperback)

k. *When I Grow Up,* Lois Lenski (Henry Z. Walck)

l. *Animal Babies,* Arthur Gregor (Harper & Row)

m. *The Little Girl and Her Mother,* Beatrice DeRegniers and Esther Gilman (Vanguard Press)

n. *The Way Mothers Are,* Miriam Schlein (Albert Whitman)

o. *Alexander and the Terrible, Horrible No-Good, Very Bad Day,* Judith Viorst (Atheneum)

p. *My Sister,* Karen Hirsh (Carolrhoda Books)

q. *Cousins Are Special,* Susan Goldman (Albert Whitman)

r. *Gorilla Wants to Be the Baby,* Barbara Hazen (Atheneum)

s. *Why Couldn't I Be an Only Kid Like You, Wigger?,* Barbara Hazen (Atheneum)

t. *It's Not Fair,* Robyn Supraner (Frederick Warne)

u. *Daddy,* Jeanette Caines (Lothrop, Lee & Shepard)

v. *My Daddy Is a Monster—Sometimes,* John Steptoe (Lippincott)

w. *Aunt Bernice,* Jack Gantos (Houghton Mifflin)

x. *Couldn't We Have a Turtle Instead?,* Judith Vigna (Albert Whitman)

y. *Family Scrapbook,* M. B. Goffstein (Farrar, Straus & Giroux)

z. *Friday Night Is Papa Night,* Ruth A. Sonneborn (Viking Press)

aa. *My Daddy Don't Go to Work,* Madeena Nolan (Carolrhoda Books)

bb. *How Your Mother and Father Met and What Happened After,* Tobi Tobias (McGraw-Hill)

cc. *It's Okay If You Don't Love Me,* Norma Klein (Dial Press)

dd. *Confessions of an Only Child,* Norma Klein (Pantheon; also paperback)

ee. *I Love My Mother,* Paul Zindel (Harper & Row)

ff. *I Want Mama,* Marjorie Sharmatt (Harper & Row)

gg. *I'm Going to Run Away,* Joan Hansen (Platt & Munk)

hh. *She Come Bringing Me That Little Baby Girl,* Eloise Greenfield (Lippincott)

ii. *The Terrible Thing That Happened at Our House,* Marge Blaine (Parents' Magazine Press)

jj. *The Ultra-Violet Catastrophe,* Margaret Mahy (Parents' Magazine Press; also paperback)

kk. *We're Very Good Friends, My Brother and I,* P. K. Hallinan (Addison-Wesley)

ll. *Me and My Family Tree,* Paul Showers (Crowell)

mm. *But What About Me?,* Sandra Love (Harcourt Brace)

nn. *My Dad Lives in a Downtown Motel,* Peggy Mann (Doubleday; also Avon paperback)

oo. *Humbug Mountain,* Sid Fleischman (Little, Brown)

pp. *Julia and the Third Bad Thing,* Barbara Wallace (Follett) qq. *Never Is a Long, Long Time,* Dick Cate (Thomas Nelson)

rr. *Somebody Else's Child,* Roberta Silman (Frederick Warne)

ss. *Without Hats, Who Can Tell the Good Guys?,* Mildred Ames (Dutton)

tt. *Feelings Between Friends,* Marcia Conta and Maureen Reardon (Raintree Publishers)

uu. *Feelings Between Brothers and Sisters,* Marcia Conta and Maureen Reardon (Raintree Publishers)

vv. *Feelings Between Kids and Parents,* Marcia Conta and Maureen Reardon (Raintree Publishers)

ww. *My Daddy Is a Cool Dude,* Karama and Mahiri Fukama (Dial Press)

17. Books About Grandparents

a. *Nana Upstairs, Nana Downstairs,* Tomie DePaola (Putnam's; also Penguin paperback)

b. *Watch Out for Chicken Feet in Your Soup,* Tomie DePaola (Prentice-Hall)

c. *Why Are There More Questions Than Answers, Grandad?,* Kenneth Mahood (Bradbury Press)

d. *Grandma's Zoo,* Shirley Gordon (Harper & Row)

e. *Granny's Fish Story,* Phyllis LaFarge (Parents' Magazine Press)

f. *Grandmother Lucy Goes on a Picnic,* Joyce Wood (Collins + World)

g. *Grandma Is Somebody Special,* Susan Goldman (Albert Whitman)

h. *Kevin's Grandma,* Barbara Williams (Dutton; also paperback)

i. *Mandy's Grandmother,* Liesel Skorpen (Dial Press)

j. *My Grandpa Died Today,* Joan Fassler (Human Sciences Press)

k. *My Grandmother and I,* Helen Buckley (Lothrop, Lee & Shepard)

l. *My Grandfather and I,* Helen Buckley (Lothrop, Lee & Shepard)

m. *Grandpa and Me,* Patricia L. Gauch (Coward, McCann)

n. *Grandma's Beach Surprise,* Ilka List (Putnam's)

o. *Grandfathers Are to Love* and *Grandmothers Are to Love,* boxed set, Lois Wyse (Parents' Magazine Press)

p. *Grandparents Around the World: Photos from 20 Lands,* Dorka Raynor (Albert Whitman)

q. *I Love My Grandma,* Steven Palay (Raintree Publishers)

r. *My Grandson Lew,* Charlotte Zolotow (Harper & Row)

s. *William's Doll,* Charlotte Zolotow (Harper & Row)

t. *Mary Jo's Grandmother,* Janice Udry (Albert Whitman)

u. *Grandfather's Story,* Mervin Marquadt (Concordia)

v. *Grandmothers,* Glenway Wescott (Atheneum)

w. *Grandpa and My Sister Bea,* Joan Tate (Addison-Wesley)

x. *Simon's Extra Gran,* Pamela Oldfield (Addison-Wesley)

y. *Grandmother Told Me,* Jan Wahl (Little, Brown)

z. *Grandpa's Indian Summer,* Jan Wahl and Jeanne Scribner (Prentice-Hall)

aa. *Grandpa,* Barbara Borack (Harper & Row)

bb. *I Have Four Names for My Grandfather*, Kathryn Lasky (Prentice-Hall)

cc. *Grandpa's Ghost Stories*, James Flora (Atheneum)

dd. *Grandpa's Farm*, James Flora (Harcourt Brace)

ee. *Grandpa Had a Windmill, Grandma Had a Churn*, Louise Jackson (Parents' Magazine Press)

ff. *Granny and the Desperadoes*, Peggy Parrish (Macmillan; also paperback)

gg. *Granny and the Indians*, Peggy Parrish (Macmillan; also paperback)

hh. *Granny and the Baby and the Big Gray Thing*, Peggy Parrish (Macmillan)

ii. *Grandmother Orphan*, Phyllis Green (Thomas Nelson)

jj. *Grandpa, Me and Our House in the Tree*, Barbara Kirk (Macmillan)

kk. *Grandpa's Maria*, Hans-Eric Hellberg (William Morrow)

18. The Community and Community Helpers

a. *I Know a Grocer*, Lorraine Henriod (Putnam's)

b. *I Know a Zoo Keeper*, Lorraine Henriod (Putnam's)

c. *I Know a Dentist*, Naomi Barnett (Putnam's)

d. *I Know a Bus Driver*, Genevieve Gray (Putnam's)

e. *I Know a Policeman*, Barbara Williams (Putnam's)

f. *I Know a Fireman*, Barbara Williams (Putnam's)

g. *I Know a Librarian*, Virginia Voight (Putnam's)

h. *I Know an Airline Pilot*, Muriel Stanek (Putnam's)

i. *I Know a Nurse*, Marilyn Schima and Polly Bolian (Putnam's)

j. *I Know a Plumber*, Polly Curren (Putnam's)

k. *Richard Scarry's Busiest People Ever*, Richard Scarry (Random House paperback)

l. *Busy Town, Busy People*, Richard Scarry (Random House)

m. *Clean Streets, Clean Water, Clean Air*, Cynthia Chapin (Albert Whitman)

n. *Nothing Ever Happens on My Block*, Ellen Raskin (Atheneum)

o. *Who Are the People in Your Neighborhood?*, a Sesame Street book (Random House)

p. *Let's Find Out About Firemen*, Martha and Charles Shapp (Franklin Watts)

q. *Let's Find Out About Neighbors*, Valerie Pitt (Franklin Watts)

r. *Let's Find Out About Hospitals*, Eleanor Kay (Franklin Watts)

s. *Ask Me What My Mother Does*, Katherine Leiner (Franklin Watts)

t. *Butcher, Baker, Cabinetmaker*, Wendy Saul (Crowell)

u. *Jobs People Do*, Jane Moncure (Child's World)

v. *People Who Help People*, Jane Moncure (Child's World)

w. *Policemen and Firemen: What They Do*, Carla Greene (Harper & Row)

x. *Truck Drivers: What They Do*, Carla Greene (Harper & Row)

y. *People in Your Neighborhood*, Jeffrey Moss (Western Publishing)

19. The Larger Community: The World

    a. *Where in the World Do You Live?*, Al Hine and John Alcorn (Harcourt Brace)

    b. *You Will Go to the Moon*, Mae and Ira Freeman (Random House)

    c. *A Book of Astronauts for You*, Franklyn Branley (Crowell)

    d. *A Book of Outer Space for You*, Franklyn Branley (Crowell)

    e. *A Book of Planet Earth for You*, Franklyn Branley (Crowell)

    f. *The World We Live In*, Arkady Leokum (Grosset & Dunlap)

    g. *The World Is Round*, Anthony Ravielli (Viking Press)

    h. *Children Everywhere*, David Harrison (Rand McNally)

    i. *Space: A Fact and Riddle Book*, Jane Sarnoff and Reginold Ruffanis (Scribner's)

20. Children's Emotions or Special Problems

    a. *Timid Timothy*, Gweneira Williams (Addison-Wesley)

    b. *Where Is Daddy? A Story of a Divorce*, Beth Goff (Beacon Press)

    c. *Will I Have a Friend?*, Miriam Cohen (Macmillan; also paperback)

    d. *Curious George Goes to the Hospital*, Margaret and H. A. Rey (Houghton Mifflin)

    e. *The Dead Bird*, Margaret Wise Brown (Addison-Wesley)

    f. *Love Is a Special Way of Feeling*, Joan Walsh Anglund (Harcourt Brace)

    g. *This Room Is Mine*, Betty Wright (Western Publishing)

    h. *The Quarreling Book*, Charlotte Zolotow (Harper & Row)

    i. *Big Sister and Little Sister*, Charlotte Zolotow (Harper & Row)

    j. *The Hating Book*, Charlotte Zolotow (Harper & Row)

    k. *The Man of the House*, Joan Fassler (Human Sciences Press)

    l. *All Alone with Daddy*, Joan Fassler (Human Sciences Press)

    m. *Don't Worry, Dear*, Joan Fassler (Human Sciences Press)

    n. *My Grandpa Died Today*, Joan Fassler (Human Sciences Press)

    o. *The Boy with a Problem*, Joan Fassler (Human Sciences Press)

    p. *The Tenth Good Thing About Barney*, Judith Viorst (Atheneum paperback)

    q. *My Mama Says There Aren't Any Zombies, Ghosts, Vampires, Creatures, Demons, Monsters, Fiends, Goblins, or Things*, Judith Viorst (Atheneum paperback)

    r. *Angry*, Susan Riley (Addison-Wesley)

    s. *Sometimes I'm Jealous*, Jane W. Watson (Western Publishing; also paperback)

    t. *Sometimes I Get Angry*, Jane W. Watson (Western Publishing; also paperback)

    u. *Sometimes I'm Afraid*, Jane W. Watson (Western Publishing; also paperback)

    v. *Sometimes I Like to Cry*, Elizabeth and Henry Stanton (Albert Whitman)

w. *I Feel*, George Ancona (Dutton)

x. *That Makes Me Mad!*, Steven Kroll (Pantheon)

y. *I Don't Care*, Marjorie Sharmatt (Macmillan)

z. *Gorilla in the Hall*, Alice Schertle (Lothrop, Lee & Shepard)

aa. *I Hate It*, Miriam Schlein (Albert Whitman)

bb. *I Won't Be Afraid*, Joan Hanson (Carolrhoda Books)

cc. *I Have Feelings*, Terry Berger (Human Sciences Press)

dd. *Was My Face Red*, Judith Conaway (Raintree Publishers)

ee. *Will I Ever Be Good Enough?*, Judith Conaway (Raintree Publishers)

ff. *I Dare You!*, Judith Conaway (Raintree Publishers)

gg. *I'll Get Even*, Judith Conaway (Raintree Publishers)

hh. *Sometimes It Scares Me*, Judith Conaway (Raintree Publishers)

ii. *Feelings Between Kids and Parents*, Marcia Conta and Maureen Reardon (Raintree Publishers)

jj. *Feelings Between Kids and Grown-ups*, Marcia Conta and Maureen Reardon (Raintree Publishers)

kk. *Dentist and Me*, Joy Schaleben-Lewis (Raintree Publishers)

ll. *I'm Running Away*, Ann Helena (Raintree Publishers)

mm. *Lie*, Ann Helena (Raintree Publishers)

nn. *Mom's New Job*, Paul Sawyer (Raintree Publishers)

oo. *Emily and the Klunky Baby and the Next Door Dog*, Joan Lexau (Dial Press)

pp. *Me Day*, Joan Lexau (Dial Press)

qq. *Mommy and Daddy Are Divorced*, Patricia Perry (Dial Press)

21. Teaching Values and Ethics to Children

a. *The Value of Believing in Yourself: Story of Louis Pasteur*, Spencer Johnson (Oak Tree Publications)

b. *The Value of Courage: Story of Jackie Robinson*, Spencer Johnson (Oak Tree Publications)

c. *The Value of Curiosity: Story of Christopher Columbus*, Spencer Johnson (Oak Tree Publications)

d. *The Value of Patience: Story of the Wright Brothers*, Spencer Johnson (Oak Tree Publications)

e. *The Value of Saving: Story of Benjamin Franklin*, Spencer Johnson (Oak Tree Publications)

f. *The Value of Caring: Story of Eleanor Roosevelt*, Ann Johnson (Oak Tree Publications)

g. *The Value of Determination: Story of Helen Keller*, Ann Johnson (Oak Tree Publications)

h. *The Value of Responsibility: Story of Ralph Bunche*, Ann Johnson (Oak Tree Publications)

22. Books About Religion

Sad to say, good books about religion for preschoolers are mighty scarce. Here are a few, but there should be more.

    a. *A Book About God,* Florence Fitch (Lothrop, Lee & Shepard)

    b. *Told Under the Christmas Tree,* Association for Childhood Education International (Macmillan)

    c. *Children's Prayers for Today,* Audrey McKim and Dorothy Logan (Association Press)

    d. Books by Mary Alice Jones

Mrs. Jones has written a series of excellent books on religion for children. Highly recommended. (Rand McNally paperbacks)

        i. *Tell Me About God*

        ii. *Tell Me About Jesus*

        iii. *Know Your Bible*

    e. *Mitzvah Is Something Special,* Phyllis Eisenberg (Harper & Row)

    f. *Wineglass: A Passover Story,* Norman Rosten (Walker & Co.)

23. The Magic of Words and the Magic of Books

    a. *Books Are Fun,* Geri Shubert (Western Publishing)

    b. *The Magic Word Book,* an Electric Company book (Random House)

    c. *CDB!,* William Steig (Simon & Schuster; also Dutton paperback)

    d. *Play on Words,* Alice and Martin Provenson (Random House)

    e. *Nailheads and Potato Eyes,* Cynthia Basil (William Morrow)

    f. *Beginning Search-a-Word Shapes,* Dawn Gerger (Grosset & Dunlap)

    g. *The Magic World of Words!* (Macmillan)

    h. *Fun with Words,* Richard Scarry (Golden Press)

    i. *Watchamacallit Book,* Bernice Hunt (Putnam's)

    j. *What a Funny Thing to Say,* Bernice Kohn (Dial Press)

    k. *I Like the Library,* Anne Rockwell (Dutton)

    l. *Rabbit and Pork: Rhyming Talk,* John Laurence (Crowell)

24. Nonsense Poems

Reading nonsense poems aloud is a good way to get a child interested in words and language at an early age. You can begin reading these books to your grandchild when he is about four years old.

    a. *The Pobble Who Has No Toes and Other Nonsense,* Edward Lear (Viking Press)

    b. *The Owl and the Pussycat,* Edward Lear (Atheneum; also paperback)

    c. *The Scroobious Pip,* Edward Lear, completed by Ogden Nash (Harper & Row)

    d. *Lear's Nonsense Omnibus,* Edward Lear (Frederick Warne)

    e. *The Book of Nonsense,* Edward Lear (Garland)

    f. *The Nutcrackers and the Sugar-Tongs,* Edward Lear (Little, Brown)

    g. *Cats and Bats and Things with Wings,* Conrad Aiken (Atheneum)

    h. *Cats and Bats and Things Like That,* Gill Beers (Moody Press)

    i. *Laughable Limericks,* edited by Sara and John Brewton (Crowell)

    j. *Poetry for Chuckles and Grins,* edited by Leland B. Jacobs (Garrard)

    k. *Nuts to You and Nuts to Me! An Alphabet of Poems,* Mary Hoberman (Knopf)

    l. *A Great Big Ugly Man Came Up and Tied His Horse to Me: A Book of Nonsense Verse,* Wallace Tripp (Little, Brown)

    m. *Father Fox's Pennyrhymes,* Clyde Watson (Scholastic paperback)

    n. *Alligator Pie,* Dennis Lee (Houghton Mifflin)

    o. *At the Top of My Voice,* Felice Holman (Scribner's)

    p. *Dinosaur Do's and Don'ts,* Jean Polhamus (Prentice-Hall)

    q. *Giant Poems,* edited by Daisy Wallace (Holiday House)

C. Fiction and Fantasy

There are enormous numbers of good nonfiction books for preschoolers. Unfortunately, the number of really excellent books of fiction for preschoolers is far, far smaller. But here is a selection of fine works of fiction and fantasy for preschoolers.

1. *Madeline,* Ludwig Bemelmans (Viking Press; also Penguin paperback). Madeline always has a good time. This time it's in Paris.

2. *The Little House,* Virginia Burton (Houghton Mifflin; also paperback). A story of urban development told on the preschool level.

3. *Mike Mulligan and His Steam Shovel,* Virginia Burton (Houghton Mifflin paperback). Kids love the story of Mike and his steam shovel. A charming modern classic.

4. *Corduroy,* Don Freeman (Viking Press; also Penguin paperback). A book that is just right for youngsters who like bears and escalators.

5. *A Rainbow of My Own,* Don Freeman (Viking Press; also paperback). A small boy looks for a rainbow to own.

6. *The Biggest House in the World,* Leo Lionni (Pantheon; also paperback). In this gorgeously illustrated picture book, a small snail has a very large wish. He wants the largest house in the world.

7. *Inch by Inch,* Leo Lionni (Astor-Honor). All of Leo Lionni's books are beautiful. This one teaches the concept of measuring.

8. *Frederick,* Leo Lionni (Pantheon; also paperback). A field mouse rescues his friends from the long, cold winter with his word pictures of sunshine and colors.

9. *Spectacles,* Ellen Raskin (Atheneum paperback). A picture book done with imagination and humor. May be useful with a child who is resisting wearing glasses.

10. *The Biggest Bear,* Lynd Ward (Houghton Mifflin; also paperback). The story of a boy and his pet bear, and the task the boy must perform.

11. *The Story of Babar; Babar and His Children; Babar the King;* and other Babar books, by Jean de Brunhoff (Random House). Children all love Babar, the wonderful elephant. These books could easily be called classics.

12. *The Five Chinese Brothers,* Claire Bishop (Coward, McCann). A most ingenious tale about five Chinese brothers who look exactly alike.

13. *Little Leo,* Leo Politi (Scribner's). A delightful story.

14. *Pedro, the Angel of Olvera Street,* Leo Politi (Scribner's). A lovely story

about a small Mexican boy who celebrates Christmas on Olvera Street, a special street of old Mexico in Los Angeles.

15. *Rain Makes Applesauce,* Julian Scheer (Holiday House). A unique picture book that a young child will want to look at again and again.

16. *Caps for Sale,* Esphyr Slobodkina (Addison-Wesley; also Scholastic paperback). A tale of a peddler, his caps, and some monkeys who get together to produce a bit of delightful monkey business.

17. *Theodore Turtle,* Ellen MacGregor (McGraw-Hill). An amusing story about a turtle who forgets where he leaves things.

18. *May I Bring a Friend?,* Beatrice Schenk DeRegniers (Atheneum; also paperback). The fantasy adventure of a little boy who visits the king.

19. *A Little House of Our Own,* Beatrice Schenk DeRegniers and Irene Haas (Harcourt Brace). Every child likes to have a small secret place of his very own.

20. *Little Toot,* Hardie Gramatky (Putnam's; also paperback). This old favorite describes the adventures of a small tugboat in New York harbor.

21. *Crow Boy,* Taro Yashima (Viking Press; also Penguin paperback). The tender story of a shy Japanese boy.

22. *The House on East 88th Street,* Bernard Waber (Houghton Mifflin; also paperback). The funny adventures of Lyle the crocodile.

23. *Lentil,* Robert McCloskey (Viking Press; also Penguin paperback). A small boy, Lentil, plays music on his harmonica and becomes a hero.

24. *Make Way for Ducklings,* Robert McCloskey (Viking Press). A children's classic about a family of ducks on Beacon Street in Boston.

25. *One Morning in Maine,* Robert McCloskey (Viking Press). A wonderful story about the loss of a tooth.

26. *Burt Dow, Deep Water Man,* Robert McCloskey (Viking Press). You have heard of adult "fish stories"—well, here is a preschool-level fish "tail."

27. *Blueberries for Sal,* Robert McCloskey (Viking Press; also Penguin paperback). More wonderful McCloskey. A little girl helps her mother pick berries, and meets a little bear.

28. *Crictor,* Tomi Ungerer (Harper & Row; also Scholastic paperback). Would you believe a boa constrictor with his own bed and a sweater for the snow? Just great!

29. *Emile,* Tomi Ungerer (Harper & Row). The story of an octopus who can do great things.

30. *The Little Auto,* Lois Lenski (Henry Z. Walck). All of Miss Lenski's books are simple and appealing to young children, and this is no exception.

31. *Where the Wild Things Are,* Maurice Sendak (Harper & Row). A little boy's dreams help other children to deal with their fears on a child's level and thus overcome them. An enormous favorite with young children.

32. *And to Think That I Saw It on Mulberry Street,* Dr. Seuss (Vanguard Press). One of Dr. Seuss's first and best—a classic.

33. *The 500 Hats of Bartholomew Cubbins,* Dr. Seuss (Vanguard Press). A fun fantasy with never-ending hats.
34. *Horton Hatches the Egg,* Dr. Seuss (Random House). Poor Horton sits on an egg while a silly bird goes away.
35. *The Story of Ferdinand,* Munro Leaf (Viking Press). Ferdinand is the famous bull who would rather smell flowers than fight in the bull ring. A classic.
36. *Timothy Turtle,* Alice Davis (Harcourt Brace; also paperback). In this delightful picture story a turtle gets turned on his back, but his friends manage to rescue him.
37. *The Snowy Day,* Ezra Jack Keats (Viking Press; also paperback). A charming, very simple, beautifully illustrated story about a small boy in the snow.
38. *Space Cat,* Ruthven Todd (Scribner's; also paperback). A cat goes by rocket ship to outer space.
39. *Casey, the Utterly Impossible Horse,* Anita Feagles (Scholastic paperback). The amusing tale of a talking horse who expects too much from his pet boy.
40. *The Alligator Case,* William Pène DuBois (Harper & Row). Fun and fantasy for young children—a little boy plays detective.
41. *Staying Home Alone on a Rainy Day,* Chihiro Iwasaki (McGraw-Hill). What to do on a rainy day? Answer: Daydream!
42. *The Happy Lion,* Louise Fatio (McGraw-Hill). A friendly lion manages to escape from the zoo in a French town, only to find that people run away from him.
43. *Switch on the Night,* Ray Bradbury (Pantheon). The famous science-fiction writer turns his hand to a children's book, with delightful results.
44. *Anatole,* Eve Titus (McGraw-Hill). The wonderful adventures of a mouse who becomes head taster for a cheese factory in Paris.
45. *A Tree Is Nice,* Janice Udry (Harper & Row). A charming story about a tree.
46. *Where Have You Been?,* Margaret Wise Brown (Hastings House). Fourteen different animals answer the same question. Your grandchild will enjoy joining in and repeating the gay poetic lines of this book as you read to him.
47. *Gilberto and the Wind,* Marie Ets (Viking Press; also Penguin paperback). A charming picture book about a little Mexican boy who has trouble with the wind.
48. *Angus and the Cat,* Marjorie Flack (Doubleday; also paperback). Angus, a feisty Scottish terrier, has trouble with a smart cat.
49. *Old MacDonald Had an Apartment House,* Judith Barrett (Atheneum paperback). A delightful fantasy of a modern-day, four-story farm.
50. *Little Pear,* Eleanor Lattimore (Harcourt Brace; also paperback). A modern classic about a little Chinese boy.
51. *Harold and the Purple Crayon,* Crockett Johnson (Harper & Row). Harold creates marvelous things with his incredible purple crayon.

52. *The Brave Cowboy,* Joan Walsh Anglund (Harcourt Brace paperback). A marvelous story about a preschool-age cowboy.

53. *Olaf Reads,* Joan Lexau (Dial Press). Learning to read can be funny, as you will discover with Olaf.

54. *A Hole Is to Dig,* Ruth Krauss (Harper & Row). A delightful story of words and their meanings as viewed by a small child.

55. *Time to Get Out of the Bath, Shirley,* John Burningham (Crowell). Shirley makes herself small and sails down the bathtub drain to an imaginary world.

56. *"Bee My Valentine!",* Miriam Cohen (Greenwillow Books). When he receives fewer valentines than some of the other children in his classroom, George retires to the coatroom and cries. His friends succeed in comforting him.

57. *Happy Birthday, Sam,* Pat Hutchins (Greenwillow Books). On his birthday, a little boy discovers that he is still too small to reach the sink where he could sail his new toy boat, but another birthday gift solves the problem.

58. *Anno's Journey,* Mitsumasa Anno (Collins + World). Full of visual puzzles, puns, and tricks, this wordless book introduces the "reader" to interesting architectural drawings and some well-known paintings.

59. *The Other Way to Listen,* Byrd Baylor (Scribner's). An old man teaches a boy the truth and beauty of simple listening.

60. *The Snowman,* Raymond Briggs (Random House). When Berkley and Calvin, who are bears but behave just like little boys, finish their beautiful snowman, an argument develops over its ownership. In the snowball fight that ensues, the snowman is ruined.

61. *Frederick's Alligator,* Esther Peterson (Crown). Frederick dreams up tales about a lion in his closet and a bear in the attic and tries, unsuccessfully, to impress his mother, teacher, and classmates with the details. Imagine their surprise when Frederick actually produces a baby alligator from under his bed!

62. *I'll Fix Anthony,* Judith Viorst (Harper & Row). A little boy dreams of turning six years old. When he is that big, he'll really be able to *fix* his mean older brother Anthony!

63. *Go and Hush the Baby,* Betsy Byars (Viking Press). Will is on his way out to play baseball when his mother asks him to take care of the crying baby. His good-natured, affectionate manner with the baby, to whom he tells a story and offers a cookie, is refreshing.

64. *Martin's Father,* Margaret Eickler (Lollipop Power Press paperback). Doing the laundry is not beneath Martin's father, nor is reading stories to his little son or playing hide-and-go-seek.

65. *The Summer Night,* Charlotte Zolotow (Harper & Row). A nonstereotyped dad spends a quiet summer evening with his little daughter.

66. *Don't You Remember?,* Lucille Clifton (Dutton). A warm book about a little black girl who wants everyone to remember her ambitions.

67. *Of Course Polly Can Ride a Bike,* Astrid Lindgren (Follett). When a four-

year-old learns to ride a two-wheeler, she is commended for her competence and bravery.

68. *Firegirl,* Gibson Rich (Feminist Press paperback). When Brenda succeeds in rescuing a forgotten pet rabbit from a burning building, her ambition to become a "fireman" is taken more seriously.

69. *My Doctor,* Harlow Rockwell (Macmillan). A little boy visits his doctor— who is a woman.

70. *Mothers Can Do Anything,* Joe Lasker (Albert Whitman). Women of all ages, engaged in jobs usually reserved for men, are the subjects of this picture book.

D. Collections of Stories, Tales, or Folktales

1. *Told Under the Green Umbrella,* Association for Childhood Education International (Macmillan)

2. *Told Under the City Umbrella* and *Told Under the Magic Umbrella,* Association for Childhood Education International (Macmillan)

3. *The Book of Greek Myths,* Edgar and Ingri D'Aulaire (Doubleday)

4. *Castles and Dragons: Read-to-Yourself Fairy Tales for Boys and Girls,* compiled by the Child Study Association of America (Crowell)

5. *Kate Greenaway Treasury,* Kate Greenaway (Collins + World)

6. *With a Deep Sea Smile,* Virginia Tashjian (Little, Brown)

7. *I Can Choose My Bedtime Story,* edited by Mary Parsley (Grosset & Dunlap)

8. *Joan Walsh Anglund Storybook,* Joan Walsh Anglund (Random House)

9. *Storybook: A Collection of Stories Old and New,* compiled by Tomi Ungerer (Franklin Watts)

10. *Fables of Aesop,* edited by Ruth Spriggs (Rand McNally)

11. *Night Noises and Other Mole and Troll Stories,* Tony Johnson (Putnam's)

E. Poetry for Preschoolers

1. *I Met a Man,* John Ciardi (Houghton Mifflin; also paperback). One of America's foremost poets proves that a poetry book written in a limited vocabulary for beginning readers doesn't have to be dull or trite.

2. *Something Special,* Beatrice Schenk DeRegniers and Irene Haas (Harcourt Brace). This book is practically guaranteed to make a preschooler love poetry. Includes rhymed verse, free verse, and a chanting game, "What Did You Put in Your Pocket?"

3. *Hailstones and Halibut Bones,* Mary O'Neill (Doubleday; also paperback). A stunning collection of poems about colors, with beautiful illustrations by Leonard Weisgard.

4. *I Can't, Said the Ant,* Polly Cameron (Coward, McCann). Your preschool-age grandchild will be delighted with this tale in verse.

5. *Sung Under the Silver Umbrella,* Association for Childhood Educational International (Macmillan). A good selection of poems for children from preschool age through third grade.

6. *Nibble, Nibble,* Margaret Wise Brown (Addison-Wesley). Poems about nature and things that fly, crawl, and swim.

7. *Where the Sidewalk Ends: Poems and Drawings,* Shel Silverstein (Harper & Row). Wonderful poems to read aloud.

8. *You Read To Me, I'll Read To You,* John Ciardi (Lippincott). A unique poetry book in which poems for adults to read aloud to children alternate with poems that children can read aloud to adults.

9. *Cricket in a Thicket,* Aileen Fisher (Scribner's; also paperback). These are poems about nature study, which is a love of young children.

10. *A Child's Garden of Verses,* Robert Louis Stevenson (Franklin Watts). Some of these poems seem a little dated, but others will never grow old. A classic.

11. *Listen, Children, Listen: An Anthology of Poems for the Very Young,* edited by Myra Cohn Livingston (Harcourt Brace). The title says it all.

12. *When We Were Very Young* and *Now We Are Six,* A. A. Milne (Dutton; also Dell paperback). These classic poems for children are just as delightful now as they were in the 1920s, when they were written.

13. *What Do You Feed Your Donkey On? Rhymes from a Belfast Childhood,* compiled by Colette O'Hare (Collins + World). A collection of rhymes, hop-skipping songs, and chants, with typically British illustrations of unsophisticated folk.

14. Other Books of Poetry

All of these are fine books of poetry to read to preschoolers. And don't forget the collections of nonsense poems I listed a few pages back, in Section B.

    a. *First Poems of Childhood,* Tasha Tudor (Platt & Munk)

    b. *A Bunch of Poems and Verses,* Beatrice Schenk DeRegniers (Seabury Press)

    c. *Honey, I Love and Other Poems,* Eloise Greenfield (Crowell)

    d. *Make a Circle, Keep Us In: Poems for a Good Day,* Arnold Adoff (Delacorte Press)

    e. *Fat Polka-Dot Cat and Other Haiku,* Betsy Maestro (Dutton)

    f. *Flower Moon Snow: A Book of Haiku,* Kazue Mizumura (Crowell)

    g. *Poems Make Pictures, Pictures Make Poems,* G. Rimanelli and Paul Rinsleur (Pantheon)

F. Nonsexist Picture Books

If children are going to grow up to be successful and complete human beings, they must learn to think of themselves and others in free, unstereotyped, nonsexist ways.

How can you help them to do this? First, you can read nonsexist books to them—books that are not contaminated by the old sexist stereotypes. In this section and the next, I provide you with the titles of a number of very good books that are excellent and truly nonsexist.

As I mentioned in Chapter 8, some feminists think you should read only completely nonsexist books to your grandchildren, and ignore any books that are tinged even in the slightest by sexism. I disagree. Many very good books listed in this appendix, particularly the older ones, are sexist. My suggestion is this: If a book is good, read it to your grandchildren. If the book is also sexist, point that out and tell them, for example, that the book is mistaken when it implies that it's bad for boys to cry, or that girls should be quiet and submissive.

1. *Mary Alice, Operator Number Nine,* Jeffrey Allen (Little, Brown; also Penguin paperback). Mary Alice tells time at the telephone company so well that when she gets sick, she cannot be replaced.

2. *I'm Bored, Ma!,* Harold Berson (Crown). Steve Rabbit has a difficult day. Mother Rabbit is a positive picture of a female who is understanding and calm with her youngster.

3. *The Steamroller,* Margaret Wise Brown (Walker & Co.). A fun fantasy in which Daisy, a girl who loves machines, gets a steamroller for Christmas.

4. *Bodies,* Barbara Brenner (Dutton). An unusual book showing how our bodies do many things. The photographs by George Ancona are a real break-through—they show small boys and girls in the nude.

5. *Will I Have a Friend?,* Miriam Cohen (Macmillan; also paperback). A little boy is taken by his father to his first day at a child-care center. This book shows that boys, too, have feelings of uncertainty, and that fathers can play active and important nurturing roles in their children's lives.

6. *Dorrie and the Amazing Elixir,* Patricia Coombs (Lothrop, Lee & Shepard). The star of this "girl witch" series guards her mother's magic recipe even though the Green Wizard turns her into a toad.

7. *Grownups Cry, Too,* Nancy Hazen (Lollipop Power Press). Stanley learns that crying is okay and that there are many reasons to cry.

8. *Max,* Rachael Isadora (Macmillan). Max joins his sister's Saturday ballet class to warm up for his baseball practice, proving that ballet is not just for "sissies." Humorous and light.

9. *Louie,* Ezra Jack Keats (Greenwillow Books). A child too shy to talk over-comes his problem through interaction with puppets.

10. *Lucky Wilma,* Wendy Kindred (Dial Press). Wilma's dad, divorced from her mother, helps Wilma learn to enjoy their Saturday outings together.

11. *Monkey Day,* Ruth Krauss (Bookstore Press). A funny, imaginative story about a girl who is a monkey lover and gives each of her monkeys a mate. First published in 1957 and amazingly nonsexist.

12. *A Bedtime Story,* Joan Goldman Levine (Dutton). Roles are reversed as a young girl bosses her parents one night and puts the exhausted and "on the brink" couple to bed.

13. *A Wise Monkey Tale,* Betsy Maestro (Crown). Animals with an equal number of males and females have humorous adventures when Monkey falls into a deep hole and has to plan her escape.

14. *Swinging and Swinging,* Fran Manushkin (Harper & Row). A marvelous fantasy about a girl who, while swinging, has special visits from a cloud, the sun, the moon, and some stars.

15. *My Mother the Mail-Carrier,* Inez Maury (Feminist Press; also paperback). In this honest book, Lupita tells about her single-parent mother, who is a

postal carrier. The story is bilingual (English and Spanish), and fun to read in either language.

16. *Around and Around Love,* Betty Miles (Knopf; also paperback). Reassuring and tender, this free-verse poem tells about the many sides of love and the many ways people show it. Illustrated with photos of people of all ages, races, and sexes.

17. *My Nursery School,* Harlow Rockwell (Greenwillow Books). Highly recommended for children about to begin nursery school, and who need reassurance. The author portrays a role-free, multiracial place where children interact with male and female teachers and students.

18. *Morris and His Brave Lion,* Helen Spelman Rogers (McGraw-Hill). In an integrated neighborhood, a little boy comes to terms with the pain the whole family feels after a divorce.

19. *The Wizard's Tears,* Anne Sexton and Maxine Kermin (McGraw-Hill). A lively tale about a twelve-year-old novice wizard who comes to Drocknock and changes people into frogs. The town has a brave lady mayor.

20. *I Am a Giant,* Ivan Sherman (Harcourt Brace). This story about a little girl giant may help to reduce a small child's fear of large, towering adults.

21. *My Special Best Words,* John Steptoe (Viking Press). A story about a warm, loving single-parent family. The parent is the father. The children's very special words are "I love you, pick me up, Daddy."

22. *Kevin's Grandma,* Barbara Williams (Dutton; also paperback). One child's grandma bakes goodies; the other child's grandma is a sky diver. Interesting comments by the kids.

23. *Betsy and the Chicken Pox,* Gunilla Wolde (Random House). Betsy's father helps her overcome her jealousy of her brother, who gets lots of attention when he is sick. This excellent book is the fourth in a series; the other titles are *This Is Betsy, Betsy's Baby Brother,* and *Betsy's First Day at Nursery School.*

24. *The Summer Night,* Charlotte Zolotow (Harper & Row). An updated version of a warm story about a father putting his daughter to sleep.

G. Nonsexist Easy Readers

This is a group of easy-to-read books that will help your grandchild to transcend the limitations of traditional sex role stereotypes.

1. *The Most Delicious Camping Trip Ever,* Alice Bach (Harper & Row; also paperback). A clever aunt teaches two bear cubs the twin arts of cooperation and accommodation on a camping trip.

2. *He Bear, She Bear,* Stanley and Janice Berenstain (Random House). Male and female bears are shown engaging in many activities.

3. *I'd Rather Stay Home,* Carol Barkin and Elizabeth James (Raintree Publishers). A little black boy expresses his worries about starting school.

4. *And I Mean It, Stanley,* Crosby Bonsall (Harper & Row). An imaginary nonfriend, Stanley, gets a lecture from an assertive little girl.

5. *Is That Your Sister? A True Story About Adoption,* Catherine and Sherry

Bunin (Pantheon). An honest, well-written book about a happy family of two white parents, their natural son, and their two adopted black daughters.

6. *Animal Fathers*, Russell Freedman (Holiday House). This book gives children a different view of sex roles in animals. It describes the involvement of fifteen animal fathers in the care of their young.

7. *Did the Sun Shine Before You Were Born?*, Sol Gordon and Judith Cohen (Okpaku Productions). Multiracial, tastefully written sex education book for young children.

8. *Delilah*, Carole Hart (Harper & Row) Good short stories about a ten-year-old girl who loves sports and lives in a family free of sex role stereotypes.

9. *New Life: New Room*, June Jordan (Crowell). When a new baby comes to an already overcrowded home, three black children who get along well work things out with the gentle help of their dad.

10. *Fiona's Bee*, Beverly Keller (Coward, McCann; also Dell paperback). A refreshing story about a shy girl's efforts to make friends. Neighborhood children marvel at her ability (accidental) to train a bee.

11. *The Missing Piece*, Shel Silverstein (Harper & Row). A humorous and clever tale about "It" looking for its missing piece. "Its" adventures, good and bad, are described with few words and simple illustrations.

12. *All Kinds of Families*, Norma Simon (Albert Whitman). Extended families, single-parent families, multiracial families—a well-written and sensitive book.

13. *Eliza's Daddy*, Ianthe Thomas (Harcourt Brace; also paperback). Eliza gets up the courage to ask to meet her daddy's new family on a Saturday (Daddy's day). His new stepdaughter turns out to be very pleasant and the three of them have a good day together.

H. Game Books

Preschool-age children love games of any kind. And these books offer a treasure trove of games that you can play with them. Many of them can be played when you travel, too, and that is a special boon.

1. *A Hole, a Box and a Stick*, Gladys Y. Cretan (Lothrop, Lee & Shepard)
2. *Jack Kent's Hop, Skip and Jump Book*, Jack Kent (Random House; also paperback)
3. *Little Boy Blue: Finger Plays Old and New*, Daphne Hogstrom (Golden Press)
4. *Two Hundred Two Things to Do*, Margaret Sedlied (Regal Press; also paperback)
5. *Finger Plays for Nursery and Kindergarten*, Emilie Poulssen (Dover Publications paperback)

I. Miscellaneous

1. Cooking for Young Children
   a. *Cool Cooking*, Esther Hautzig (Lothrop, Lee & Shepard)
   b. *Kids Cooking Without a Stove: A Cookbook for Young Children*, Aileen Paul (Doubleday)

    c. *Kids Cooking: A First Cookbook for Children,* Aileen Paul and Arthur Hawkins (Archway paperback)

    d. *I Am a Cookbook,* Em Riggs and Barbara Darpinion (J. P. Tarcher)

    e. *Teddybears' Cookbook,* Susanna Greta (Doubleday)

2. "Open Books" for Adults and Children

These books by Sara Stein have a story that can be read aloud to a child, and a text running beside the story for the parents or grandparents. This text explains the childhood fears that are being dealt with in the story, the questions a child might have at a given point, and how an adult can further explore the story with the child through questions and discussion. (Walker & Co.)

    a. *That New Baby*

    b. *Making Babies*

    c. *A Hospital Story*

    d. *About Dying*

    e. *Who'll Take Care of Me?*

3. Western Publishing Read-Together Paperback Books

This is another series of books specially designed for parents or grandparents to read aloud to their preschoolers. The authors are Jane Werner Watson, Dr. R. E. Switzer, and Dr. J. C. Hirschberg. (Western Publishing)

    a. *My Body—How It Works*

    b. *My Friend, the Babysitter*

    c. *Sometimes I'm Jealous*

    d. *Sometimes I'm Afraid*

    e. *Sometimes I Get Angry*

IV. Middle Childhood (approximately the sixth to the eleventh birthday)

It is particularly important at this stage that you not take the suggested year levels for a book too literally. When a publisher puts year levels or grade levels on a book (or when I do the same in this bibliography), they represent only good guesses about the "average child" and his ability to read the book. But, of course, there is no such thing as an "average child." And middle childhood children may be very highly motivated to read books on subjects that especially interest them. This means that a nine-year-old girl who loves horses may be able, because of her high motivation, to read very advanced (even adult-level) books on horses, while in general she reads at an "average" nine-year-old level.

At this stage, let your grandchildren read anything they like. Even reading comic books will develop their reading ability.

Many youngsters spend the first three grades of elementary school not only learning the mechanics of reading, but also learning to feel comfortable about reading so that they can truly enjoy it. Most children do not really "explode" into reading for enjoyment until the fourth or fifth grade. So don't worry too much if your grandchild doesn't become an avid and voracious reader in his first three grades at school. Be patient: If you keep taking the youngster to the library and the bookstore, as I have suggested, the appeal of television will gradually lessen, and an interest in reading will take over.

A. "Double-Duty" Beginning to Read Books

The first list of good nonfiction books for the six-year-old, and in some cases for the seven- or eight-year-old as well, consists of the same books I listed in Section A for preschoolers. These are excellent books to offer your grandchild when he or she is learning to read. If you have already read these books aloud to your grandchild, so much the better.

Here are some additional nonfiction books that are excellent for the middle childhood stage.

1. Franklin Watts: First Book series (ages eight to eleven)
    a. *How to Run a Meeting,* David Powers (paperback)
    b. *Facts and How to Find Them,* David Whitney
    c. *How to Write a Report,* Sue Brandt (paperback)
    d. *The Ancient Maya,* Barbara Beck
    e. *The Aztecs,* Barbara Beck
    f. *The Incas,* Barbara Beck
    g. *Ancient Rome,* Charles Robinson
    h. *Ancient Egypt,* Charles Robinson
    i. *Ancient Greece,* Charles Robinson
    j. *Women's Rights,* Janet Stevenson (paperback)
    k. *Women of the West,* Dorothy Levenson (paperback)
    l. *American Negroes,* Margaret Young (paperback)
    m. *Ecology,* John Hoke
    n. *Snakes,* John Hoke
    o. *Volcanoes and Earthquakes,* Rebecca Marcus
    p. *Air,* David Knight
    q. *Deserts,* David Knight
    r. *The Earth,* Irene Sevrey
    s. *Fishing,* John Waters
    t. *Electricity,* Sam and Beryl Epstein
    u. *Camping,* E. C. Janes
    v. *Chess,* Joseph Lemming
    w. *Magic,* Edward Stoddard
2. Franklin Watts: Human Body series (ages eight to eleven)
    a. *The Brain,* Kathleen Elgin
    b. *The Ear,* Kathleen Elgin
    c. *The Eye,* Kathleen Elgin
    d. *The Heart,* Kathleen Elgin
    e. *The Digestive System,* Kathleen Elgin
3. Franklin Watts: "They Lived Like This" series (ages eight to eleven)

This excellent series by Marie Neurath introduces young readers to cultural anthropology in a fascinating way. Each book provides a glimpse into the everyday life of a particular ancient culture—the author describes homes, clothing, beliefs and ceremonies, farming and manufacturing techniques, and ways of communicating.

    a. *Ancient China*
    b. *Ancient Rome*
    c. *Old Japan*
    d. *Chaucer's England*
    e. *The Ancient Maya*
    f. *The Old Stone Age*

4. Franklin Watts: "Colonial Americans" series (ages eight to eleven)

Leonard Fisher writes and illustrates this series, which deals with the tools, techniques, and extraordinary skill of pioneer Americans.

    a. *The Doctors*
    b. *The Schoolmasters*
    c. *The Printers*
    d. *The Shipbuilders*
    e. *The Shoemakers*
    f. *The Silversmiths*
    g. *The Homemakers*

5. Grosset & Dunlap: How and Why Wonder Books (ages eight to eleven)

    a. *Air and Water,* Claire Cuniff
    b. *Ants and Bees*
    c. *Airplanes*
    d. *The Human Body,* Martin Keen
    e. *Let's Experiment,* Martin Keen
    f. *Science Experiments,* Martin Keen
    g. *Prehistoric Mammals,* Martin Keen
    h. *Microscopes,* Martin Keen
    i. *Beginning Science,* Jerome Notkin and Sydney Galkin
    j. *Ecology,* Shelley Grossman and Mary L. Grossman
    k. *Basic Inventions,* Irving Robbin
    l. *Explorations and Discoveries,* Irving Robbin
    m. *Primitive Man,* Donald Barr
    n. *Atomic Energy,* Donald Barr
    o. *Sea Shells,* Donald Low

6. John Day: "Reason Why" books (ages eight to twelve)

Written by two splendid science writers, Irving Adler and Ruth Adler, these books provide "in-depth" explanations of science fundamentals.

    a. *Atomic Energy*
    b. *Atoms and Molecules*
    c. *Hot and Cold*
    d. *Houses: From Cave to Skyscraper*
    e. *Your Eyes*
    f. *Taste, Touch, and Smell*
    g. *Why: A Book of Reasons*

   h. *Magic House of Numbers*
   i. *Why and How: A Second Book of Reasons*

7. William Morrow: Science books by Herbert Zim (ages eight to eleven)

Zim, a distinguished scientist, is one of our most gifted writers on science for children. I recommend his books most enthusiastically.

   a. *What's Inside of Animals?*
   b. *What's Inside of Engines?*
   c. *Your Heart and How It Works*
   d. *What's Inside the Earth?*
   e. *Our Senses and How They Work*
   f. *Alligators and Crocodiles*
   g. *Goldfish*
   h. *Sharks*
   i. *Monkeys*
   j. *Snakes*
   k. *Sun*
   l. *Your Brain and How It Works*
   m. *Life and Death* (written with Sonia Bleeker)
   n. *Armored Animals*
   o. *Great Whales*
   p. *The Universe* (also paperback)

8. Putnam's: Science books (ages eight to twelve)

   a. *How the Indians Really Lived,* Gordon Baldwin (Berkley paperback)
   b. *Hurricanes, Storms, Tornadoes,* James Winchester
   c. *Robots in Space,* Michael Chester
   d. *I Was Born in a Tree and Raised by Bees,* Jim Arnosky
   e. *Metric Is Here,* William Moore

9. Books for Late-Starting Readers

These books by Ed Radlauer are designed to appeal to older middle childhood children who have been slow to learn to read. (Childrens Press; Elk Grove Books paperbacks)

   a. *CB Radios*
   b. *Model Airplanes*
   c. *Model Cars*
   d. *Motorcycle Mania*
   e. *Ready, Get Set, Whoa!*
   f. *Skateboard Mania*
   g. *Soapbox Racing*
   h. *Soccer*
   i. *Wild Wheels*

10. Books for Reluctant Readers

A series of books designed to appeal especially to older middle childhood and preadolescent children (grades five to ten) who are not very interested in reading. (Troll Associates)

    a. *Baja Run: Racing Fury,* Don Smith
    b. *Surfing: The Big Wave,* Don Smith
    c. *Bobsledding: Down the Chute,* Stephen Gregory
    d. *Racing to Win: The Salt Flats,* Stephen Gregory
    e. *Challenge! The Big Thunderboats,* Jane Stone
    f. *Diving the Great Barrier Reef,* Lucy Ferrier
    g. *Danger! White Water,* Otto Penzler
    h. *Hang Gliding: Riding the Wind,* Otto Penzler
    i. *Hunting the Killer Shark,* Otto Penzler

B. General Nonfiction
  1. Biography
    a. *Buffalo Bill,* Ingri and Edgar P. D'Aulaire (Doubleday)
    b. *The Story of Ben Franklin,* Eve Merriam (Scholastic paperback)
    c. *Meet Martin Luther King, Jr.,* James T. DeKay (Random House)
    d. *Lincoln's Birthday,* Clyde Bulla (Crowell)
    e. *George Washington: A Talk with His Grandchildren,* Dorothy Richards (Child's World)
    f. *Charles Lindbergh: Hero Pilot,* David Collins (Garrard)
    g. *John Muir: Friend of Nature,* Margaret Clark (Garrard)
    h. *The Great Houdini,* Anne Edwards (Putnam's)
    i. *Muhammad Ali,* Beth Wilson (Putnam's)
    j. *Theodore Roosevelt: Man of Action,* James Beach (Garrard)
    k. *Walt Disney: Master of Make-Believe,* Elizabeth R. Montgomery (Garrard)
    l. *Anne Sullivan,* Mary Malone (Putnam's)
    m. *Annie Oakley: The Shooting Star,* Charles Graves (Garrard)
  2. Books on Religion
    a. *One God: The Ways We Worship Him,* Florence Fitch (Lothrop, Lee & Shepard). This book is outstanding for this age group. It describes the religious beliefs of Protestants, Catholics, and Jews, and the ways they worship.
    b. *The Children's Bible* (Golden Press). Well-illustrated. For children from kindergarten to sixth grade.
  3. Mathematics
    a. *Liter,* William Shirnek (Lerner Publications)
    b. *Meter,* William Shirnek (Lerner Publications)
    c. *Math Games and Puzzles,* Xerox Educational Publications (Grosset & Dunlap paperback)
    d. *Math Puzzles,* Irving and Peggy Adler (Franklin Watts)
  4. Science
    a. *A First Look at Fish,* Millicent Selsam and Joyce Hunt (Walker & Co.; Scholastic paperback)

b. *A First Look at Birds,* Millicent Selsam and Joyce Hunt (Walker & Co.)

c. *A First Look at Frogs, Toads and Salamanders,* Millicent Selsam and Joyce Hunt (Walker & Co.)

d. *A First Look at Mammals,* Millicent Selsam and Joyce Hunt (Scholastic paperback)

e. *A First Look at Insects,* Millicent Selsam and Joyce Hunt (Walker & Co.)

f. *A First Look at Snakes, Lizards and Other Reptiles,* Millicent Selsam and Joyce Hunt (Walker & Co.; Scholastic paperback)

g. *Great Whales,* Patricia Lauber (Garrard)

h. Scientific Discovery Series written by Isaac Asimov, a fine science writer (Walker & Co.)

    i. *How Did We Find Out About Atoms?*

    ii. *How Did We Find Out About Dinosaurs?*

    iii. *How Did We Find Out About Energy?*

    iv. *How Did We Find Out About Germs?*

    v. *How Did We Find Out About Nuclear Power?*

    vi. *How Did We Find Out About Outer Space?*

i. *Small Worlds Close Up,* Lisa Grillone and Joseph Gennaro (Crown)

j. *Time After Time,* Melvin Berger (Coward, McCann)

k. *Exploring Animal Homes,* T. R. Entwistle (Franklin Watts)

l. *Exploring Animal Journeys,* T. R. Entwistle (Franklin Watts)

5. Great Unsolved Mysteries

a. *The Abominable Snowman,* Barbara Antonopulos (Raintree Publishers)

b. *The Bermuda Triangle,* Jim Collins (Raintree Publishers)

c. *Unidentified Flying Objects,* Jim Collins (Raintree Publishers)

d. *Bigfoot: Man, Monster or Myth?,* Carrie Carmichael (Raintree Publishers)

e. *The Case of the Ancient Astronauts,* I. J. Gallagher (Raintree Publishers)

f. *Killer Bees,* Melinda Blau (Raintree Publishers)

g. *Mysteries of the Mind,* Joann Lawless (Raintree Publishers)

h. *Secrets of Tut's Tomb and the Pyramids,* Stephanie Reiff (Raintree Publishers)

i. *Terror in the Tropics: The Army Ants,* Tom Lisker (Raintree Publishers)

j. *Bigfoot,* Ian Thorpe (Crestwood House)

k. *UFOs,* Ian Thorpe (Crestwood House)

6. Babies and Sex Education

a. *A Baby Is Born,* Milton Levine, M.D., and Jean H. Seligman (Golden Press)

b. *Nobody Asked Me If I Wanted a Baby Sister,* Martha Alexander (Dial Press)

c. *Hi, New Baby: A Book to Help Your Child Learn About the New Baby,* Andrew Andry (Simon & Schuster)

      d. *The Berenstain Bears' New Baby,* Stanley and Janice Berenstain (Random House)

      e. *Did the Sun Shine Before You Were Born?,* Sol Gordon and Judith Cohen (Third Press)

C. Books of Fascinating Facts

Middle childhood children are intrigued by books of fascinating facts, and the weirder the facts the better. At this age children love to regale their peers with such intriguing tidbits as "Did you know that the extinct tribe of Wakishi Indians on the west coast of Mexico ate dirt for breakfast?" Knowing such incredible facts increases a child's standing with his peer group. So these books have a psychological reward built in!

1. *Anything You Might Ask Almanac,* Pappy Kilma (Platt & Munk)
2. *Felton and Fowler's Best, Worst and Most Unusual,* Bruce Felton and Mark Fowler (Crowell)
3. *First Facts and Feats,* Bill Adler (Grosset & Dunlap)
4. *Greatest Quiz Book Ever,* Rog Dickson (Bantam paperback)
5. *It's an Odd World,* Paul Hazerman (Sterling)
6. *Would You Believe . . . ?,* Deidre Sanders (Sterling)
7. *Would You Believe This, Too?,* Deidre Sanders (Sterling)
8. *The Giant Walt Disney Word Book,* Walt Disney (Western Publishing; also paperback)
9. *The World Almanac and Book of Facts,* (Newspaper Enterprise Association)
10. *Information Please Almanac, Atlas, and Yearbook* (Viking Press)
11. *Guinness Book of World Records,* edited and compiled by Norris McWhirter (Sterling)

All of the following books are also compiled by Norris and Ross McWhirter and published by Sterling:

12. *Guinness Book of Amazing Achievements*
13. *Guinness Book of Astounding Feats and Events*
14. *Guinness Book of Exceptional Experiences*
15. *Guinness Book of Extraordinary Exploits*
16. *Guinness Book of Phenomenal Happenings*
17. *Guinness Book of Startling Acts and Facts*
18. *Guinness Book of Surprising Accomplishments*
19. *Guinness Book of Young Record Breakers*

D. Books of Activities

1. *Art Activities for the Very Young,* F. L. Hoover (Davis Publications paperback)
2. *Puppet Party,* Goldie Chernoff (Walker & Co.). Illustrated instructions for making puppets from materials such as paper cups and kitchen utensils.
3. *Clay Dough, Play Dough,* Goldie Chernoff (Walker &Co.)
4. *Masks,* Chester Alkema (Sterling). Instructions, accompanied by clear black-and-white photographs and color illustrations, help the child master the "how-to" of mask-making.

5. *Starting with Papier-Maché,* Chester Alkema (Sterling)
6. *Eric Plants a Garden,* Jean Hudlow (Albert Whitman). The planning, planting, cultivating, and harvesting of crops by young gardeners are depicted in clear photographs.
7. *Perplexing Puzzles and Tantalizing Teasers,* Martin Gardner (Archway paperback). A good book of puzzles for this age group.
8. *More Perplexing Puzzles and Tantalizing Teasers,* Martin Gardner (Archway paperback)
9. *Look Again!,* Tana Hoban (Macmillan). Beautiful photographs, first seen through a small square "peephole" and then viewed in their entirety, lead to interesting analysis and discussion.
10. *Yarn: The Things It Makes and How to Make Them,* Carolyn Meyer (Harcourt Brace). Knitting, weaving, macrame, and crocheting are explained carefully and clearly. The left-handed child will find explicit instructions, too.
11. *Here Is Your Hobby,* Bill Neumann (Putnam's)
12. *Lens and Shutter: An Introduction to Photography,* Harvey Weiss (Young Scott Books). Information and helpful suggestions for the young, inexperienced photographer.
13. *You're a Good Dog, Joe: Knowing and Training Your Puppy,* Kurt Unkelback (Prentice-Hall)
14. *How to Raise a Puppy: A Child's Book of Pet Care,* Sara B. Stein (Random House)
15. *Draw 50 Airplanes, Aircraft and Spacecraft,* Lee J. Ames (Doubleday)
16. *Draw 50 Boats, Ships, Trucks and Trains,* Lee J. Ames (Doubleday). Easy, step-by-step instructions for drawing things that are fascinating to children, but are sometimes difficult for them to draw.
17. *Let's Play Cards,* John Belton and Joella Cramblit (Raintree Publishers). This book gives simple directions for several card games to play. Large, clear illustrations.
18. *Arts and Crafts You Can Eat,* Vicki Cobb (Lippincott). Art doesn't always have to be permanent. It can be in the form of "stained glass" cookies or sculptured Duchess potatoes meant to be consumed by hungry appreciators!
19. *The Crowell Book of Arts and Crafts for Children,* Arnold Arnold (Crowell). Instructions for all kinds of projects—from simple to complex—using leather, wood, paper, foil, and plastic.
20. *Cardboard Carpentry,* Janet and Alex D'Amato (Lion Books). This well-illustrated book suggests things to do with boxes, shirt cardboard, milk cartons, egg cartons, oatmeal cartons, and corrugated cardboard.
21. *Mr. Mysterious's Secrets of Magic,* Sid Fleischman (Little, Brown). Instructions for performing twenty-one magic tricks—some classic and some original with the author. Humorous illustrations.
22. *Tricks with Your Fingers,* Harry Helfman (William Morrow). Simple to understand and perform, these tricks, done with ten fingers and a few common objects, are really impressive.

23. *Black Within and Red Without: A Book of Riddles,* compiled by Lillian Morrison (Crowell). It's always fun to stump a friend or member of your family with a good riddle.
24. *The Everything Book,* Eleanor Graham Vance (Golden Press; Western Publishing paperback). If you are a grandparent with just funds enough for one good grandparent aid, this may be it! Chock full of good ideas for things to make and things to do, it even has one whole "Grandmother Chapter" (for Grandfather, too).
25. *Holiday Cards for You to Make,* Susan Purdy (Lippincott). Instructions for personalized Mother's Day cards, birthday cards, and others.
26. *Little Witch Presents a Monster Joke Book,* Linda Grovach and Charles Keller (Prentice-Hall)
27. *Little Witch's Black Magic Book of Games,* Linda Grovach (Prentice-Hall)
28. *Little Witch's Hallowe'en Book,* Linda Grovach (Prentice-Hall)
29. *Making Easy Puppets,* Shari Lewis (J. P. Tarcher)
30. *Tell-It-Make-It Book,* Shari Lewis (J. P. Tarcher)
31. *Kids Only Club Book,* Shari Lewis (J. P. Tarcher)
32. *Folding Paper Toys,* Shari Lewis and Lillian Oppenheimer (Stein & Day)
33. *Easy-to-Make Contraptions,* Roland Berry (Harvey House)
34. *Let's Make a Kite!,* Jack Stokes (David McKay paperback)
35. *From Seed to Salad,* Hannah Johnson (Lothrop, Lee & Shepard)
36. *Taking Pictures,* Nina Leen (Holt, Rinehart & Winston)
37. *Ed Emberley's Great Thumbprint Drawing Book,* Ed Emberley (Little, Brown)
38. *How To Make Snop-Snappers and Other Fine Things,* Robert Lopshire (Greenwillow Books)
39. *A Pop-Up Book of Fun and Easy Things to Make,* James Razzi (Random House)
40. *I Did It,* Harlow Rockwell (Macmillan)
41. *Exciting Things to Make with Paper,* Ruth Thomson (Lippincott)
42. *Exciting Things to Make with Wool, String and Thread,* Rosalind May and Sheila Brull (Lippincott)
43. *Exciting Things to Do with Nature Materials,* Judy Allen (Lippincott)
44. *Star-Spangled Fun! Things to Make, Do and See from American History* (Parents' Magazine Press)
45. Cookbooks
    a. *The Outdoor Cookbook,* Marjorie P. Blanchard (Franklin Watts)
    b. *The Boys' Cookbook,* Helen Evans Brown and Philip S. Brown (Doubleday)
    c. *Love at First Bite,* Jane Cooper (Knopf; also paperback)
    d. *Peter Rabbit's Natural Foods Cookbook,* Arnold Dobrin (Frederick Warne)
    e. *The Bread Book,* Carolyn Meyer (Harcourt Brace Jovanovich)
    f. *Let's Start to Cook,* Nell B. Nichols (Doubleday)

g. *Hallowe'en Cookbook,* Susan Purdy (Franklin Watts)

h. *Wide World Cookbook,* Rebecca Shapiro (Little, Brown)

E. Game Books

1. *Games for All Seasons,* Alida Thacker (Raintree Publishers)

2. *Sidewalk Games,* Lani Van Ryzin (Raintree Publishers)

3. *Can You Walk the Plank?,* June Behrens (Addison-Wesley)

4. *Card Games,* John Belton and Joella Cramblit (Raintree Publishers)

5. *Dice Games,* John Belton and Joella Cramblit (Raintree Publishers)

6. *Great Indoor Games from Trash and Other Things,* Judith Conaway (Raintree Publishers)

7. *Great Outdoor Games from Trash and Other Things,* Judith Conaway (Raintree Publishers)

8. *Magic, Magic,* Betty and Douglas Kobs (Raintree Publishers)

9. *Guinness Game Book,* Norris and Ross McWhirter (Sterling)

10. *Anytime, Anywhere, Anybody Games,* Andrea DiNoto (Western Publishing; also paperback)

11. *Bike, Skate and Skateboard Games,* (Western Publishing; also paperback)

12. *Card and Coin Tricks* (Western Publishing; also paperback)

13. *Frisbee Fun,* Margaret Poynter (Archway paperback)

14. *Make-It, Play-It Game Book,* Roz Abisch (Walker & Co.)

15. *Illustrated Chess for Children,* Harvey Kidder (Doubleday)

16. *Chess for Children, Step by Step,* William and Betty Marshall-Lombardy (Little, Brown; also paperback)

17. *Games to Learn,* Muriel Mandell (Sterling). Stimulating ideas for music, art, language, math, and science games.

F. Personal Relationships and the Self

1. Books About Grandparents

Middle childhood children will continue to enjoy many of the books about grandparents that I listed in Section B for preschoolers. Here are some additional good books about grandparents:

a. *Grandma Didn't Wave Back,* Rose Blue (Franklin Watts)

b. *At Grandmother's House,* John Lim (Tundra Books)

c. *Grandma Moses,* Charles Graves (Garrard)

d. *Grandmother Comes from Dworitz: A Jewish Story,* Ethel Vineberg (Tundra Books paperback)

e. *Grandmother Oma,* Ilse Kleberger (Atheneum)

f. *Grandfather's Land,* Bob and Lynne Fitch (Creative Education)

g. *Grandpa and Frank,* Janet Majerus (Lippincott; also paperback)

2. Lerner Publications: Awareness Series

a. *Look at Adoption,* Margaret S. Purcell

b. *Look at Birth,* Margaret S. Purcell

c. *Look at Divorce,* Margaret S. Purcell

    d. *Look at the Environment,* Margaret S. Purcell

    e. *Look at Alcoholism,* Rebecca Anders

    f. *Look at Death,* Rebecca Anders

    g. *Look at Drug Abuse,* Rebecca Anders

    h. *Look at Prejudice and Understanding,* Rebecca Anders

3. Divorce

    a. *A Book for Jordan,* Marcia Newfield (Atheneum)

    b. *Ice River,* Phyllis Green (Addison-Wesley)

    c. *Me and Mr. Stenner,* Evan Hunter (Lippincott)

    d. *No Place for Mitty,* Marian Young (Scholastic paperback)

    e. *To Live a Lie,* Anne Alexander (Atheneum)

    f. *Talking About Divorce: A Dialogue Between Parent and Child,* Earl Grollmen (Beacon Press paperback)

    g. *Boys' and Girls' Book About Divorce,* Dr. Richard Gardner (Bantam paperback)

4. Death

    a. *Beat the Turtle Drum,* Constance Greene (Viking Press)

    b. *Come Again in the Spring,* Richard Kennedy (Harper & Row)

    c. *Oliver Hyde's Dishcloth Concert,* Richard Kennedy (Little, Brown)

    d. *Summer to Die,* Lois Lowry (Houghton Mifflin)

    e. *Taste of Blackberries,* Doris Smith (Crowell)

5. Choosing Careers

    a. *Women at Their Work,* Betty English (Dial Press)

    b. *What Can She Be? A Farmer,* Gloria Goldreich and Esther Goldreich (Lothrop, Lee & Shepard)

    c. *What Can She Be? A Film Producer,* Gloria Goldreich and Esther Goldreich (Lothrop, Lee & Shepard)

    d. *What Can She Be? A Geologist,* Gloria Goldreich and Esther Goldreich (Lothrop, Lee & Shepard)

    e. *What Can She Be? A Lawyer,* Gloria Goldreich and Esther Goldreich (Lothrop, Lee & Shepard)

    f. *What Can She Be? A Legislator,* Gloria Goldreich and Esther Goldreich (Lothrop, Lee & Shepard)

    g. *What Can She Be? A Newscaster,* Gloria Goldreich and Esther Goldreich (Lothrop, Lee & Shepard)

    h. *What Can She Be? A Musician,* Gloria Goldreich and Esther Goldreich (Lothrop, Lee & Shepard)

    i. *What Can She Be? A Police Officer,* Gloria Goldreich and Esther Goldreich (Lothrop, Lee & Shepard)

    j. *What Can She Be? A Veterinarian,* Gloria Goldreich and Esther Goldreich (Lothrop, Lee & Shepard)

    k. *What Can She Be? An Architect,* Gloria Goldreich and Esther Goldreich (Lothrop, Lee & Shepard)

    l. *In a Fire Department,* Margaret Reuter (Raintree Publishers)

    m. *In a Police Station,* Margaret Reuter (Raintree Publishers)

    n. *In a Hospital,* Joy Schaleben-Lewis (Raintree Publishers)

    o. *In an Airport,* Gary Paulsen (Raintree Publishers)

    p. *A Day in the Life of a Veterinarian,* William Jasperson (Little, Brown)

6. Handling Money Wisely

    a. *What Is Money?,* Elizabeth James and Carol Barkin (Raintree Publishers)

    b. *Managing Your Money,* Elizabeth James and Carol Barkin (Raintree Publishers)

    c. *Money Isn't Everything,* Kathlyn Gay (Delacorte Press)

    d. *Kids' Guide to the Economy,* Manfred Kudel (Prentice-Hall)

    e. *Kids' Money-Making Book,* Jean and Jim Young (Doubleday)

    f. *Money of Your Own,* Grace Weinstein (Dutton)

G. Fiction and Fantasy

The number of fine nonfiction books for this age group far surpasses the number of good books of fiction and fantasy. But here are some excellent ones.

1. Grosset & Dunlap: Illustrated Junior Library of Classics for Children (ages nine to eleven)

    a. *The Adventures of Tom Sawyer,* Mark Twain (also Scholastic paperback)

    b. *The Adventures of Huckleberry Finn,* Mark Twain (also Penguin paperback)

    c. *Black Beauty,* Anna Sewell (also paperback)

    d. *Andersen's Fairy Tales,* Hans Christian Andersen

    e. *Aesop's Fables*

    f. *Alice in Wonderland* and *Through the Looking Glass,* Lewis Carroll (also paperback)

    g. *Gulliver's Travels,* Jonathan Swift

    h. *Heidi,* Johanna Spyri (also paperback)

    i. *Call of the Wild and Other Stories,* Jack London (also Scholastic paperback)

    j. *Kidnapped,* Robert Louis Stevenson (also Washington Square Press paperback)

    k. *Treasure Island,* Robert Louis Stevenson (also Airmont paperback)

    l. *The Jungle Book,* Rudyard Kipling (also Airmont paperback)

    m. *Little Women,* Louisa May Alcott (also paperback)

    n. *Robinson Crusoe,* Daniel Defoe (also Scholastic paperback)

    o. *The Wizard of Oz,* L. Frank Baum

    p. *Swiss Family Robinson,* Johann Wyss (also Airmont paperback)

    q. *The Wind in the Willows,* Kenneth Grahame (also paperback)

    r. *Pinocchio,* Carlo Collodi (also paperback)

    s. *The Little Lame Prince,* Dinah Craik

    t. *King Arthur and His Knights,* Sidney Lanier and Howard Pyle (also Penguin paperback)

2. All of a Kind Family series by Sydney Taylor (Follett; also Dell paperback)
   a. *All of a Kind Family*
   b. *All of a Kind Family Downtown*
   c. *All of a Kind Family Uptown*
3. The Malone Family series by Lenora Weber (Crowell)
   a. *Meet the Malones*
   b. *Beany Malone*
   c. *Beany Has a Secret Life*
4. The Borrowers series by Mary Norton (Harcourt Brace)
   a. *The Borrowers*
   b. *The Borrowers Afloat*
   c. *The Borrowers Aloft*
5. The Black Stallion series by Walter Farley (Random House; also paperback)
   a. *The Black Stallion*
   b. *The Black Stallion and Flame*
   c. *The Black Stallion Mystery*
   d. *The Black Stallion's Courage*
6. The Bagthorpe Saga series by Helen Cresswell (Macmillan)
   a. *Ordinary Jack*
   b. *Absolute Zero*
   c. *Bagthorpes Unlimited*
7. Rally Books series by Ed Radlauer (Childrens Press)
   a. *Minibike Challenge*
   b. *Dragstrip Challenge*
   c. *Karting Challenge*
   d. *Motorcycle Challenge*
8. Mystery series by Enid Blyton (Atheneum)
   a. *Five Caught in a Treacherous Plot*
   b. *Five Fall into Adventure*
   c. *Five Find a Secret Way*
   d. *Five on a Treasure Island*
9. Additional mystery stories by Enid Blyton (British Book Centre)
   a. *The Mystery of Banshee Towers*
   b. *The Mystery of Holly Lane*
   c. *The Mystery of the Strange Message*
   d. *The Mystery of the Disappearing Cat*
   e. *The Mystery of the Invisible Thief*
10. Putnam's: See and Read storybook series (ages eight to ten)
    a. *Andrew's Amazing Boxes*, Unada
    b. *Brave Betsy*, Miriam Dreifus
    c. *Bottles of Pop*, James Holding
    d. *The Horse That Liked Sandwiches*, Vivian Thompson
    e. *Ida the Bareback Rider*, Syd Hoff
    f. *The Little Sponge Fisherman*, Florence Rowland

     g. *The Lucky Little Porcupine,* Patricia Martin

     h. *Night Outdoors,* Naomi Buchheimer

  11. Horse stories by Marguerite Henry

Not a series, but a group of fine books by a very gifted author. These stories appeal especially to girls aged eight to eleven. (Rand McNally)

     a. *Misty of Chincoteague* (also paperback)

     b. *Stormy, Misty's Foal* (also paperback)

     c. *Sea Star, Orphan of Chincoteague* (also paperback)

     d. *White Stallion of Lipizza*

     e. *Brighty of the Grand Canyon* (also paperback)

  12. Henry Huggins books by Beverly Cleary

The hilarious adventures of an irrepressible boy and his friends. Real favorites with the eight-to-eleven set. (William Morrow)

     a. *Henry Huggins*

     b. *Henry and Beezus*

     c. *Ramona, the Pest*

     d. *The Mouse and the Motorcycle*

     e. *Henry and the Clubhouse*

     f. *Ramona the Brave*

  13. Miscellaneous Fiction

I mentioned some of these titles in the lists of books for preschoolers. But don't hesitate to offer a middle childhood child a book you have already read aloud to her. The fact that she knows the story may make your young granddaughter all the more interested in reading the book to herself.

     a. *June 7!,* Aliki (Macmillan). A picture book that shows an ever-expanding crowd of relatives gathering in a city apartment to celebrate a birthday.

     b. *Little Runner of the Longhouse,* Betty Baker (Harper & Row). A humorous Iroquois Indian story about Little Runner, who ultimately receives the reward of maple sugar in the New Year rites.

     c. *We Are Having a Baby,* Viki Holland (Scribner's). Skillfully examines the confused reactions of a young child confronted by the appearance of a new baby in the family.

     d. *A Pocketful of Cricket,* Rebecca Caudill (Holt, Rinehart & Winston; also paperback). A pet cricket goes to school with Jay on his first day in the "awesome institution."

     e. *Nobody Listens to Andrew,* Elizabeth Guilfoile (Follett; also Scholastic paperback). Andrew tries frantically to tell everyone that there is a bear in his bed!

     f. *A Bargain for Frances,* Russell Hoban (Harper & Row; also paperback). The latest book in a series about a small badger whose antics are amusing and very childlike.

     g. *The New Teacher,* Miriam Cohen (Macmillan, also paperback). When the first-grade teacher leaves to have a baby, the members of her class speculate about what her replacement will be like.

h. *Emily, the Klunky Baby and the Next Door Dog,* Joan Lexau (Dial Press). When Mother, who is divorced and has increased chores as a result, cannot play with her, Emily sets off for Daddy's apartment.

i. *Ira Sleeps Over,* Bernard Waber (Houghton Mifflin; also Sandpiper Books paperback). When Ira is invited to spend the night with his next-door neighbor, he cannot decide whether to take his teddy bear or not.

j. *If I Built a Village,* Kazue Mizumura (Crowell). Wishing is the theme of this gentle book, which gives a child's view of environmental spoilage.

k. *Alexander and the Terrible, Horrible, No-Good, Very Bad Day,* Judith Viorst (Atheneum). Everything goes wrong for Alexander, and he vows to move to Australia. Mother assures him, however, that "some days are like that"—even in Australia!

l. *The Tenth Good Thing About Barney,* Judith Viorst (Atheneum). When a boy's cat dies, his mother helpfully suggests that he think of ten good things to tell about Barney during the funeral.

m. *A Father Like That,* Charlotte Zolotow (Harper & Row). A fatherless boy describes the kind of father he would like to have. His mother reassures him that he himself can grow up to be just that kind of man!

n. *Mop Top,* Don Freeman (Viking Press; also Penguin paperback). If promoting haircuts is a problem in your family, read this story about a boy whose hair resembles a floppy red mop.

o. *Grasshopper on the Road,* Arnold Lobel (Harper & Row). An up-to-date version of the ant and grasshopper fable, this is the story of a persistent insect on the road to high adventure.

p. *Indian Hill,* Clyde Bulla (Crowell). Moving from an Indian reservation to an apartment in a big city traumatizes a Navaho family.

q. *Surprise for a Cowboy,* Clyde Bulla (Crowell). A city boy wants desperately to become a cowboy and live on a ranch.

r. *Then Again, Maybe I Won't,* Judy Blume (Bradbury Press; also Dell paperback). A boy is upset about his family's changed attitudes when they become well-to-do, and by his first sexual stirrings.

s. *Andy's Mountain,* Bianca Bradbury (Houghton Mifflin).

t. *Humbug Mountain,* Sid Fleischmann (Little, Brown). A "tall tale" of recent vintage, this outlandish, fast-paced story tells of a down-on-their-luck family who inadvertently start a gold rush. Good to read aloud.

u. *My Mother Is Not Married to My Father,* Jean Davies Okimoto (Putnam's). Cynthia's parents are divorced, and she pours out her sixth-grade views on things like weekends at her dad's apartment and her mother's first date as a "single" to the family cat. Refreshingly funny.

v. *My Dad Lives in a Downtown Motel,* Peggy Mann (Doubleday; also Avon paperback). When Joey's parents separate, it hurts inside his stomach because he thinks maybe it's his fault. After suffering anger, frustration, and grief, Joey finds out that each of his parents has very tender feelings about him.

w. *Beanie,* Ruth and Latrobe Carroll (Henry Z. Walck). The Smoky Mountains serve as the setting for a warm, happy family story.

x. *The House of Sixty Fathers,* Meindert DeJong (Harper & Row). A story set in China about a boy looking for his lost family.

y. *The Grizzly,* Annabel and Edgar Johnson (Harper & Row; also Scholastic paperback). Since his parents' separation, David has had little opportunity to get to know his father. During a fishing trip, David tries to overcome his fear of both his father and the natural elements.

z. *Rabbit Hill,* Robert Lawson (Viking Press; also Dell paperback). Georgie, a happy little rabbit boy, and his old Uncle Analdas move engagingly through this story, in which a new family moves into the neighborhood.

aa. *Ben and Me,* Robert Lawson (Little, Brown). The life of Benjamin Franklin as told by a little mouse.

bb. *Gull #737,* Jean George (Crowell). A sea gull is being studied by Dr. Rivers, a scientist father who is self-centered and closed-minded. When his son Luke offers logical, creative ideas, it's the beginning of true communication between father and son.

cc. *Onion John,* Joseph Krumgold (Crowell; also paperback). At first, Andy's father dominates him completely, but as Andy grows more independent, his father becomes more understanding.

dd. *Rough Ice,* Beaman Lord (Henry Z. Walck). A young boy tries to equal the skill of his father, who was a champion hockey player.

ee. *The Lion, the Witch, and the Wardrobe,* C. S. Lewis (Macmillan; also paperback). The children in this story become involved in a number of conflicts between good and evil, which are symbolized by a kindly lion and a wicked witch.

ff. *Little House in the Big Woods,* Laura Ingalls Wilder (Harper & Row; also paperback). This book and seven others (*Little House on the Prairie, Little Town on the Prairie,* etc.) tell warm family stories of American pioneer life. All are based on the author's vivid memories of her own nineteenth-century childhood. Modern classics for children.

gg. *Homer Price,* Robert McCloskey (Viking Press; also Penguin paperback). A series of funny stories about a lively boy, this book was one of the first to spoof comic books.

hh. *Harriet the Spy,* Louise Fitzhugh (Harper & Row; also Dell paperback). Harriet has a secret notebook that she fills with painfully honest comments about her parents, neighbors, and classmates. Every day on her "spy route" she observes and jots down anything of interest to her.

    ii. *Bed-Knobs and Broomsticks,* Mary Norton (paperback). As Miss Price is studying to become a witch, she is discovered by the Wilson children. Interesting things happen when she gives the children "special magic" to keep them quiet about her activities.

    jj. *Miracles on Maple Hill,* Virginia Sorenson (Harcourt Brace; also paperback). Father has been in a prisoner-of-war camp and the family moves to the country hoping that he will regain his health.

    kk. *Little Rascal,* Sterling North (Dutton). The heartening story of a raccoon and a lonely boy.

14. Science Fiction

    a. *The Carnival Kidnap Caper,* Fitzhugh Dodson and Paula Reuben (Oak Tree Publications)

    b. *Danny Dunn and the Universal Glue,* Jay Williams and Raymond Abrashkin (McGraw-Hill)

    c. *Danny Dunn, Invisible Boy,* Jay Williams and Raymond Abrashkin (Archway paperback)

    d. *Dragonfall 5 and the Empty Planet,* Brian Earnshaw (Lothrop, Lee & Shepard)

    e. *Dragonfall 5 and the Space Cowboys,* Brian Earnshaw (Lothrop, Lee & Shepard)

    f. *Miss Pickerell and the Earthquake Rescue,* Ellen McGregor and Dora Pantell (McGraw-Hill)

    g. *Miss Pickerell Meets Mr. H.U.M.,* Ellen McGregor and Dora Pantell (McGraw-Hill)

    h. *Empty World,* John Christophen (Dutton)

    i. *Fat Men from Space,* Daniel M. Pinkwater (Dodd, Mead)

    j. *My Robot Buddy,* Alfred Slote (Lippincott)

    k. *My Trip to Alpha I,* Alfred Slote (Lippincott)

    l. *Next Stop, Earth,* William Butterworth (Walker & Co.)

    m. *The Furious Flycycle,* Jan Wahl (Delacorte Press)

    n. *SOS Bobo-Mobile: The Further Adventures of Melvin Spitznagle and Professor Mickimecki,* Jan Wahl (Delacorte Press)

15. Newbery Medal Winners

The Newbery Medal is awarded annually by the Children's Services Division of the American Library Association to the book that it chooses as the outstanding contribution to children's literature for the preceding year. Here is a complete list of Newbery winners. Not all of these books can be read by a middle childhood youngster, but the list can serve as a guide to outstanding books for older children as well.

    1979 *The Westing Game,* Ellen Raskin (Dutton)

    1978 *Bridge to Terabithia,* Katherine Paterson (Crowell)

    1977 *Roll of Thunder, Hear My Cry,* Mildred D. Taylor (Dial Press)

    1976 *Grey King,* Susan Cooper (Atheneum)

    1975 *M. C. Higgins, the Great,* Virginia Hamilton (Macmillan)

1974   *The Slave Dancer*, Paula Fox (Bradbury Press)

1973   *Julie of the Wolves*, Jean Craighead George (Harper & Row)

1972   *Mrs. Frisby and the Rats of NIMH*, Robert C. O'Brien (Atheneum)

1971   *Summer of the Swans*, Betsy C. Byars (Viking Press)

1970   *Sounder*, William H. Armstrong (Harper & Row)

1969   *The High King*, Lloyd Alexander (Holt, Rinehart & Winston)

1968   *From the Mixed-Up Files of Mrs. Basil F. Frankweiler*, E. M. Konigsburg (Atheneum)

1967   *Up a Road Slowly*, Irene Hunt (Follett)

1966   *I, Juan de Pareja*, Elizabeth B. Trevino (Farrar, Straus & Giroux)

1965   *Shadow of a Bull*, Maia Wojciechowska (Atheneum)

1964   *It's Like This, Cat*, Emily Cheney Neville (Harper & Row)

1963   *A Wrinkle in Time*, Madeleine L'Engle (Farrar, Straus & Giroux)

1962   *The Bronze Bow*, Elizabeth G. Speare (Houghton Mifflin)

1961   *Island of the Blue Dolphins*, Scott O'Dell (Houghton Mifflin)

1960   *Onion John*, Joseph Krumgold (Crowell)

1959   *The Witch of Blackbird Pond*, Elizabeth G. Speare (Houghton Mifflin)

1958   *Rifles for Watie*, Harold Keith (Crowell)

1957   *Miracles on Maple Hill*, Virginia Sorensen (Harcourt Brace)

1956   *Carry On, Mr. Bowditch*, Jean L. Latham (Houghton Mifflin)

1955   *The Wheel on the School*, Meindert DeJong (Harper & Row)

1954   *And Now Miguel*, Joseph Krumgold (Crowell)

1953   *Secret of the Andes*, Ann N. Clark (Viking Press)

1952   *Ginger Pye*, Eleanor Estes (Harcourt Brace)

1951   *Amos Fortune, Free Man*, Elizabeth Yates (Dutton)

1950   *The Door in the Wall*, Marguerite De Angeli (Doubleday)

1949   *King of the Wind*, Marguerite Henry (Rand McNally)

1948   *The Twenty-One Balloons*, William Pène Du Bois (Viking Press)

1947   *Miss Hickory*, Carolyn S. Bailey (Viking Press)

1946   *Strawberry Girl*, Lois Lenski (Lippincott)

1945   *Rabbit Hill*, Robert Lawson (Viking Press)

1944   *Johnny Tremain*, Esther Forbes (Houghton Mifflin)

1943   *Adam of the Road*, Elizabeth J. Gray (Viking Press)

1942   *The Matchlock Gun*, Walter D. Edmonds (Dodd, Mead)

1941   *Call It Courage*, Armstrong Sperry (Macmillan)

1940   *Daniel Boone*, James Daugherty (Viking Press)

1939   *Thimble Summer*, Elizabeth Enright (Holt, Rinehart & Winston)

1938   *The White Stag*, Kate Seredy (Viking Press)

1937   *Roller Skates*, Ruth Sawyer (Viking Press)

1936   *Caddie Woodlawn*, Carol R. Brink (Macmillan)

1935   *Dobry*, Monica Shannon (Viking Press)

1934   *Invincible Louisa*, Cornelia Meigs (Little, Brown)

1933   *Young Fu of the Upper Yangtze*, Elizabeth F. Lewis (Holt, Rinehart & Winston)

1932 *Waterless Mountain,* Laura A. Armer (David McKay)

1931 *The Cat Who Went to Heaven,* Elizabeth Coatsworth (Macmillan)

1930 *Hitty, Her First Hundred Years,* Rachel Field (Macmillan)

1929 *The Trumpeter of Krakow,* Eric P. Kelly (Macmillan)

1928 *Gay-Neck,* Dhan Gopal Mukerji (Dutton)

1927 *Smoky, the Cow Horse,* Will James (Scribner's)

1926 *Shen of the Sea,* Arthur Bowie Chrisman (Dutton)

1925 *Tales from Silver Lands,* Charles Finger (Doubleday)

1924 *The Dark Frigate,* Charles Hawes (Little, Brown)

1923 *The Voyages of Doctor Dolittle,* Hugh Lofting (Lippincot

1922 *The Story of Mankind,* Hendrik Van Loon (Liveright)

16. Caldecott Medal Winners

The Caldecott Medal is also awarded annually by the Children's Services Division of the American Library Association. It goes to the artist who has produced the most distinguished picture book for children published during the preceding year. Here is a complete list of the books and illustrators that have won Caldecott Medals. Some of these books are for middle childhood readers; others are more suitable for preschoolers.

1979 *The Girl Who Loved Wild Horses,* Paul Goble (Bradbury Press)

1978 *Noah's Ark: Story of the Flood,* Peter Spier (Doubleday)

1977 *Ashanti to Zulu: African Traditions,* Diane Dillon & Leo Dillon (Dial Press)

1976 *Why Mosquitos Buzz in People's Ears,* Diane Dillon & Leo Dillon (Dial Press)

1975 *Arrow to the Sun,* Gerald McDermott (Viking Press)

1974 *Duffy and the Devil,* Margot Zemach (Farrar, Straus & Giroux)

1973 *The Funny Little Woman,* Blair Lent (Dutton)

1972 *One Fine Day,* Nonny Hogrogian (Macmillan)

1971 *A Story—A Story,* Gail E. Haley (Atheneum)

1970 *Sylvester and the Magic Pebble,* William Steig (Windmill Books)

1969 *The Fool of the World and the Flying Ship,* Uri Shulevitz (Farrar, Straus & Giroux)

1968 *Drummer Hoff,* Ed Emberley (Prentice-Hall)

1967 *Sam, Bangs, and Moonshine,* Evaline Ness (Holt, Rinehart & Winston)

1966 *Always Room for One More,* Nonny Hogrogian (Holt, Rinehart & Winston)

1965 *May I Bring a Friend?,* Beni Montresor (Atheneum)

1964 *Where the Wild Things Are,* Maurice Sendak (Harper & Row)

1963 *The Snowy Day,* Ezra Jack Keats (Viking Press)

1962 *Once a Mouse,* Marcia Brown (Scribner's)

1961 *Baboushka and the Three Kings,* Nicholas Sidjakov (Parnassus Press)

1960 *Nine Days to Christmas,* Marie Hall Ets (Viking Press)

1959 *Chanticleer and the Fox,* Barbara Cooney (Crowell)

1958 *Time of Wonder,* Robert McCloskey (Viking Press)

1957   *A Tree Is Nice*, Marc Simont (Harper & Row)

1956   *Frog Went A-Courtin'*, Feodor Rojankovsky (Harcourt Brace)

1955   *Cinderella*, Marcia Brown (Scribner's)

1954   *Madeline's Rescue*, Ludwig Bemelmans (Viking Press)

1953   *The Biggest Bear*, Lynd Ward (Houghton Mifflin)

1952   *Finders Keepers*, Nicolas Mordvinoff (Harcourt Brace)

1951   *The Egg Tree*, Katherine Milhous (Scribner's)

1950   *Song of the Swallows*, Leo Politi (Scribner's)

1949   *The Big Snow*, Berta & Elmer Hader (Macmillan)

1948   *White Snow, Bright Snow*, Roger Duvoisin (Lothrop, Lee & Shepard)

1947   *The Little Island*, Leonard Weisgard (Doubleday)

1946   *The Rooster Crows*, Maud & Miska Petersham (Macmillan)

1945   *Prayer for a Child*, Elizabeth Orton Jones (Macmillan)

1944   *Many Moons*, Louis Slobodkin (Harcourt Brace)

1943   *The Little House*, Virginia Burton (Houghton Mifflin)

1942   *Make Way for Ducklings*, Robert McCloskey (Viking Press)

1941   *They Were Strong and Good*, Robert Lawson (Viking Press)

1940   *Abraham Lincoln*, Ingri & Edgar Parin D'Aulaire (Doubleday)

1939   *Mei Li*, Thomas Handforth (Doubleday)

1938   *Animals of the Bible*, Dorothy P. Lathrop (Lippincott)

17. Personalized Books

Every once in a while a truly original idea hits the field of children's books. The personalized book is such an idea.

A personalized book is about the child who is reading it; it uses the child's own name and address, the names of brothers and sisters or friends, the names of pets. The bookplate is also personalized—it says, "This book was written especially for [whatever the child's name is]. With love and kisses from [whoever is giving the book]." The book is printed by computer; the computer is programmed to insert the personal information in more than seventy places throughout a standardized story.

Research findings by reading consultants at the University of Southern California show that the personalized book—"a book written all about me!"—has a tremendous impact on a young child. Mediocre readers have been found to do as well as excellent readers with the personalized book.

These personalized books are called "Me-Books." The person buying the book fills out a form, giving the child's name and address, the first names of up to three brothers, sisters, or friends, the names of the child's pets, and the child's birthdate. After you have ordered the book, it will be mailed to your bookstore, where you can pick it up. If your local bookstore does not sell Me-Books, you can get them by mail from Me-Books Publishing, 10635 Vanowen Street, Burbank, California 91505.

Me-Books are for children reading at the kindergarten or first-grade level. If you buy your grandchild one of these marvelous books, be sure to present the book to the child yourself. You won't want to miss the expression on your little grandson's face when he discovers that the book is all about him!

Me-Books are thirty-two pages long. Here is a partial list of the titles available:

    a. *My Friendly Giraffe*

    b. *My Jungle Holiday*

    c. *My Birthdayland Adventure*

    d. *My Special Christmas*

    e. *My Circus Story*

    f. *My Holiday Adventure*

    g. *Me and the Sad Clay Dragon*

    h. *Sesame Street ABC Hunt*

    i. *My Adventure in Mother Goose Land*

    j. *Spelling My Name Is a Game*

    k. *Flintstones Alphabet*

    l. *Me and the Yellow-Eyed Monster*

18. All-Time Favorites

And now I want to conclude this section of books of fiction and fantasy for middle childhood with a dozen of my own personal favorites for this age group.

    a. *Winnie-the-Pooh,* A. A. Milne (Dutton; also Dell paperback). Be sure to get the original edition of this book and not the watered-down Walt Disney version. Originally created by A. A. Milne for his own son, Christopher Robin, this is one of the most wonderful children's classics ever written.

    b. *Charlie and the Chocolate Factory,* Roald Dahl (Knopf; also Bantam paperback). Five children get to see the mysterious machinery in the marvelous chocolate factory of Mr. Willy Wonka.

    c. *James and the Giant Peach,* Roald Dahl (Knopf). Another delightful fantasy by Roald Dahl. "Fabulous unbelievable things" happen to James inside the giant peach.

    d. *Stuart Little,* E. B. White (Harper & Row; also paperback). The whimsical first sentence of this book reads, "When Mrs. Frederick C. Little's second son arrived, everybody noticed that he was not much bigger than a mouse." In fact, he *was* a mouse! The rest of the book describes his fascinating adventures. A modern classic.

    e. *Charlotte's Web,* E. B. White (Harper & Row; also paperback). Another wonderful tale of whimsy and imagination by E. B. White.

    f. *The Wind in the Willows,* Kenneth Grahame (Scribner's; also paperback). This marvelous children's classic is the story of Mole, Badger, Rat, and Toad, and their life along the banks of the Thames River.

    g. *The Twenty-One Balloons,* William Pène Du Bois (Viking Press; also Dell paperback). This is the book that I, personally, most enjoyed reading to my children. Professor William Waterman Sherman goes adventuring in a flying balloon that lands on the amazing island of Krakatoa, where twenty families live in secluded luxury. The inventions of the families of Krakatoa will delight both children and grandparents.

    h. *Just So Stories,* Rudyard Kipling (Grosset & Dunlap; also Scholastic paperback). Another children's classic. A delightful collection of humorous animal fantasy tales, such as "How the Leopard Got His Spots" and "How the Whale Got His Throat."

    i. *Mary Poppins,* P. L. Travers (Harcourt Brace). Walt Disney's wonderful movie *Mary Poppins* has spread the fame of the fabulous nursemaid of the Banks children. Wherever Mary Poppins goes, magic is sure to be in the air.

    j. *The Enormous Egg,* Oliver Butterworth (Little, Brown; also Dell paperback). A twelve-year-old boy finds a huge egg that hatches into a dinosaur.

    k. *Mr. Popper's Penguins,* Richard and Florence Atwater (Little, Brown; also Dell paperback). Mr. Popper, a paperhanger with a passion for the Antarctic, is given a penguin by an explorer. The one penguin becomes twelve, and the twelve penguins proceed to turn the lives of the entire Popper family upside down. Hilarious whimsy.

    l. *Chitty Chitty Bang Bang, the Magical Car,* Ian Fleming (Random House). Walt Disney has also popularized this book, which tells the story of Commander Crackpot and his marvelous car that can swim, fly, and communicate with people.

V. Preadolescence and Adolescence

I have decided not to include any book lists for preadolescents and adolescents, for several reasons. One is that preadolescents will continue to enjoy many of the books I've listed for middle childhood. But the main one is that preadolescents and adolescents are no longer really children, and they usually have strong tastes in reading material. In many ways, their reading tastes are similar to those of adults. So you will need to tune in on your grandchildren's unique, idiosyncratic preferences. (For example, if your grandson is interested in fishing, hot rods, and motorcycles, a list of excellent books of biography for adolescents will not be of much help as a guide to buying him books.) Give your grandchildren books that fit their reading preferences, and they will be happy with them. *Don't* select books that you think your preadolescent or adolescent grandchild "ought" to read!

VI. Buying an Encyclopedia for Your Grandchild

I believe that when your grandchild arrives midway in the stage of middle childhood (fourth, fifth, or sixth grade, depending on the child), you should get him or her an encyclopedia if you can afford it. I say "if you can afford it," because an encyclopedia is a major investment. (I won't even attempt to specify in dollars what that means, because with today's alternately creeping and galloping inflation, the figures would probably be out of date by the time they were printed.)

Because an encyclopedia will be costly, you need to choose carefully. One of the best ways to compare encyclopedias is to visit your library and browse through the different encyclopedias there. Look up a topic on which you are pretty well informed.

Ask yourself, "Is the topic easy to locate? Is the writing interesting? Is it so far as you know accurate?" Ask your librarian's help, and get her views on which encyclopedias are best.

Two encyclopedias are generally recommended by librarians for grades four through six and up:

1. Compton's Encyclopedia (twenty-six volumes for grades four to twelve), published by F. E. Compton Company, a division of Encyclopedia Britannica, 425 North Michigan Avenue, Chicago, Illinois 60611.

2. The World Book Encyclopedia (twenty-one volumes for grades four to twelve), published by Field Enterprises Educational Corporation, 510 Merchandise Mart Plaza, Chicago, Illinois 60654.

I will stick my neck out and say that I, personally, believe the World Book Encyclopedia is the best for this age group.

Encyclopedias can only be bought through salesmen, not in department stores or bookstores. However, it is sometimes possible to buy used sets, or sets a few years old. You may find used encyclopedias in a bookstore, or it may be possible to buy one from a salesman, or from a library that has replaced its old set with a newer one.

Most of the information in an encyclopedia stays up to date for a number of years, so if you happen to find a set that is a few years old, give it a careful inspection. You may find you've got yourself a good buy.

In any case, don't just buy an encyclopedia and present it "cold" to your grandchild. You will need to teach the child how to use it so it will not be a forbidding set of strange volumes to her. For instance, help your granddaughter think of a topic that interests her. Then show her how to look it up. Explain how to use the index to the encyclopedia, and how to follow cross-references to other articles. Above all, show her how to find the main points in an encyclopedia article. This way, she will not be like many students, who do their homework by mechanically copying all or part of an encyclopedia article.

VII. Magazines for Children

I would be remiss if I closed this appendix without some mention of good magazines for children. Children get so little mail that it is always a thrill when a magazine arrives for them. They will beg you to read these magazines to them in the preschool years, and they will read them themselves in the years of middle childhood. They also enjoy doing the puzzles, cutouts, and other activities in the magazines. Here are the magazines I recommend:

A. For Preschoolers
1. *Humpty Dumpty's Magazine* (Parents' Magazine Enterprises, 52 Vanderbilt Avenue, New York, New York 10017). Ages three to seven.

2. *Jack and Jill* (1100 Waterway Boulevard, Box 567B Indianapolis, Indiana 46206). Ages five to twelve.
3. *Highlights for Children* (2300 West Fifth Avenue, Columbus, Ohio 43216). Ages two to twelve.
4. *Sesame Street Magazine* (Children's Television Workshop, 1 Lincoln Plaza, New York, New York 10023). Text in English and Spanish. Ages three to five.

B. For Middle Childhood Children
1. *Electric Company Magazine* (1 Lincoln Plaza, New York, New York 10023). For graduates of *Sesame Street*. Ages six to eleven.
2. *Ranger Rick's Nature Magazine* (National Wildlife Federation; available only to members who pay the annual dues of six dollars. Write to *Ranger Rick's Nature Magazine* Membership Services, 1412 16th Street NW, Washington, D.C. 20036). Ages six to ten.
3. *Golden Magazine for Boys and Girls* (Golden Press, Inc., 850 Third Avenue, New York, New York 10022). Ages eight to twelve.
4. *Boys' Life* (Boy Scouts of America, North Brunswick, New Jersey 08902). For boys aged eight to eighteen.
5. *American Girl* (Girl Scouts of America, 830 Third Avenue, New York, New York 10022). For girls aged eleven to seventeen.
6. *Pack-O-Fun* (Clapper Publishing Company, 14 Main Street, Park Ridge, Illinois 60068). Craft projects for ages eight to fourteen.
7. *Mystery and Science Fiction Magazine* (1100 Waterway Boulevard, Box 567B, Indianapolis, Indiana 46206). For children up to fourteen.
8. *Cricket: The Magazine for Children* (Box 100, LaSalle, Illinois 61301). Ages six to twelve.
9. *National Geographic World* (Department 00778, 17th and M Streets NW, Washington, D.C. 20036). Ages seven to twelve.
10. *Young World* (1100 Waterway Boulevard, Box 567B, Indianapolis, Indiana 46206). Ages eight to twelve.
11. *Stone Soup* (Children's Art Foundation, Box 83, Santa Cruz, California 95063). Ages eight to thirteen.
12. *Now Voyager* (193 Beacon Street, Boston, Massachusetts 02116). Short stories for ages eight to fourteen.
13. *Young Miss* (Parents' Magazine Enterprises, 52 Vanderbilt Avenue, New York, New York 10017). For girls aged ten to fourteen.

❧ *Appendix C* ❧
A Grandparent's Guide to Children's Records

If you drop in at your local record and tape shop or the music section of your local department store, chances are you will find a reasonably good selection of records and tapes for adolescents and adults. But you will usually find much less for younger children. And those few records and tapes will probably be banal, trite, and "cutesy." Unless you live in a large metropolitan area or near an exceptionally good record or music store, you probably are not aware at all of how many truly fine records and cassettes there are for children. You probably do not know the great names in children's music today—Sam Hinton, Hap Palmer, Pete Seeger, Ella Jenkins, Marcia Berman, Patty Zeitlin, Ann Barlin, Tom Glazer.

I am very fortunate, because I live in a suburb of Los Angeles and have literally thousands of excellent children's records and cassettes to choose from. I can find them simply by driving over to the Children's Book and Music Center in Santa Monica and browsing through their extensive collection of records and cassettes.

If you cannot find a recommended record or cassette in your local music store or record shop, you can mail-order it from this excellent source. Write to the Children's Book and Music Center, 2500 Santa Monica Boulevard, Santa Monica, California 90404; or phone (213) 829-0215. Ask them to send you their free catalog, which lists not only the records and cassettes in this appendix, but many more that space limitations prevented me from listing. Or if you want a particular kind of record or cassette for a particular child, describe your needs in a letter and the staff will suggest something appropriate. I cannot recommend the services of this store too highly. In this age of stores run on the high-speed principle of "Hurry-up-and-get-him-out-of-here-so-we-can-get-to-the-next-customer," the Children's Book and Music Center is an oasis of old-fashioned personalized service.

Compared with toys and books, records and cassettes are an unknown land for many grandparents. You may be unaware of how valuable they are as learning devices, especially for preschool-age children. A good record or cassette can be used for developing listening skills, training the memory, teaching logical thinking, building the vocabulary, and providing a child with information.

When you play a record for a preschool child, don't just put the record on and play it "cold." Warm the child up and prepare her to hear the record.

Suppose you are getting ready to play a record of "The Three Little Pigs" for your granddaughter. Tell her in a generalized way what the record is about. After she has heard it, have a conversation with her about it. Ask questions like "What kind of homes did the three little pigs live in? Do you think they lived in a big city or a small town? Which pig was the best builder? What kind of voice did the big bad wolf use when he first knocked on the door? Can you imitate it?" Questions such as these will give your grandchild experience in listening to a record actively, rather than passively.

Since many people still have record players rather than cassette or tape players, I have listed a selection of the excellent children's *records* that are available. But more and more children's cassettes are being made. So if you are ordering by mail and want a cassette rather than a record, indicate your preference. (Practically no eight-track tapes are available in the children's field, so I have not bothered to list any of these.)

I. Infancy and Toddlerhood (from birth to approximately the second birthday)

A. A Child's First Records

These recordings are simple, uncluttered, and rhythmic. The concepts are simple and basic. Instrumentation is clear and musical. They encompass sensory, physical, vocal, and emotional responses. I recommend all of them highly for the earliest years.

1. "Music for One's and Two's," Tom Glazer (CMS)
2. "A Child's First Record," Frank Luther (Vocalion)
3. "Songs to Grow On for Mother and Child," Woody Guthrie (Folkways)
4. "Lullabies from 'Round the World," Marilyn Horne and Richard Robinson (Rhythm Productions)
5. "Songs and Play Time with Pete Seeger," Pete Seeger (Folkways)
6. "Golden Slumbers: Lullabies from Near and Far," Pete Seeger, Oscar Brand, et al. (Caedmon)
7. "Lullabies and Other Children's Songs," Nancy Raven (Pacific Cascade)
8. "Thoroughly Modern Mother Goose," Nancy Raven (Pacific Cascade)
9. "Seagulls: Music for Rest and Relaxation," Hap Palmer (Educational Activities)
10. "Folk Song Carnival," Hap Palmer (Educational Activities)
11. "Children's Creative Playsongs," volume I, Teddy Bears (Stepping Tones)
12. "Activity Songs," Marcia Berman (Tom Thumb)
13. "I'm Not Small," Marcia Berman and Patty Zeitlin (Educational Activities)
14. "You'll Sing a Song and I'll Sing a Song," Ella Jenkins (Folkways)
15. "Best of The Baby Sitters," The Baby Sitters (Vanguard)
16. "Fiddle–EE–Fee," Ruth White and Terry Gris (Tom Thumb)
17. "Loving and Learning from Birth to Three," Diane Hartman Smith (Joy)
18. "Little Favorites," male and female voices (Bowmar)
19. "Nursery and Mother Goose Songs," male and female voices (Bowmar)

B. Music of Many Cultures for Infants

Only recently has research shown us how sensitive babies are to their environment, how much they can see, hear, and smell. I believe it is a very good thing for parents and grandparents to play music of other cultures to young children. Although the baby may make no outward response, the music is being filed away in the computer brain of that lovely little head, for use later on.

1. "El Mejor Mariachi del Mundo," volume I, Mariachi Tecatitlan (Arcano)
2. "Bailes Folkloricos de Mexico" (Peerless)
3. "The Four Suns and Selections from *Piramide*" (Mexico), Carlos Chavez (Columbia)
4. "Fiesta Mexicana," Javier de Leon (Monitor)
5. "Juegos Infantiles de Mexico," volume I (RCA)
6. "El Autentico Tamborazo Zacatecano" (Mexico) (Orefon)
7. "The Sound of the Sun" (Trinidad), The Westland Steel Band (Nonesuch)
8. "Jatari!!" (South America) (Monitor)
9. "Lilacs Out of the Dead Land" (Greece), Manos Hadjidakis (Philips)
10. "Israeli Folk Dances," Martha Schlamme and Mort Freeman (Israel)
11. "Hora-Songs and Dances of Israel," Geula Gill (Elektra)
12. "Jazayer" (Egypt) (Jazayer Co.)
13. "Russian Folk Dances of the Moiseyev Dance Company" (Monitor)
14. "Olatunji! Drums of Passion" (Africa) (Columbia)
15. "African Drum, Chant and Instrumental Music" (Nonesuch)
16. "Musical Instruments of Africa, volume I: Strings" (Kaleidophone)
17. "Flower Dance" (Japan; includes koto, shamisen, drums) (Nonesuch)
18. "Flower Drum and Other Chinese Folk Songs" (Monitor)
19. "Songs and Dances of Vietnam" (Monitor)
20. "International Folk Dance Mixer" (includes music from Africa, Denmark, Israel, Italy, Russia, Scotland) (Gateway)

II. First Adolescence and the Preschool Stage (approximately the second to the sixth birthday)

A. Activity Records

These recordings encourage free body movement and rhythmic activities. They may be used with the help of adults or alone by the children. All are upbeat and lively and invite young children to create and move.

1. "Dance-a-Story" records, Ann Barlin (RCA)

A series of eight storybook and record combinations designed to inspire creative rhythm play, pantomime, dramatization, and storytelling. One side of each record is narrated, describing possible movements to go with the melody. The reverse side has music alone, and children are free to interpret the music as they feel it. An excellent series.

    a. "Little Duck"
    b. "Noah's Ark"
    c. "Magic Mountain"
    d. "Balloons"
    e. "Brave Hunter"
    f. "Flappy and Floppy"
    g. "The Toy Tree"
    h. "At the Beach"

2. "Rainy Day Dances, Rainy Day Songs," Marcia Berman, Patty Zeitlin, and Anne Barlin (Educational Activities)
3. "Castle in My City," Patty Zeitlin (Educational Activities)
4. "We All Live Together," volumes I and II, Youngheart Music Education Group (Youngheart Records)
5. "Machines and Things That Go," Jon Frommer (Pacific Cascade)
6. "Action Songs for Indoor Days," David White and Terry Gris (Tom Thumb)
7. Recordings by Ella Jenkins (Folkways)
    a. "And One and Two"
    b. "Call and Response"
    c. "Early Early Childhood Songs"
    d. "Growing Up with Ella Jenkins"
    e. "Jambo and Other Call and Response Songs and Chants"
    f. "Little Johnny Brown"
    g. "Play Your Instruments and Make a Pretty Sound"
    h. "Rhythm and Game Songs for Little Ones"
    i. "This-a-Way That-a-Way"
    j. "Travelin' with Ella Jenkins"
8. Recordings by Hap Palmer (Educational Activities)
    a. "Folk Song Carnival"
    b. "Creative Movement and Rhythmic Expression"
    c. "Getting to Know Yourself"
    d. "Movin' "
    e. "Ideas, Thoughts, and Feelings"
    f. "Pretend"
    g. "Homemade Band"
    h. "Modern Tunes for Rhythms and Instruments"
    i. "Mod Marches"
    j. "Seagulls: Music for Rest and Relaxation"
    k. "Feelin' Free"
    l. "Witches' Brew"
    m. "Easy Does It"
9. "The Small Dancer" (Bowmar)
10. "Moving Makes Me Magic," Yvonne Johnson and Betty Mosley (Folkways)
11. "Say Hi," Soundpiper Music (Soundpiper Records)
12. "I Like Sunny Days," Soundpiper Music (Soundpiper Records)

13. "Getting Bigger Every Day," Soundpiper Music (Soundpiper Records)
14. "Activity and Game Songs for Children," volumes I and II, Tom Glazer (CMS)

B. Recordings by TV Personalities
   1. Mister Rogers
      a. "Come On and Wake Up" (Pickwick)
      b. "Let's Be Together" (Pickwick)
      c. "A Place of Our Own" (Pickwick)
      d. "Won't You Be My Neighbor?" (Pickwick)
      e. "You Are Special" (Pickwick)
   2. Sesame Street
      a. "Sesame Street Original Cast Record" (CTW)
      b. "Pete Seeger and Brother Kirk Visit Sesame Street" (CTW)
      c. "Aren't You Glad You're You?" (CTW)
      d. "Sesame Street Fever" (CTW)
      e. "Sesame Street Disco" (CTW)

C. Records to Promote Positive Self-Concepts
These recordings inspire a positive self-image and deal with different aspects of self-esteem. They help children to grow both socially and emotionally.
   1. "Free to Be You and Me," Marlo Thomas and Friends (Arista)
   2. "Candy Band Sings 'Play Me a Song,'" Candy Band (Folkways)
   3. "Songs Between Friends," Wanda May and Tom Guy (T.G.I.D. Publications)
   4. "I Have a Friend in You" (Wise Owl)
   5. "Who Am I?" (Wise Owl)
   6. "Everybody Cries Sometimes," Marcia Berman and Patty Zeitlin (Educational Activities)
   7. "Won't You Be My Friend?," Marcia Berman and Patty Zeitlin (Educational Activities)
   8. "Sing a Song of Neighbors" (Bowmar)
   9. "Getting to Know Myself," Hap Palmer (Educational Activities)
   10. "I've Got a Reason to Sing," Ruth White and David White (Tom Thumb)
   11. "It's a Happy Feeling," Ruth White and David White (Tom Thumb)
   12. "Mommy . . . Gimme a Drinka Water," Danny Kaye (Capitol)

D. Nonsexist Records
These are recordings that motivate children to build new concepts and healthier self-images, free from sex role stereotypes.
   1. "My Mommy Is a Doctor," Patty Zeitlin (Educational Activities)
   2. "Action Songs for Indoor Days," David White and Terry Gris (Tom Thumb)
   3. "Hurray for Captain Jane" (stories), Tammy Grimes (Caedmon)
   4. "Free to Be You and Me," Marlo Thomas and Friends (Arista)
   5. "When I Grow Up I Want to Be," Bob Kay (Stallman)

E. Story Records

The stories on these records are not too long and will hold the youngest listener's attention. Books are available to accompany the recordings. Children like to see the pictures as they are listening to the story on the record.

1. "The Little Engine That Could" (also "Winnie-the-Pooh"), Paul Wing (RCA Educational)
2. "Peter Rabbit, Goldilocks, and Other Great Tales for Growing Boys and Girls," Paul Wing (RCA Educational)
3. "Happy Stories for Gloomy Days," Frank Luther (Vocalion)
4. "Stories for Rainy Days," Frank Luther (Vocalion)
5. "Winnie-the-Pooh and Christopher Robin," Frank Luther (MCA)
6. Dr. Seuss stories read by Marvin Miller (Pickwick)
   a. "If I Ran the Zoo / Dr. Seuss's Sleep Book"
   b. "The Sneetches / Horton Hatches the Egg"
   c. "Fox in Socks / Green Eggs and Ham"
7. "Babar the King / Babar and Zephyr," Louis Jourdan (Caedmon)
8. "Caps for Sale" on "Listening to Picture Books" (Classroom Materials)
9. "Curious George" (three stories), Julie Harris (Caedmon)
10. "Curious George Learns the Alphabet" (plus two other stories), Julie Harris (Caedmon)
11. "Frances Stories," Glynis Johns (Caedmon)
12. "Frederick" (plus several other stories), Carol Channing (Caedmon)
13. "Madeline" (four stories), Carol Channing (Caedmon)
14. "Madeline and the Gypsies" (plus three other stories), Carol Channing (Caedmon)
15. "Winnie-the-Pooh," Carol Channing (Caedmon)
16. "Grimm's Fairy Tales," Joseph Schildkraut (Caedmon)
17. "Higglety Pigglety Pop," Tammy Grimes (Caedmon)
18. "Where the Wild Things Are," Tammy Grimes (Caedmon)
19. "Just So Stories," Boris Karloff (Caedmon)
20. "The Three Little Pigs and Other Fairy Tales," Boris Karloff (Caedmon)
21. "Little Toot Stories," Hans Conreid (Caedmon)
22. "Lyle, Lyle, Crocodile," Gwen Verdon (Caedmon)
23. "Story of Ferdinand," Gwen Verdon (Caedmon)
24. "Why Mosquitos Buzz in People's Ears and Other Tales," Ruby Dee and Ossie David (Caedmon)
25. "Catch a Little Rhyme," Eve Merriam (Caedmon)

The following records all come packaged with books:

26. "The Bears' Picnic," the Berenstains (Caedmon)
27. Scholastic record and book sets (seven-inch long-playing record and paperback book)
   a. "Amelia Bedelia"
   b. "Bigger Giant"
   c. "Birth of a Foal"

    d. "Bread and Jam for Frances"
    e. "Bremen-Town Musicians"
    f. "City Mouse and Country Mouse"
    g. "Clifford Gets a Job / Clifford Takes a Trip"
    h. "The Elves and the Shoemaker"
    i. "The Emperor's New Clothes"
    j. "The Frog Prince"
    k. "Half a Kingdom"
    l. "Hansel and Gretel"
    m. "The Harmonica Man"
    n. "Life and Words of Martin Luther King, Jr."
    o. "Little Red Hen"
    p. "Old MacDonald Had a Farm"
    q. "A Picture for Harold's Room"
    r. "Stone Soup"
    s. "Tale of Peter Rabbit"
    t. "Tell Me a Mitzi"
    u. "That's What Friends Are For"
    v. "The Three Bears"
    w. "Three Billy Goats Gruff / Gingerbread Man"
    x. "Tikki Tikki Tembo"
    y. "What Do You Do with a Kangaroo?"
28. "Storyteller series (Storyteller Company) (cassette and book packages)
    a. "Cinderella"
    b. "Hansel and Gretel"
    c. "Tom Thumb"
    d. "Jack and the Beanstalk"
    e. "Aladdin"
    f. "Rumpelstiltskin"
    g. "Sleeping Beauty"
    h. "Snow White"
    i. "Little Red Riding Hood"
    j. "Pinocchio"
    k. "Ugly Duckling"
    l. "The Elves and the Shoemaker"

F. Foreign Languages

These records help a child learn a foreign language through music.
1. "Songs in French for Children," Lucienne Vernay (Columbia)
2. "Songs in Spanish for Children," Elena Travesi (Columbia)
3. "Building Spanish Vocabulary Through Music," volumes I and II, Eddie Cano (CP Records)
4. "Folksongs for Children of All Ages" (Spanish-American children's songs), Jenny Vincent (Cantemos)
5. "Canasta Musical," Linda Giles (Spanish) (Educational Activities)

6. "Canciones para el Recreo," Suni Paz (Spanish) (Folkways)
7. "Lo Mejor de Cri-Cri" (Spanish) (Arcano)

G. Folk Songs
1. "Abiyoyo and Other Story Songs for Children," Pete Seeger (Folkways)
2. "Birds, Beasts, Bugs and Little Fishes," Pete Seeger (Folkways)
3. "Birds, Beasts, Bugs and Bigger Fishes," Pete Seeger (Folkways)
4. "American Folk Songs for Children," Pete Seeger (Folkways)
5. "Folk Songs for Young People," Pete Seeger (Folkways)
6. "Whoever Shall Have Some Good Peanuts," Sam Hinton (Scholastic)
This is my single favorite record for preschoolers, done in Sam Hinton's inimitable
style.
7. "Through Children's Eyes," The Limelighters (RCA)
8. "Rhythms of Childhood," Ella Jenkins (Folkways)
9. "Children's Greatest Hits," volumes I and II, Tom Glazer (CMS)
10. "Little White Duck," Burl Ives (Columbia)
11. "Peter, Paul, and Mommy," Peter, Paul, and Mary (Warner Bros.)
12. "Really Rosie," Carole King (Ode)
13. "Songs to Grow On," Woody Guthrie (Folkways)

H. Music of Other Cultures
1. "It's a Small World" (Disneyland)
2. "It Could Be a Wonderful World" (Motivation)
3. "Songs of the Jewish People," Esther Lawrence (Jakob)
4. "Marn Ling Sees the Chinese Lion Dance" (International Telecom)
5. "Favorite Songs of Japanese Children" (Bowmar)
6. "Singing Games from Ghana" (M & M)
7. "Children's Songs of Mexico" (Bowmar)

I. Music Appreciation
1. "Tubby the Tuba," Danny Kaye (MCA)
2. "A Child's Introduction to the Orchestra" (Golden)
3. "Rusty in Orchestraville" (Capitol)
4. "Sparky's Music Mix-up" (Capitol)
5. "The Small Listener" (Bowmar)

J. Intellectual Stimulation
1. "Noisy and Quiet, Big and Little," Tom Glazer (RCA)
2. "Now We Know: Songs to Learn By," Tom Glazer and Paul Tripp (Columbia)
3. "Dance, Sing and Listen with Miss Nelson and Bruce" (Dimension 5)
4. "Learning Basic Skills Through Music," volumes I, II, and III, Hap Palmer
(Educational Activities)

5. "Math Readiness, Vocabulary and Concepts," Hap Palmer (Educational Activities)
6. "Math Readiness: Addition and Subtraction," Hap Palmer (Educational Activities)
7. "Acting Out the ABC's: A Child's Primer of Alphabet, Counting and Acting Out Songs" (Disneyland)
8. "14 Numbers, Letters and Animal Songs," Alan Mills (Folkways)
9. "All About Numbers and Counting," Ray Heatherton (Miller-Brody)
10. "Musical Math: Beginning Concepts," Ruth White and David White (Rhythm Productions)
11. "Alphabet in Action" (consonants and vowels taught through songs and motor activities), Michael Gallina (Kimbo)
12. "Sing a Song of Sounds" (developing auditory perception through songs, sound games, and motor activities), Michael Gallina (Kimbo)
13. "Slim Goodbody—Inside Out" (science), John Burstein (Grapefruit Records)
14. "Slim Goodbody Presents the Inside Story," John Burstein (Grapefruit Records)
15. "Songs of Safety / Manners Can Be Fun," Frank Luther (Vocalion)
16. "Children's Basic Concepts Through Music," Bob Kay (Stallman)
17. "Counting Games and Rhythms for Little Ones," Ella Jenkins (Folkways)
18. "Singing Sounds," volumes I and II (simplified phonics set to music) (Bowmar)
19. Musical math records (Tom Thumb)
    a. "Addition / Subtraction"
    b. "Multiplication"
20. Ballads for the Age of Science (Motivation)

This series of records is superb. They introduce science concepts to preschoolers in a delightful, clear way.

    a. "Weather and Climate"
    b. "Nature Songs"
    c. "More Nature Songs"
    d. "Space Songs"
    e. "Energy and Motion Songs"
    f. "Science Experiment and Activity Songs"

III. Middle Childhood (approximately the sixth to the eleventh birthday)

A. Folk Songs, Activities
   1. "Camp Songs," Pete Seeger, et al. (Folkways)
   2. "American Folk Songs for Children," Mike and Peggy Seeger (Rounder)
   3. "Spin, Spider, Spin," Marcia Berman and Patty Zeitlin (Educational Activities)
   4. "Our Dinosaur Friends," volumes I and II (EMU)
   5. "The Best of Burl's for Boys and Girls," Burl Ives (MCA)

6. "Magical Songs," Malvina Reynolds (Cassandra)
7. "Honey on Toast," Sandy Offenheim (Berandol)
8. "Are We There Yet?," Sandy Offenheim (Berandol)
9. "If Snowflakes Fell in Flavors," Sandy Offenheim (Berandol)

B. Recorded Literature
Books are available to go along with these records.
   1. "The Happy Prince / The Star Child," Robert Morley (Argo)
   2. "The Selfish Giant," Robert Morley (Argo)
   3. "The Wizard of Oz," sound track with Judy Garland and Ray Bolger (MGM)
   4. "Paddington—A Disappearing Trick," Michael Bond (Caedmon)
   5. "James and the Giant Peach," Roald Dahl (Caedmon)
   6. "Charlie and the Chocolate Factory," Roald Dahl (Caedmon)
   7. "Jacob Two-Two Meets the Hooded Fang," Christopher Plummer (Caedmon)
   8. "Bambi," Glynis Johns (Caedmon)
   9. "Story of Peter Pan," Glynis Johns (Caedmon)
  10. "American Tall Tales: Johnny Appleseed and Paul Bunyan," Ed Begley (Caedmon)
  11. "Rip Van Winkle," Ed Begley (Caedmon)
  12. "Tom Sawyer," Ed Begley (Caedmon)
  13. "Paul Bunyan in Story and Song," Ed Begley and Oscar Brand (Caedmon)
  14. "Heidi," Claire Bloom (Caedmon)
  15. "Alice in Wonderland," Joan Greenwood (Caedmon)
  16. "Rootabaga Stories," Carl Sandburg (Caedmon)
  17. "Ghost Stories for Young People," John Allen (Golden)
  18. "A Coven of Witches' Tales," Vincent Price (Caedmon)
  19. "Hornbook for Witches," Vincent Price (Caedmon)
  20. "A Child's Garden of Verses," Judith Anderson (Caedmon)

C. Music Appreciation
   1. Meet the Classics series (Sine Qua Non)
      a. "Bartok"
      b. "Berlioz"
      c. "Dvorak"
      d. "Stephen Foster"
      e. "Gershwin"
      f. "Grieg"
      g. "Handel"
      h. "Scott Joplin"
      i. "Paganini"
      j. "Prokofiev"
      k. "Rachmaninoff"
      l. "Ravel"
      m. "Rossini"

n. "Schumann"
o. "Sousa"
p. "Johann Strauss"
q. "Verdi"
r. "Vivaldi and Corelli"
s. "Wagner"
2. "Peter and the Wolf," Leonard Bernstein (Columbia)
3. "Major Classics for Minors" (RCA)
4. "Story of Babar and the Little Tailor," Peter Ustinov (Angel)
5. "Rhythms of the World," Langston Hughes (Folkways)
6. "Story of Jazz," Langston Hughes (Folkways)
7. "Young Person's Guide to the Orchestra," Henry Chapin (Columbia)

D. Intellectual Stimulation
1. "Learning to Read with Phonics" (Educational Insights)
2. "It's About Time" (Miller-Brody)
3. "Magnificent Multiplication," Chip Fields (Wise Owl)
4. "Multiplication Rock" (Capitol)
5. "Sing a Sum or Remainder" (Educational Activities)
6. "Singing Multiplication Tables," Hap Palmer (Educational Activities)

E. Electronic Music
Electronic music is made with purely electronic sounds, or with tapes of natural sounds that are speeded up or slowed down, filtered, and cut. Many middle childhood children find this music fascinating. Here are some good recordings of electronic music.
1. "The Electronic Record for Children," Bruce Haack and Esther Nelson (Dimension 5)
2. "The In Sound from Way Out!," Perry Kingsley (Vanguard)
3. "Snowflakes Are Dancing" (electronic recordings of music by Debussy), Tomita (RCA)
4. "Switched-On Bach" (Columbia)

IV. Preadolescence and Adolescence
Once again, I will list no suggestions for these age groups. When your grandchildren become preadolescents and, later, adolescents, their taste in music becomes very individualized. They may well become intensely interested in rock music; they will probably be increasingly interested in adult records and cassettes. If you wish to give your preadolescent or adolescent grandson a record or cassette as a gift, ask him what kind of music he likes. Rock? Folk? Disco? Maybe even classical? Get as many details as you can and, armed with this information, proceed to your local record or music shop. If you need help in finding the right thing, the staff there will probably be able to help you—chances are they are young people who are "into" the same kind of music.

✍§ *Appendix D* ɜ🙡
Books on Parenting for Grandparents

The books in this appendix are written not for grandparents, but for parents. However, they may be of interest to you as a grandparent in the new extended family for one or more of these reasons:

In special circumstances—for example, if you have a divorced working daughter (or daughter-in-law)—you may become a full-time parent to your grandchildren during the day.

In order to better understand your grandchildren and enjoy them fully, you may want to have more information on children than the average grandparent has.

You may not understand some of your adult children's modern views on child-raising. These books will help you to understand the reasons behind the new approaches to child-raising.

A. Books on Child Psychology

These books deal mainly with the stages of psychological development from birth to age twenty-one.

1. *How to Parent,* Fitzhugh Dodson (New American Library paperback). A comprehensive guide to both the emotional and the intellectual development of the child in the first five years of life. It gives both parents and grandparents tips on how to stimulate children intellectually.
2. *How to Father,* Fitzhugh Dodson (New American Library paperback). Even though this book is directed at fathers, it has been read with enjoyment and profit by many, many mothers. It covers the psychological development of the child from birth to age twenty-one. You are not meant to read and absorb the information in this book all at once. Use *How to Father* to follow your grandchild along, year by year, in his development.
3. *Your Two Year Old,* Louise Ames and Frances Ilg (Delacorte Press)
4. *Your Three Year Old,* Louise Ames and Frances Ilg (Delacorte Press)
5. *Your Four Year Old,* Louise Ames and Frances Ilg (Delacorte Press)
6. *Your Five Year Old,* Louise Ames and Frances Ilg (Delacorte Press)
7. *Your Six Year Old,* Louise Ames and Frances Ilg (Delacorte Press)

These five books by Ames and Ilg would be a valuable addition to any grandparent's (or parent's) library. They are basically updated versions of the justly famous Gesell studies. Each one is full of helpful background information on the age group under discussion.

8. *Infant and Child in the Culture of Today,* Arnold Gesell, Frances Ilg, Louise Bates Ames (Harper & Row). This is an updated version of a book that

278

has had a great influence on American psychology, psychologists, and parents. And rightly so. It covers the development of the child from birth to age five. The typical traits and growth trends of each age are summarized in a behavior profile and a "behavior day." The profile is a thumbnail sketch of the behavior and growth forces of a child of a particular age. The "behavior day" describes a typical day in the life of a youngster of that age in terms of eating, sleeping, and play habits, and a number of other characteristic activities.

9. *The Child from Five to Ten,* Arnold Gesell, Frances Ilg, Louise Ames (Harper & Row). An updated version of the earlier book by the same name, following the basic format established in *Infant and Child in the Culture of Today*.

10. *Youth: The Years from Ten to Sixteen,* Arnold Gesell, Frances Ilg, Louise Ames (Harper & Row). The authors take their developmental studies of children up to age sixteen, using the same research methods and psychological categories established in the two earlier books.

11. *The First Three Years of Life,* Burton White (Avon paperback). Dr. White has written an impressive book dealing with the importance of the first three years of life. Much of the book is based upon the results of the Harvard Preschool Project, of which Dr. White was the director. He speaks very forthrightly and lets the psychological chips fall where they may on such topics as methods of dealing with children, good toys for children, and so forth.

12. *The Magic Years,* Selma Fraiberg (Scribner's paperback). A unique book written to help grandparents or parents understand the mind of the young child. It is written strictly from the psychoanalytic point of view, but within that limitation, the book is excellent in describing the psychological development of the child from birth to six.

B. Books on Discipline

1. *How to Discipline with Love,* Fitzhugh Dodson (New American Library paperback). This book describes nineteen different discipline techniques, and contains examples of how to apply these techniques in typical situations. The range of techniques covers all the developmental stages from birth to age twenty-one. This book also discusses subjects not usually mentioned in other books on discipline—the rights of parents, how to teach ethics and morality to children, how to desensitize yourself to a child's behavior through the use of "negative thinking." There are chapters on the special discipline situations of working parents, single parents, and stepparents.

2. *Parent Effectiveness Training,* Thomas Gordon (New American Library, Plume paperback). The book deals in great detail with Dr. Gordon's active listening technique and his "no-lose" method of solving problems between parents and children. I think every grandparent and parent should read this book.

3. *Between Parent and Child,* Haim Ginott (Avon paperback). This book, which covers ages six to ten, is psychologically sound, and clear and forceful in its writing. It is a classic in its field, but as up-to-date as the day it was written. It is particularly helpful in teaching parents and grandparents how to translate the "coded language" of a child's words and behavior. However, Dr. Ginott is not as effective as Dr. Gordon in communicating to adults how to use the "reflection of feelings" technique in dealing with children.

4. *Between Parent and Teenager,* Haim Ginott (Avon paperback). Despite its title, this book does not really come to grips with the current teenage scene. But it is still well worth reading, if you apply its insights to younger children. Think of it as an expanded version of *Between Parent and Child* and you will get a great deal out of it.

C. Books to Help You Understand How to Stimulate Children Intellectually

1. *How to Raise a Brighter Child,* Joan Beck (Pocket Books paperback). This book is clear, down-to-earth, and interesting. It describes in great detail how a parent or grandparent can provide a stimulating intellectual environment for a child during the first five years of life. I recommend it highly.

2. *Give Your Child a Superior Mind,* Siegfried and Therese Engelmann (Simon & Schuster). This is a very important book for grandparents or parents who are anxious to help in the intellectual development of their children during the preschool years. This book, like Beck's, concentrates exclusively on the intellectual development of the child. The Engelmanns give very specific advice on such things as teaching a child arithmetic and math concepts, science concepts, and how to print and read. They avoid extravagant promises and misleading claims. Probably the best single book to help parents and grandparents maximize the intellectual development of their children.

3. *Thinking Is Child's Play,* Evelyn Sharp (Avon paperback). The first part of this book gives an overview of how young children learn to think. The second part contains forty games with which parents and grandparents can teach logical thinking to young children using ordinary materials such as playing cards, paper plates, string, and spools. An excellent book.

4. *A Parent's Guide to Children's Education,* Nancy Larrick (Pocket Books paperback). The single best guide to what a child will be learning in the elementary grades at school, and how you can help him at home. What a child is learning at school is a mystery to most grandparents and parents, but this book will clear up the mystery. No wonder it has become a classic in the field!

5. *A Parent's Guide to Children's Reading,* Nancy Larrick (Pocket Books paperback). This classic work by Dr. Larrick is every bit as good in its own way as her education guide. Dr. Larrick writes clearly and interestingly about children and books, and gives a comprehensive bibliography for children up to the age of twelve.

D. Books to Guide You in Playing with Children
  1. *Your Child's Play,* Arnold Arnold (Essandess paperback). This excellent, down-to-earth book will help any grandparent better understand the play of his grandchild and participate in it. I recommend it highly.
  2. *The Complete Book of Children's Play,* Ruth Hartley and Robert Goldenson (Crowell paperback). If you want to buy just one book as a complete guide to understanding children's play from birth to adolescence, this is the one to get. Very few grandparents are aware of the existence of this magnificent book, and that's a pity. It is a treasure trove, covering all aspects of your grandchild's play. You will consult it again and again.
  3. *Play and Playthings for the Preschool Child,* Elizabeth Matterson (Penguin paperback). This book emphasizes the importance of play for the emotional and intellectual development of preschool children. Mrs. Matterson stresses how natural materials and improvised playthings in the home are superior to "gimmicky" store-bought toys.
  4. *A Parent's Guide to Children's Play and Recreation,* Alvin Schwartz (Collier Books paperback). Schwartz emphasizes play that is creative and absorbing but not expensive. He discusses play materials, trips, children's parties, games, and music.
  5. *How to Fly a Kite, Catch a Fish, Grow a Flower,* Alvin Schwartz (Pocket Books paperback). Schwartz is a father of four himself, and he knows his way around children's play activities. This book covers just about everything a grandparent and grandchild could do together: swimming, boating, fishing, camping, bike riding; hobbies, pets, magic; and more.
  6. *The Rainy Day Book,* Alvin Schwartz (Simon & Schuster paperback). Another fine book by Alvin Schwartz. This one is a complete guide to rainy day activities for children, as well as a survival guide for harassed parents or grandparents. The book describes quiet games of all kinds, science experiments, nature projects, arts and crafts projects, and active indoor games for letting off steam.

E. Books on Raising Black Children
  It took some time for books on parenting to catch up with the racial facts of life in the United States. For many years, child-raising books tacitly assumed that the children being raised and the parents or grandparents raising them were white. Now, finally, we have two excellent books for black parents or grandparents to use in raising their children.
  1. *The Black Child: A Parent's Guide,* Phyllis Harrison-Ross and Barbara Wyden (David McKay). A unique book, intended for both black and white parents. It deals with the special problems of the black child, but it also offers guidance to white parents and grandparents to help them raise children with an acceptance of both racial differences *and* racial similarities. An excellent book.

2. *Black Child Care,* James Comer and Alvin Poussaint (Pocket Books paperback). This superb book traces the development of a hypothetical black child from birth through adolescence. Psychologically sound and eminently readable.

F. Other Helpful Books
Two books to help grandparents understand drugs and the drug scene:
1. *You, Your Child, and Drugs,* by the staff of the Child Study Association of America (Child Study Press). A booklet that packs a great deal of helpful information on drugs into seventy-two pages. Contains specific information on various drugs, and discusses why youngsters misuse drugs and where to go for help.
2. *Marijuana, a Signal of Misunderstanding: The Official Report of the National Commission on Marijuana and Drug Abuse* (New American Library paperback). This report of the National Commission, prepared for the President and Congress, deals with more than fifty studies conducted all over the world on every aspect of the marijuana problem. It speaks to such questions as "Who smokes marijuana, and why? Is it a sexual stimulant? What is the effect of marijuana on driving ability? Does the use of marijuana trigger crime?" This thorough and well-documented book should be of help to every grandparent in understanding this controversial drug and discussing it intelligently with his teenage grandchild.

And finally, a book to help grandparents understand today's parenting scene:
3. *Becoming Parents,* Sandra Jaffe and Jack Viertel (Atheneum). Books on parenting abound, but too many of them have the smell of the library upon them. This book has the smell of real life: parents loving, worrying, getting upset, crying, quarreling, kicking a hole in the wall out of sheer frustration, discovering that children sometimes get in the way of sex, laughing, and finding fulfillment. It is a splendid book. Read it yourself and then pass it along to your grown children.

Notes

Quotes for chapter headings in Chapters 1 to 20:
Richard and Helen Exley, *To Grandma and Grandpa* (New York: Houghton Mifflin Company, 1979).

Chapter 1
1. Leontine Young, *The Fractured Family* (New York: McGraw-Hill, 1973).
2. Ibid.
3. Ibid.
4. Ibid.
5. Ibid.
6. Ibid.
7. Ibid.
8. Robert C. Sorensen, *Adolescent Sexuality in Contemporary America* (New York: World, 1973).
9. Ruth Goode, *A Book for Grandmothers* (New York: Macmillan Company, 1976).
10. Ibid.
11. Ibid.

Chapter 9
1. Barbara Biber, "The School Years," in *The New Encyclopedia of Child Care and Guidance,* ed. Sidonie Matsner Gruenberg (New York: Doubleday & Company, 1968).

Chapter 10
1. Arnold Gesell, Frances Ilg, and Louise Bates Ames, *Youth* (New York: Harper & Row, Publishers, 1956).

Chapter 11
1. Ogden Nash, *Verses from 1929 On* (Boston: Little, Brown & Company, 1947).

~§ Index §~